Overview Map Key

T0152360

STANDS OF MATURE SAGUAROS ARE ESPECIALLY THICK ON THE FREEMAN HOMESTEAD TRAIL (HIKE 3, PAGE 44).

Tucson

38 Spectacular Hikes Around the Old Pueblo

2ND EDITION

ROB RACHOWIECKI

MENASHA RIDGE PRESS
Your Guide to the Outdoors Since 1982

Five-Star Trails: Tucson

Copyright © 2014 and 2020 by Rob Rachowiecki
All rights reserved
Published by Menasha Ridge Press
Distributed by Publishers Group West
Printed in the United States of America
Second edition, fourth printing 2022

Project editor: Kate Johnson
Cover design: Scott McGrew
Text design: Annie Long
Cover and interior photos: Rob Rachowiecki except where noted
Cartography and elevation profiles: Rob Rachowiecki and Scott McGrew
Proofreader: Emily Beaumont
Indexer: Rich Carlson

Cover: Sabino Canyon Trail © Nelson Sirlin/Shutterstock

Library of Congress Cataloging-in-Publication Data

Names: Rachowiecki, Rob, 1954– author.
Title: Five-star trails : Tucson / Rob Rachowiecki.
Description: Second edition. | Birmingham, AL : Menasha Ridge Press, [2019]
Summary: "Each trail has been thoroughly researched, recently hiked,
  and includes detailed descriptions, trail profiles and maps. At-a-glance
  categorical ratings, such as scenery, trail condition, difficulty, solitude,
  and kid-friendliness, let you quickly select a trail that fits your tastes
  and ability. Other key information such as fees, restrictions for dogs
  as well as advice on when to visit offers you the best information so you
  can plan your trip with ease"— Provided by publisher.
Identifiers: LCCN 2019018571 | ISBN 9781634041003 (paperback)
  ISBN 9781634041010 (ebook)
Subjects: LCSH: Hiking—Arizona—Tucson Region—Guidebooks.
  Trails—Arizona—Tucson Region—Guidebooks. | Tucson Region
  (Ariz.)—Guidebooks.
Classification: LCC GV199.42.A72 T8357 | DDC 796.5109791/776—dc23
LC record available at https://lccn.loc.gov/2019018571

 MENASHA RIDGE PRESS
An imprint of AdventureKEEN
2204 First Ave. S, Ste. 102
Birmingham, AL 35233
menasharidge.com

DISCLAIMER This book is meant only as a guide to select trails in and around Tucson, Arizona, and does not guarantee hiker safety in any way—you hike at your own risk. Neither Menasha Ridge Press nor Rob Rachowiecki is liable for property loss or damage, personal injury, or death that may result from accessing or hiking the trails described in this guide. Be especially cautious when walking in potentially hazardous terrains with, for example, steep inclines or drop-offs. Do not attempt to explore terrain that may be beyond your abilities. Please read carefully the introduction to this book, as well as safety information from other sources. Familiarize yourself with current weather reports and maps of the area you plan to visit (in addition to the maps provided in this guidebook). Be cognizant of park regulations, and always follow them. While every effort has been made to ensure the accuracy of the information in this guidebook, land and road conditions, phone numbers and websites, and other information are subject to change.

Contents

Santa Catalina Foothills   137

Saguaro National Park West, Tucson Mountains, and Tortolita Mountains   181

Madera Canyon Area   227

Dedication

For Audrey, as always

 # Acknowledgments

Without knowing I was researching a guidebook, many hikers I met provided me with friendly tips and valuable insights. It's remarkable how the whole hiking community looks out for one another on the trails.

I'm equally indebted to the volunteers, rangers, and staff of Saguaro National Park, Coronado National Forest, and Catalina State Park, who likewise were a fine source of information. Again, I rarely revealed my authorship, preferring to receive the same kind of support any other hiker would.

A shout-out to Jay Rochlin, who turned me on to the trails of Tortolita Mountain Park, which are now featured in this second edition.

Lastly, I thank my editor, Kate Johnson, and my cartographer, Scott McGrew, for putting up with my rants about GPS units—though I still don't know why my parked car was 30 feet lower at the end of my hike than it was when I started.

—*Rob Rachowiecki*

Preface

The highlights of my earliest visits to Tucson in the 1970s were sweeping views of stands of saguaro cactus, those many-armed icons of the desert Southwest. I never took those initial trips in summer, so when the vagaries of life brought me to settle permanently in Tucson in 1989, I discovered that seemingly endless days of 100°F weather were as much part of the picture as the fabulous desert scenery.

Having been born and raised in England and then having spent a good chunk of my late 20s, 30s, and 40s hiking and climbing in the Andes, I was not very well prepared for blistering summers. Happily, I discovered I could escape into the mountain ranges surrounding Tucson, where lovely forests and temperatures in the 70s provided ideal conditions for enjoying the outdoors.

Perhaps the area's greatest attraction is being able to hike year-round in superb scenery, with gorgeous desert in winter and nearby temperate mountains in summer always providing close-to-perfect weather. Although it is dry in the lowlands, with Tucson averaging a total annual rainfall of barely 12 inches, the mountains form their own microclimates and typically attract two to three times as much rainfall, thus supporting thriving forests.

Mount Lemmon is one of the "sky islands" of southern Arizona. Driving from Tucson to near its summit in the Santa Catalina Mountains is the equivalent of driving from the Mexican border to the Canadian border in terms of ecosystems. It takes just an hour to drive Mount Lemmon Road (also known as the Catalina Highway or General Hitchcock Highway) from saguaro cactus lowlands through high desert grasslands and on to oak and mesquite woodlands, ending in pine, fir, and spruce highlands. Meanwhile, the temperature drops by 20°–30°F. It's no wonder, then, that Tucsonans enjoy picnicking and hiking in the mountains to get away from 100°F summer temperatures in the city.

**THERE ARE MANY LONG DESCENTS ON THE WILDERNESS OF ROCK LOOP—
BUT YOU HAVE TO CLIMB BACK UP!**

This guidebook includes detailed descriptions of all the best-known routes, ranging from relaxing jaunts of a couple of hours to tough all-day ascents, as well as a number of lesser-known hikes, some of which are rarely described in other books. By no means is this an exhaustive list: avid hikers are encouraged to discover more possibilities. No overnight backpacking trips are included, although I've suggested a few as extensions or combinations of the day hikes. I've also provided details about campsites that you can use as a base for hiking without having to carry a full pack. But every hike in this book can be accomplished from your home or hotel room in one day or less.

Recommended Hikes

All the hikes in this book are recommended on some level; the following list serves merely as a starting point. There is much overlap among categories, and many hikes could easily fit in several of them. I haven't included a Best for Scenery category, as every hike in the Tucson area has great scenery in abundance. Enjoy it!

Best for City Views, Far and Near

Best for Geological Features

Best for Historical Remnants

Best for Kids

Best for Mountain Summits

Best for Nature

Best for Railroad Views

Best for Ridge Hiking

Best for Seasonal Water Features

Best for Wheelchair Adventurers

RAPPEL ROCK FROM THE UPPER REACHES OF THE WILDERNESS OF ROCK LOOP (HIKE 18, PAGE 131)

Introduction

About This Book

Tucson lies within the Basin and Range Province, a physiographic region that covers much of the western United States and is distinguished by lowland areas alternating with abrupt, high ridges. It's tough country, with vast deserts, precipitous canyons, and steep mountains challenging the original native settlers, early pioneers, and today's travelers.

At an elevation of roughly 2,500 feet, Tucson sits in a basin surrounded by mountains to the north, south, east, and west, some of which rise to more than 9,000 feet and many of which are protected within the Coronado National Forest. In addition, Tucson's fabulous desert scenery earns it two national-park sectors on its doorstep, with Saguaro National Park's east and west districts bookending town. Each district has a visitor center, a scenic driving loop, picnic sites, and numerous desert and mountain trails, but no lodges or drive-in campgrounds.

With more than 500,000 inhabitants and a metro-area population of more than a million, The Old Pueblo is a casual city where shorts or jeans and T-shirts or cowboy hats are seen in restaurants, casinos, and theaters. Tucson's cultural quotient is high, however: It's America's first city to be named a UNESCO city of gastronomy; it's home to the acclaimed University of Arizona; it has a world-class outdoor museum; and it features thriving arts districts and more than 20 performing-arts organizations,. It also consistently ranks atop "best places for bicycling" lists and enjoys 350 days of sunshine a year—perfect for hiking.

The hikes in this book are arranged in roughly doughnut fashion around The Old Pueblo, beginning on the east side and circling counterclockwise.

SAGUARO NATIONAL PARK EAST AND EASTERN TUCSON The city's east side is bounded by the Rincon Mountains, which rise to more than 8,000 feet. Much of this range lies within Saguaro National Park East, the site of numerous lowland hikes. Two trails that climb into the mountains are described in this book. (The highest peak, 8,666-foot Mica Mountain, is reached by an approximately 26-mile out-and-back hike, not included here.)

SABINO CANYON This is Tucsonans' favorite canyon. Lying at the northeastern end of the city and the southeastern part of the Santa Catalina Mountains, it merits its own recreation-area designation within the Coronado National Forest. The many trails here include some of the best views and most favored water destinations near Tucson. Note that the large parking area can fill early on spring and fall weekends, when an overflow parking area is opened almost 0.5 mile to the north.

MOUNT LEMMON This 9,157-foot peak is the highest in the Santa Catalina Mountains, which abut Tucson's north side and are the city's favored highland-recreation site. The paved 27.6-mile Santa Catalina Highway leaves from Tucson's far northeast side and goes almost to the summit, giving access to numerous hiking trails, picnic areas, campgrounds, a ski area, and the village of Summerhaven. This is the highest road in the Tucson area.

SANTA CATALINA FOOTHILLS Locals simply call this area The Foothills. Upscale, view-filled housing covers the acreage up to the border with the Coronado National Forest. To the north of this boundary lie some of Tucson's steepest and most difficult trails, climbing beautiful canyons high above the city and into the Pusch Ridge area of the Santa Catalina Mountains.

SAGUARO NATIONAL PARK WEST, TUCSON MOUNTAINS, AND TORTOLITA MOUNTAINS The city's western horizon comprises the low Tucson Mountains, dominated by Wasson Peak, a panoramic 4,687-foot hiking destination reached by various trail combinations within Saguaro National Park West. My two favorite routes are described in complete detail, and two others are referenced with enough information for hikers to be able to find and follow them to the summit. This range stretches southeast into Tucson Mountain Park, with outlying hills, such as Sentinel Peak, overlooking downtown.

To the far northwest of Tucson lie the equally low Tortolita Mountains, a sprawling range where an excellent trail system has been developed in recent years and which is a new feature in this edition (see Wild Burro Loop, page 219).

MADERA CANYON AREA The Santa Rita Mountains on the far south side are the highest and most distant from Tucson. The best and easiest way to explore them is to drive to Madera Canyon, which has a wide variety of trails, as well as picnic sites and places to stay. Trails vary from wheelchair-accessible routes to ascents of Mount Wrightson, which, at 9,453 feet, is the highest peak in the Tucson area. This canyon is also a favored spot for bird-watchers, who come to see the elegant trogon and other species.

How to Use This Guidebook

The following section walks you through this book's organization, making it easy and convenient to plan great hikes.

Overview Map, Map Key, and Map Legend

Use the overview map on the inside front cover to assess the general location of each hike's primary trailhead. Each hike's number appears on the overview map, on the map key facing the overview map, and in the table of contents. As you flip through the book, a hike's full profile is easy to locate by watching for the hike number at the top of each page. The book is organized by region, as indicated in the table of contents. A map legend that details the symbols found on trail maps appears on the inside back cover.

Trail Maps

In addition to the overview map on the inside cover, a detailed map of each hike's route appears with its profile. On each of these maps, symbols indicate the trailhead, the complete route, significant features, facilities, and topographic landmarks such as creeks, overlooks, and peaks.

To produce the highly accurate maps in this book, I used a handheld GPS unit to gather data while hiking each route and then sent that data to Menasha Ridge Press's expert cartographers. Be aware, though, that your GPS device is no substitute for sound, sensible navigation that takes into account the conditions that you observe while hiking.

Further, despite the high quality of the maps in this guidebook, the publisher and I strongly recommend that you always carry an additional map, such as the ones noted in each profile opener's "Maps" entry.

Elevation Profile (Diagram)

This graphical element accompanies hikes with significant changes in elevation. Each entry's key information lists the elevation at the

LOOKING DOWN AT FINGER ROCK FROM ABOVE THE PIMA SADDLE TURNOFF (HIKE 23, PAGE 161)

trailhead, along with elevations such as the high or low points of the trail, trail ends, or summits.

The elevation profile represents the rises and falls of the trail as viewed from the side, over the complete distance of that trail in miles. On the diagram's vertical axis, or height scale, the number of feet between each tick mark lets you visualize the climb. Varying height scales provide an accurate image of each hike's climbing challenge. For example, the Sentinel Peak hike (see page 201) begins west of downtown Tucson at 2,499 feet, while the Old Baldy and Super Trails (pages 246 and 252, respectively) reach the summit of Mount Wrightson at 9,453 feet, the highest elevation in southern Arizona.

The Hike Profile

Each profile opens with the hike's star ratings, GPS trailhead coordinates, and other key at-a-glance information—from the trail's distance and configuration to contacts for local information. Each profile also includes a map (see "Trail Maps," page 3). The main text for each profile includes four sections: Overview, Route Details, Nearby Attractions, and Directions (for driving to the trailhead area).

Star Ratings

Each hike in this book was assigned a one- to five-star rating in each of the following categories: scenery, trail condition, suitability for children, level of difficulty, and degree of solitude. This being Tucson, none of the hikes have one- or two-star ratings for scenery—most rate four or five stars. Equally, with trails surrounding a metropolitan area of more than a million inhabitants, it's rare to find a five-star (positively tranquil) rating for solitude. If I can go for an hour without seeing another hiker, I'll rate the hike four stars (spurts of isolation), which is usually as good as it gets. Other categories tend to have more variety among the hikes, but whichever hike you choose, you'll find that it gets four or five stars in at least one rating group, and usually in two or more.

FOR SCENERY:

★ ★ ★ ★ ★	Unique, picturesque panoramas
★ ★ ★ ★	Diverse vistas
★ ★ ★	Pleasant views
★ ★	Unchanging landscape
★	Not selected for scenery

FOR TRAIL CONDITION:

★ ★ ★ ★ ★	Consistently well maintained
★ ★ ★ ★	Stable, with no surprises
★ ★ ★	Average terrain to negotiate
★ ★	Inconsistent, with good and poor areas
★	Rocky, overgrown, or often muddy

FOR CHILDREN:

★ ★ ★ ★ ★	Babes in strollers welcome
★ ★ ★ ★	Fun for anyone past the toddler stage
★ ★ ★	Good for young hikers with proven stamina
★ ★	Not enjoyable for children
★	Not advisable for children

FOR DIFFICULTY:

★ ★ ★ ★ ★	Grueling
★ ★ ★ ★	Strenuous
★ ★ ★	Moderate: won't beat you up—but you'll know you've been hiking
★ ★	Easy, with patches of moderate
★	Good for a relaxing stroll

FOR SOLITUDE:

★ ★ ★ ★ ★	Positively tranquil
★ ★ ★ ★	Spurts of isolation
★ ★ ★	Moderately secluded
★ ★	Crowded on weekends and holidays
★	Steady stream of individuals and/or groups

GPS TRAILHEAD COORDINATES

As noted in "Trail Maps" (page 3), I used a handheld GPS unit to obtain geographic data and sent the information to the cartographers at Menasha Ridge Press. In the opener for each hike profile, the coordinates—the intersection of latitude (north) and longitude (west)—will orient you from the trailhead. In some cases, you can drive within viewing distance of a trailhead. Other hiking routes require a short walk to the trailhead from a parking area. (One trail is reached by a motorized shuttle.)

You will also note that this book uses the degree–decimal minute format for presenting the latitude and longitude GPS coordinates:

N32° 13.247' W110° 43.570'

The latitude–longitude grid system is likely quite familiar to you, but here's a refresher, pertinent to visualizing the coordinates:

Imaginary lines of latitude—called parallels and approximately 69 miles apart from each other—run horizontally around the globe. The equator is established to be 0°, and each parallel is indicated by degrees from the equator: up to 90°N at the North Pole, and down to 90°S at the South Pole.

Imaginary lines of longitude—called meridians—run perpendicular to lines of latitude and are likewise indicated by degrees. Starting from 0° at the Prime Meridian in Greenwich, England, they continue to the east and west until they meet 180° later at the International Date Line in the Pacific Ocean. At the equator, longitude lines also are approximately 69 miles apart, but that distance narrows as the meridians converge toward the North and South Poles.

To convert GPS coordinates given in degrees, minutes, and seconds to degrees and decimal minutes, divide the seconds by 60. For more on GPS technology, visit usgs.gov.

DISTANCE AND CONFIGURATION

Distance indicates the length of the hike round-trip, from start to finish. If the hike description includes options to shorten or extend the hike, those round-trip distances are also factored here. Where the distances shown on maps and trail signs differ from those I've measured by GPS, I usually favor the former and mention the latter in "Comments" (see page 10).

YUCCA AND GRASSLANDS ALONG THE MOLINO BASIN TRAIL (PAGE 126)

Configuration defines the type of route—for example, an out-and-back (which takes you in and out the same way), a point-to-point (a one-way route), a figure-eight, or a balloon.

HIKING TIME

The second edition of this book was published as the author was signing up for Medicare and wondering how 65 years danced by so quickly. Throw in a couple of back and knee surgeries, and I find myself taking 10 hours to hike a trail that was a 6-hour workout a couple of decades ago. Therefore, the hiking times here are geared to my slow pace. Many of you will undoubtedly find my times easy to beat—go for it!

My rule of thumb for hiking these trails is 1.5 miles per hour, a pace that typically allows time for taking photos, dawdling and admiring views, and tackling alternating stretches of hills and descents. Flatter, easier trails can be hiked at 2-plus miles per hour, while some of the steepest, rockiest routes might drop to less than 1.5 miles per hour.

I don't see the point of hiking much faster than 2 or so miles an hour: I prefer to look at the scenery rather than constantly keep my eyes on my feet. I remember hiking off-trail about 10 yards to watch a deer that was munching on a shrub. Several hikers breezed past without noticing me or the deer—their eyes were on the trail. Of course, you don't want to fall, but there is a sweet spot between keeping your eyes on the trail and looking around at the scenery.

Finally, when planning to hike a particular trail, consider your general physical condition, experience, expectations, weather, and energy level on a given day.

HIGHLIGHTS

This section lists features that draw hikers to the trail: mountain, canyon, or forest views; water features; historical sites; and the like.

ELEVATION

In each hike's key information, you will see the elevation (in feet) at the trailhead and another figure for the high (or low) point on the trail. Where appropriate, a third elevation, such as the trail's end, is also listed. Most hikes also include an elevation diagram (see page 4).

ACCESS

Trail-access hours are listed here, along with any fees or permits required to hike the trail. (*Note:* The Coronado National Forest is proposing a parking fee increase at some of its sites from the current $5/$10/$20 for day/week/year to a proposed $8/$20/$40. Campsites may go up from $10 to $20 per night. If the proposal is successful, expect to see it implemented in winter 2019–20.)

MAPS

Resources for maps, in addition to those in this guidebook, are listed here. As noted earlier, we recommend that you carry more than one map—and that you consult those maps before heading out on the trail, to resolve any confusion or discrepancy.

FACILITIES

Includes visitor centers, restrooms, water, picnic tables, and other basics at or near the trailhead. In some cases, facilities may be limited to just a small parking area.

WHEELCHAIR ACCESS

Paved sections or other areas where one can safely use a wheelchair are noted here.

COMMENTS

Here you'll find assorted nuggets of information, such as whether dogs, horses, or mountain bikes are allowed on the trails. I also mention here whether hiking distances listed on maps or signs differ from my GPS measurements.

CONTACTS

Listed here are phone numbers and websites for checking trail conditions and gleaning other day-to-day information.

OVERVIEW, ROUTE DETAILS, NEARBY ATTRACTIONS, AND DIRECTIONS

These four elements compose the heart of the hike. "Overview" gives you a quick summary of what to expect on that trail; "Route Details" guides you on the hike, from start to finish; and "Nearby Attractions" suggests appealing adjacent sites, such as restaurants, museums, and other trails (note that not every hike profile has these). "Directions" will get you to the trailhead from a well-known road or highway.

Weather

When Tucson gets rain, it tends to be in the form of scattered showers or focused thunderstorms, and one of the numerous weather stations throughout the city may report twice the daily rain total of another station a few miles away. Tucson's main rainfall occurs during the monsoon season, officially June 15–September 30. Realistically, it rarely rains in June, and the first of numerous monsoon thunderstorms usually falls in the first half of July.

Monsoons also bring thunder-and-lightning storms, especially in the afternoon. Try to avoid summits, ridges, and flat, open areas at these times. If lightning is followed by a thunderclap within 5 seconds, the lightning is dangerously close—within a mile or less. To minimize your chances of being struck, crouch down and tuck your head into your hands. Don't stand tall, and don't lie flat. If you're hiking with someone else, keep 20 or 30 yards apart so that you don't both get struck.

These storms can also cause flash floods, which wreak brief havoc on roadways that rarely see rain and have poor drainage; some roads may be closed for a few hours following a storm. Don't attempt to drive across a closed road. Every year, foolish drivers are swept away by monsoon floods—not all of them survive, and those who do incur hefty fines and rescue fees.

Streams in the lowlands often have water flowing during and after the monsoon, and also in the spring as the snow melts in the highlands. Ski Valley, just above Summerhaven, is the southernmost ski area in the United States; it receives an average of 65 inches of snow in winter. Snowmelt can keep Sabino Creek running into May.

Summer temperatures average 100°F in June and July, but many days are much hotter. June is the area's hottest and driest month. Tucson's record high of 117°F was recorded June 26, 1990, and 116°F was reached on June 20, 2017. Many Tucsonans escape the heat by driving up nearby Mount Lemmon, but they should be prepared for violent thunderstorms, especially in July and August. Fortunately, these usually occur in the afternoon, making a pleasant hike possible in the morning.

Tucson rarely gets snow, and when it falls it rarely settles, usually melting within minutes.

AN AGAVE STALK ON BLACKETT'S RIDGE TRAIL (PAGE 74)

Every few years, conditions might be right to "bury" the city in 2 or 3 inches of snow. Snow-laden branches break, happy schoolchildren get a snow day, and bewildered drivers slide around.

When it comes to avoiding heat, lowland-desert hiking is best from October to April, although nature is somewhat subdued during late fall and into winter. Desert wildflowers are best from late February to mid-April, and depending on winter weather patterns, a spectacular bloom may occur every few years, with golden, white, and blue flowers carpeting the ground. Cacti flower reliably from April through early June, although the large fishhook barrel cactus will often bloom as late as August and even September. Trees noted for their blooms include palo verdes, which are covered in tiny yellow blossoms in April and May. Migrant birds boost avian populations around April, and lizards and other reptiles begin to appear around then.

During the summer, desert hikers need to make very early starts to avoid the heat. "It's a dry heat" is Tucson's summer mantra, and it is true that dry desert air doesn't hold heat as well as moist air does: there is often a temperature difference of 30°F between 4 p.m. and 4 a.m. If predawn wake-ups aren't your thing, drive into the mountains, where flowers bloom well into the summer.

Fall in the mountains brings splashes of color, with the aspens at the bottom of Ski Valley providing one of several reliable shows during the annual Oktoberfest held there. By Thanksgiving, the first snows may have fallen in the high mountains, and it's time to hike in the desert again.

The following tables illustrate the huge variation in climate between Tucson in the lowland deserts and Summerhaven near the summit of Mount Lemmon. For each month, "Hi Temp" shows the average daytime high, "Lo Temp" gives the average nighttime low, and "Rain" lists the average precipitation.

TUCSON INTERNATIONAL AIRPORT			
MONTH	HI TEMP	LO TEMP	RAIN
January	66°F	40°F	0.94"
February	69°F	42°F	0.89"
March	74°F	46°F	0.73"
April	82°F	52°F	0.31"
May	92°F	61°F	0.23"
June	100°F	69°F	0.20"
July	100°F	75°F	2.25"
August	97°F	73°F	2.39"
September	95°F	69°F	1.29"
October	85°F	57°F	0.89"
November	74°F	46°F	0.57"
December	65°F	39°F	0.93"

Source: usclimatedata.com

SUMMERHAVEN			
MONTH	HI TEMP	LO TEMP	RAIN
January	49°F	23°F	3.15"
February	48°F	22°F	1.69"
March	53°F	26°F	1.17"
April	61°F	32°F	0.50"
May	69°F	37°F	0.25"
June	76°F	44°F	0.62"
July	77°F	50°F	4.41"
August	74°F	50°F	6.99"
September	70°F	45°F	3.39"
October	62°F	36°F	3.05"
November	56°F	30°F	1.75"
December	51°F	24°F	2.60"

Source: usclimatedata.com

Water

A hiker walking steadily in 90°F heat needs about 10 quarts of fluid per day—that's 2.5 gallons. A good rule of thumb is to hydrate prior to your hike, carry (and drink) 6 ounces of water for every mile you plan to hike, and hydrate again after the hike. On a hot day, you could easily double this amount. Almost every year recreational hikers die of heat exhaustion on popular Tucson trails—there were three fatalities in June 2016 and another in May 2017, all on trails described in this book. The reason: they weren't carrying enough water.

For most people, the pleasures of hiking make carrying water a relatively minor burden, so pack more water than you anticipate needing, even for short hikes. If you don't like drinking tepid water on a hot day, freeze a couple of bottles overnight. It's also a good idea to carry a bottle of sports drink such as Gatorade; the electrolytes replace essential salts that you sweat out.

If you find yourself tempted to drink found water, proceed with extreme caution. Many ponds and lakes you'll encounter are fairly stagnant, and the water tastes terrible. Drinking such water presents inherent risks for thirsty trekkers. Giardia parasites contaminate many water sources and cause the absolutely awful intestinal ailment giardiasis, which can last for weeks after onset. For more information, visit the Centers for Disease Control and Prevention website: cdc.gov/parasites/giardia.

In any case, effective treatment is essential before you use any water source found along the trail. Boiling water for 2–3 minutes is always a safe measure for camping, but day hikers can consider iodine tablets, approved chemical mixes, filtration units rated for giardia, and ultraviolet filtration. Some of these methods (for example, filtration with an added carbon filter) remove bad tastes typical in stagnant water, while others add their own taste. As a precaution, carry a means of water purification in case you underestimate your consumption needs.

Clothing

Weather, unexpected trail conditions, fatigue, extended hiking duration, and wrong turns can individually or collectively turn a great outing into a very uncomfortable one at best and a life-threatening one at worst. Thus, proper attire plays a key role in staying comfortable and, sometimes, in staying alive. Some helpful guidelines:

★ Choose silk, wool, or synthetics for maximum comfort in all of your hiking attire, from hats to socks. Cotton is fine if the weather remains dry and stable, not so much if that material gets wet.

★ Always wear a hat, or at least tuck one into your day pack or hitch it to your belt. Hats offer all-weather sun and wind protection, as well as warmth if it turns cold.

★ Be ready to layer up or down as the day progresses and the mercury rises or falls. Today's outdoor wear makes layering easy, with such designs as jackets that convert to vests and zip-off or button-up legs.

★ Wear hiking boots paired with good socks to avoid blisters. Flip-flopping along a paved urban greenway is one thing, but you should never hike a trail in open sandals or casual sneakers. Your bones and arches need support, and your skin needs protection from cacti along the trail. Rattlesnakes, while rarely encountered, can't bite through hiking boots.

★ Even if the day dawns clear and sunny, don't leave rainwear behind during Tucson's wet months, especially on mountain hikes. Tuck into your day pack, or tie around your waist, a jacket that is breathable and either water-resistant or waterproof. Investigate different choices at your local outdoors retailer. If you're a frequent hiker, ideally you'll have more than one rainwear weight, material, and style in your closet to protect you in all seasons.

Essential Gear

Today you can buy outdoor vests that have up to 20 pockets shaped and sized to carry everything from toothpicks to binoculars. Or, if you don't aspire to feel like a burro, you can neatly stow all these items in your day pack or backpack. The following is a list of never-hike-without-them items—in alphabetical order, as all are important:

★ *Extra clothes:* depending on the season, raingear, a warm hat, and gloves

★ *Extra food:* trail mix, granola bars, or other high-energy snacks

★ *Flashlight or headlamp* with extra bulb and batteries, for getting back to the trailhead if you take longer than expected (which I often do!)

★ *Hiking poles:* OK, these aren't absolutely essential, but I never hike without them. (European hikers almost always use them.) They take a few miles to get used to, but they help transfer weight from your legs to your shoulders so you can go farther, and they help you balance in tricky spots like creek crossings. Their wrist loops enable you to take a photo or a swig from a bottle without having to ditch the sticks. Try them!

★ *Insect repellent:* Mosquitoes breed during monsoon months.

★ *Maps and a high-quality compass:* Unless you know the trail like the back of your hand, don't leave home without these tools. And, as previously noted, bring other maps in addition to those in this guidebook, and consult your maps prior to the hike. If you're GPS-savvy, bring that device, too, but don't rely on it as your sole navigational tool—battery life is limited, after all—and be sure to check its accuracy against that of your maps and compass.

★ *Pocketknife* and/or multitool

★ *Sun protection:* Bring sunglasses with UV protection, a sunhat with a wide brim, and sunscreen. Tucson has 350 sunny days per year and ranks second in the world for skin-cancer rates. (Queensland, Australia, is first.) Apply sunscreen 30 minutes before you begin hiking, and reapply it after heavy sweating or a dip in a pool or stream. Use a product with an SPF of at least 30, and check the expiration date on top of the tube or bottle. Experienced "desert rats" (as some Tucsonans call themselves) wear light-colored long pants and long-sleeved shirts to protect themselves from the sun, even on the hottest days.

★ *Toilet paper* and a zip-top plastic bag to pack it out in

★ *Water:* Again, bring more than you think you'll drink. Depending on your destination, you may want to bring a container and iodine or a filter for purifying water in case you run out.

★ *Whistle:* It could become your best friend in an emergency.

★ *Windproof matches and/or a lighter,* for real emergencies—please don't start a forest fire.

First Aid Kit

In addition to the preceding items, those that follow may seem daunting to carry along for a day hike. But any paramedic will tell you that the products listed here—again, in alphabetical order because all are important—are just the basics. The reality of hiking is that you can be out for a week of backpacking and acquire only a mosquito bite. Or you can hike for an hour, slip, and suffer a cut or broken bone. Fortunately, the items listed pack into a very small space. You may also purchase convenient prepackaged kits at your pharmacy or online.

★ Adhesive bandages

★ Antibiotic ointment (such as Neosporin)

★ Aspirin, acetaminophen (Tylenol), or ibuprofen (Advil)

★ Athletic tape

★ Blister kit (moleskin or an adhesive variety such as Spenco 2nd Skin)

★ Butterfly-closure bandages

★ Diphenhydramine (Benadryl), in case of allergic reactions

★ Elastic bandages (such as Ace) or joint wraps (such as Spenco)

★ Epinephrine in a prefilled syringe (EpiPen), typically by prescription only, for people known to have severe allergic reactions to hiking mishaps such as bee stings

★ Gauze (one roll and a half-dozen 4-by-4-inch pads)

★ Hydrogen peroxide or iodine

Note: Consider your intended terrain and the number of hikers in your party before you exclude any article listed above. A short stroll may not inspire you to carry a complete kit, but anything beyond that warrants precaution. When hiking alone, you should always be prepared for a medical need. And if you're a twosome or with a group, one or more people in your party should be equipped with first aid supplies.

General Safety

The following tips may have the familiar ring of your mother's voice as you take note of them.

★ *Always let someone know* where you'll be hiking and how long you expect to be gone. It's a good idea to give that person a copy of your route, particularly if you're headed into an isolated area. Let him or her know when you return.

★ *Always sign in and out of any trail registers provided.* Don't hesitate to comment on the trail condition if space is provided; that's your opportunity to alert others to any problems you encounter.

★ *Don't count on a mobile phone for your safety.* Reception may be spotty or nonexistent on the trail, even on an urban walk—especially one embraced by towering trees.

★ *Always carry food and water, even for a short hike.* And bring more water than you think you'll need. (We can't emphasize this enough!)

★ *Ask questions before you set out.* Public-land employees are on hand to help. It's a lot easier to solicit advice before a problem occurs, and it will help you avoid a mishap away from civilization when it's too late to amend an error.

★ *Stay on designated trails.* Even on the most clearly marked trails, you usually reach a point where you have to stop and consider which direction to head. If you become disoriented, don't panic. As soon as you think you may be off-track, stop, assess your current direction, and then retrace your steps to the point where you went astray. Using a map, a compass, and this book, and keeping in mind what you've passed thus far, reorient yourself, and trust your judgment on which way to continue. If you become absolutely unsure of how to continue, return to your vehicle the way you came in. Should you become completely lost and have no idea how to find the trailhead, remaining in place along the trail and waiting for help is most often the best option for adults, and always the best option for children.

★ *Always carry a whistle*—another precaution we can't overemphasize. It may become a lifesaver if you get lost or hurt.

★ *Be especially careful when crossing streams.* Whether you're fording the stream or crossing on a log, make every step count. If you have any doubt about maintaining your balance on a log, ford the stream instead: use a trekking pole or stout stick for balance, and face upstream as you cross. If a stream seems too deep to ford, turn back. Whatever is on the other side isn't worth risking your life for.

★ *Be careful at overlooks.* While these areas may provide spectacular views, they are potentially hazardous. Stay back from the edge of outcrops, and make absolutely sure of your footing—a misstep can mean a nasty and possibly fatal fall.

★ *Standing dead trees and storm-damaged living trees pose a significant hazard to hikers.* These trees may have loose or broken limbs that could fall at any time. While walking beneath trees, and when choosing a spot to rest or enjoy your snack, look up!

★ *Know the symptoms of subnormal body temperature, or hypothermia.* Shivering and forgetfulness are the two most common indicators of this stealthy killer. Hypothermia can occur at any elevation, even in the summer, especially when the hiker is wearing lightweight cotton clothing. If symptoms develop, get to shelter, hot liquids, and dry clothes as soon as possible.

★ *Likewise, know the symptoms of heat exhaustion, or hyperthermia.* Lightheadedness and loss of energy are the first two indicators. If you feel these symptoms, find some shade, drink your water, remove as many layers of clothing as practical, and stay put until you cool down. Marching through heat exhaustion leads to heatstroke—which can be deadly. If you should be sweating and you're not, that's the signature warning sign. Your hike is over at that point: Heatstroke is a life-threatening condition that can cause seizures, convulsions, and eventually death. If you or a companion reaches that point, do whatever you can to cool down, and seek medical attention immediately.

★ *Most important, take along your brain.* A cool, calculating mind is the single most important asset on the trail. Think before you act. Watch your step. Plan ahead. Avoiding accidents before they happen is the best way to ensure a rewarding and relaxing hike.

Watchwords for Flora and Fauna

Hikers should remain aware of the following concerns regarding plant life and wildlife, described in alphabetical order. Almost all of these are very rarely seen; if you're interested in a close-up view, visit the outdoor Arizona-Sonora Desert Museum (2021 N. Kinney Road, Tucson; 520-883-2702, desertmuseum.org).

AFRICANIZED BEES So-called killer bees are found throughout the Tucson area, though not in abundance. They don't attack unless their hive is threatened, so if you see a colony, stay far away. In rare cases, an attack can be deadly, as happened in May 2013 when a rock climber was found dead on his rope, covered with hundreds of stings.

Most hikers will be able to run away, which is the recommended course of action if you're attacked. Try to cover your face and head as much as possible, don't agitate the bees more by swatting, run into the wind if it's blowing, and move as fast as you can. If you reach shelter, such as your car at the trailhead, get in. (Water is not a shelter—the swarm will be waiting when you come up for air.) Bees will follow you for several hundred yards but will give up when you are 0.3–0.5 mile away from their hive. If you get stung, don't try to pluck the stinger out, as this will squeeze the venom deeper into your skin. Instead, scrape it off with your fingernails or a credit card immediately because the venom sac will continue injecting even after the bee is gone. Get medical attention if you've been stung multiple times or you're allergic to bees.

BLACK BEARS You won't find them inhabiting the desert; however, a small but healthy black-bear population lives in the forests of the high mountain ranges, especially the Santa Ritas. Though bear attacks are uncommon, the sight or approach of a bear can give anyone a start. If you encounter one while hiking, remain calm and avoid running or playing dead. Make loud noises to scare off the bear, and back away slowly.

In primitive and remote areas, assume bears are present; in more-developed sites, check on the current bear situation before your hike. Most encounters are food-related, as bears have an exceptional sense of smell and not particularly discriminating tastes. While this is of greater concern to backpackers and campers, on a day hike you may be planning a lunchtime picnic or munching on an energy bar or other snack from time to time. So remain aware and alert.

CACTI Obviously, you'll see many species of cacti in prolific numbers. The ones to watch out for are chollas (below), often nicknamed "jumping cacti" because their pads break off and adhere to a passing animal or hiker at the slightest touch. Their spines are barbed and difficult to remove. Carry a comb to pull off the pads without prick-

TEDDY BEAR CHOLLA
Photographed by Isabel Eve/Shutterstock

ing your fingers. Tweezers on your pocketknife are useful for removing spines. Also watch out for small pincushion cacti on the ground. They're easy to miss—and no fun to sit on while taking a break.

GILA MONSTERS These are the only venomous lizards in the United States. They are unmistakable, their fat bodies ranging from 12 to more than 20 inches long and covered with beady pink, orange, and black scales arranged in rough stripes. They spend much of their lives in underground burrows, but they come out to feed and mate from April to September, and you might see one on a desert trail if you're lucky. Gila monsters move slowly by lizard standards, and they don't attack. The only way to get bitten is to handle the animal or

GILA MONSTER Photographed by JayPierstorff/Shutterstock

accidentally reach under a rock where one happens to be resting—very rare and unlikely. When a Gila monster bites, it hangs on to its prey, allowing the poison to sink in, and is difficult to remove. You literally have to pry the jaws off, and then get medical attention. The bite can be very painful, but the last recorded death was in 1915.

JAVELINA Photographed by Dennis W Donohue/Shutterstock

JAVELINAS These piglike animals live in small herds in the washes surrounding the Tucson suburbs. They've become accustomed to people and their pets, and though they can seem cute and cuddly when young, they have been known to bite. Never feed a javelina (or any other wild animal, for that matter). On trails away from the city, your chances of coming across a herd are low, and the javelinas are likely to run away.

MOSQUITOES In some areas, mosquitoes are known to carry West Nile virus, so take extra care to avoid their bites. Pima County, where most of the hikes in this book are located, recorded its first case of the virus in 2003. However, mosquitoes are not especially dense on Tucson trails, even in the monsoon months, so I carry insect repellent but rarely use it until I hear that obnoxious whine.

MOUNTAIN LIONS Also known as pumas or cougars, these big cats are stealthy and rarely seen, but several dozen are estimated to live in the Tucson area. They have occasionally (every year or two) been sighted on popular trails in Sabino Canyon but are more likely to slink into the undergrowth before you see them. If you do encounter one, leave it alone and it will probably go away. If it doesn't, don't run away—it may chase you, thinking you're prey. Instead, make yourself as large as possible: facing the animal, raise your arms and hiking sticks, open your jacket, and pick up small children. Stare the mountain lion down (remove your sunglasses to make eye contact), and speak loudly but calmly so it identifies you as human. Back away slowly while facing the animal. In the unlikely event that you're attacked, fight back with everything you have available: sticks, rocks, packs, swinging camera, bare hands. Keep standing—you're most vulnerable if you crouch.

POISON IVY, OAK, AND SUMAC While you won't find these plants in the desert, they do grow in riparian and forested areas, though not as abundantly as in wetter parts of the country. Nevertheless, you need to watch out for them.

Recognizing and avoiding poison ivy, oak, and sumac is the most effective way to prevent the painful, itchy rashes associated with them. Poison ivy occurs as a vine or ground cover, 3 leaflets to a leaf; poison oak occurs as either a vine or shrub, also with 3 leaflets; and poison sumac flourishes in swampland, each leaf having 7–13 leaflets. Urushiol, the oil in the sap of these plants, is responsible for the rash. Within 14 hours of exposure, raised lines and/or blisters will appear on your skin, accompanied by a terrible itch. Try to refrain from scratching, though, because bacteria under your fingernails can cause an infection. Wash and dry the affected area thoroughly, applying calamine lotion to help dry out the rash. If the itching or blistering is severe, seek medical attention. To keep from spreading

POISON IVY Photographed by Tom Watson

the misery to someone else, wash not only any exposed parts of your body but also any oil-contaminated clothes, hiking gear, and pets. Long pants and a long-sleeved shirt may offer the best protection.

SCORPIONS Of the estimated 30 species in Arizona, one, the bark scorpion is venomous and potentially lethal (only two deaths have been reported in Arizona since 1968). Light tan in color, this scorpion is barely 1.5 inches long and is most often encountered in woodpiles, under tree bark, or on the undersides of rocks, either near houses or in riparian areas. So don't poke around in fallen wood or pick up rocks or sticks without kicking them over (wearing a hiking boot)

first. A sting from this scorpion is not only dangerous but also extremely painful. Fortunately, an antivenin is available, so if you think you've been stung by a bark scorpion, call the national Poison Help Line at 800-222-1222 or visit webpoisoncontrol.org for advice. The bark scorpion has a slender stinger and pincers; other scorpions tend to be stockier and larger, and their bites less painful. Scorpions hibernate from November to March and are most active at night in warm months.

BARK SCORPION
Photographed by Ernest Cooper/Shutterstock

SNAKES In the Tucson region, you will possibly encounter rattlesnakes or corals, which typically hibernate from November to March. Rattlesnakes like to bask in the sun and won't bite unless threatened. Dry scales at the end of their tails produce the well-known rattle—once you've heard that buzzy, low-pitched sound, you won't forget it! If you encounter a rattler, move away from it; the majority of snakebites are caused by people trying to get too close. If you get bitten, loosen tight clothing (including shoes) on the affected limb, remove jewelry, try to elevate and immobilize the limb, and get help. Admittedly, this isn't

THE HARMLESS KING SNAKE (TOP) AND THE VENOMOUS CORAL SNAKE (BOTTOM)
Photographed by Matt Jeppson/Shutterstock (top) and jokerbethyname/Shutterstock (bottom)

easy to do if you're far from a trailhead, in which case don't attempt to slash and suck—that only makes it worse. Do your best to get to a medical facility, and call 911 or 800-222-1222 for help.

The Arizona coral snake is banded black, white, red, white, and black. The similar-looking but nonvenomous Sonoran mountain king snake is banded white, black, red, black, and white. In other words, if the red band is surrounded by black bands, the snake is harmless. In fact, the snakes you'll most likely see while hiking are nonvenomous species. The best rule is to leave all snakes alone, give them a wide berth as you hike past, and make sure any hiking companions (including dogs) do the same.

When hiking, stick to well-used trails, and wear over-the-ankle boots and loose-fitting long pants. Don't step or put your hands beyond your range of detailed visibility, and avoid wandering around in the dark. Step onto logs and rocks, never over them, and be especially careful when climbing rocks. Avoid walking through dense brush or willow thickets whenever possible.

SPIDERS The fearsome black widow, brown recluse, and tarantula can all deliver a nasty bite, but they tend to live in or near buildings rather than on trails. So keep your eyes open when entering restrooms and other facilities near trailheads. If you get bitten, wash the bite with soap and water to prevent infection, and call 800-222-1222 for advice. The spiders you see on trails are most likely benign.

TICKS These arachnids may be found in brush and tall grass, especially during monsoon season. In the Tucson area, ticks rarely attach themselves to humans but frequently bite dogs, so if your pet is scratching, check it for ticks. Remove ticks that are already embedded, using tweezers made especially for this purpose. Treat the bite with disinfectant solution.

Hunting

Both districts of Saguaro National Park and the Sabino Canyon area prohibit hunting. Other areas see relatively few hunters. Hunting, often limited to archery, is permitted with a license in some parts of the Coronado National Forest and Tucson Mountain Park during certain short seasons. Some lakes are stocked for anglers with licenses. Contact the Arizona Game and Fish Department for detailed information: 602-942-3000, azgfd.com.

Regulations

Many hikes have information boards at their trailheads informing visitors whether horses, mountain bikes, or dogs are allowed on the trails. Some trails are for hikers only. Where dogs are permitted, they must be leashed. Specific rules are listed in the "Comments" section preceding each hike, but these are subject to change, so check ahead.

A few trailheads close after dark. This could present a problem if you can't drive out, like in Saguaro National Park East, which is gated at night.

During the dry months preceding the monsoon season, fire restrictions are often enforced. Campfires are prohibited, as are charcoal grills in picnic areas. Hikers wanting to end their trip with a picnic should bring cold food or use a campstove with a shutoff valve. Smoking is restricted to designated smoking areas. If you hike many of the trails in this book, you'll soon appreciate the damage forest fires have created.

Mountain sheep used to be common in the Santa Catalinas, especially the Pusch Ridge area, but they died out in the 1990s. In November 2013, 30 sheep from the Yuma Mountains, in the south-western corner of the state, were reintroduced to Pusch Ridge. More have been introduced since then, and some births as well as deaths have been reported, but it remains to be seen if a viable population can be established. Dating from before the new herd, signs at trail-heads leading toward Pusch Ridge prohibit dogs and limit humans to developed trails during lambing season.

Trail Etiquette

Always treat trails, wildlife, and fellow hikers with respect. Here are some reminders.

★ *Plan ahead in order to be self-sufficient at all times.* For example, carry necessary supplies for changes in weather or other conditions. A well-planned trip brings satisfaction to you and to others.

★ *Hike on open trails only.*

★ *In seasons or construction areas where road or trail closures* are a possibility, use the websites or phone numbers listed in the "Contacts" section of each hike profile to check conditions before you head out. And don't try to circumvent such closures.

★ *Don't trespass on private land, and obtain all permits and authorization as required.* Leave gates as you found them or as directed by signage.

★ *Be courteous to other hikers, bikers, equestrians, and others* you encounter on the trails.

★ *Never spook wild animals or pets.* An unannounced approach, a sudden movement, or a loud noise startles most critters, and a surprised animal can be dangerous to you, to others, and to itself. Give animals plenty of space.

★ *Observe the yield signs around the region's trailheads and back-country.* Typically they advise hikers to yield to horses, and bikers to yield to both horses and hikers. Observing common courtesy on hills, hikers and bikers should yield to any uphill traffic. When encountering mounted riders or horse packers, hikers can courteously step off the trail, on the downhill side if possible. So that horses can see and hear you, calmly greet their riders before they reach you, and don't dart behind trees. Also resist the urge to pet horses unless you are invited to do so.

★ *Stay on the existing trail,* and don't blaze any new trails.

★ *Practice Leave No Trace principles.* Leave the trail in the same shape you found it in, if not better. Visit lnt.org for more information.

Tips on Hiking the Tucson Area

★ If you're here in midwinter, you're in luck. Apart from an occasional overnight freeze and a rare snow flurry, the desert is perfect for hiking all winter long.

★ If you're here in midsummer, don't despair. Even in the months when temperatures consistently soar over 100°F, you'll enjoy cool hikes in the Santa Catalina Mountains or rise at dawn when the dry desert air is 30°F cooler than the afternoon highs. Sun protection is essential, so use a broad-brimmed hat, sunglasses, and sunscreen. Skin cancer is a bummer.

★ Always carry water. Even in cooler months, the dry air will dehydrate you. In summer, I like to freeze a couple of bottles of water to put in my bag, in addition to cold water. Treat yourself to ice water as the day progresses.

★ Desert trails tend to be rough and rocky, with prickly plants at the ready. Tennis shoes or sandals won't cut it. Wear hiking boots. Merino wool socks are best for keeping your feet cool.

★ The saguaro scenery is uniquely wonderful. Slow down and give yourself time to enjoy it.

★ Undocumented immigrants and drug smugglers may be encountered near the US–Mexico border. This is generally not an issue in the areas covered by this book, but the Santa Ritas south of Madera Canyon and close to the border are best avoided.

HUTCH'S POOL (HIKE 9, PAGE 79)

Saguaro National Park East and Eastern Tucson

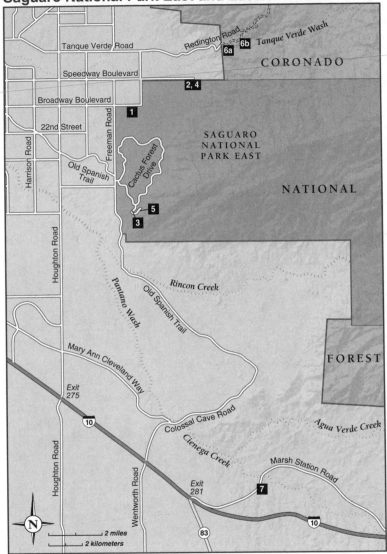

Saguaro
National Park East
and Eastern Tucson

YOU MAY SEE TRAINS PASSING THROUGH ON THE ARIZONA TRAIL (HIKE 7, PAGE 67).

Saguaro National Park East:
Cactus Forest Trail—Mica View Loop

SCENERY: ★ ★ ★
TRAIL CONDITION: ★ ★ ★ ★
CHILDREN: ★ ★ ★ ★
DIFFICULTY: ★ ★
SOLITUDE: ★ ★ ★

SAGUAROS AND OTHER CACTI MIX WITH OCOTILLOS AND MESQUITE TREES ALONG THE TRAIL.

GPS TRAILHEAD COORDINATES: N32° 13.247' W110° 43.570'

DISTANCE & CONFIGURATION: 10.4-mile out-and-back, 10.5 miles via alternate loop

HIKING TIME: 4.25 hours

HIGHLIGHTS: Varied cactus scenery and views of surrounding mountain ranges

ELEVATION: 2,760' at trailhead, 3,100' at high point

ACCESS: Trailhead open daily, 24/7; park open daily, 7 a.m.–sunset. Admission: $20/$15/$10 per car/motorcycle/bicycle or pedestrian, payable at the visitor center (4 miles away) and valid for 1 week in both Saguaro National Park districts; $40 for 1-year car pass. All National Park Service annual passes accepted. Admission passes can be purchased through the QR code posted on the information board at the trailhead. Note that entrance fees may increase by $5 each in 2020.

MAPS: National Geographic–Trails Illustrated 237–*Saguaro National Park*, Green Trails Map 2910S–*Saguaro;* free trail map available at visitor center

FACILITIES: Parking for about 15 vehicles at Broadway Trailhead; no restrooms or fee station

WHEELCHAIR ACCESS: None

COMMENTS: Horses permitted; mountain bikes permitted on Cactus Forest Loop Drive only; no dogs allowed

CONTACTS: SNP Rincon Mountain District Visitor Center, 520-733-5153, nps.gov/sagu

Overview

This gentle stroll crosses almost the entire girth of Saguaro National Park East from north to south. For a quick look at the desert, you can just take the Mica View Loop (1.9 miles). The northern part of the Cactus Forest Trail intersects several other short trails that can be explored with a map. The main trail intersects the Cactus Forest Loop Drive at two points; mountain bikes are allowed on the 2.6-mile-long section of trail between those points. The remains of late-19th-century lime kilns lie along this section.

Route Details

At the trailhead you'll find a register, a map board with a QR code to buy entrance passes, and a signed trail fork. Take the fork bearing left (south-southeast), and after 100 yards take the right fork (south-east) onto the Cactus Forest Trail itself. After about 0.6 mile, you'll cross the sandy Javelina Wash. Surface water rarely flows, but there's enough underground moisture to support a mesquite bosque and numerous low creosote bushes with small, shiny leaves.

Creosote is a tough desert plant with small yellow flowers that bloom after early-spring rains, resulting in cottony white fruits. The plant is nicknamed greasewood because it contains many resins, waxes, and oils that repel insects and grazing animals and give off a distinct pungent fragrance after the first monsoonal rains wash them out. Tucsonans patiently endure the scorching, parched early summer to celebrate that special smell signaling the first cooling rains of late July: "The desert smells like rain!"

A short way past the wash, the Cholla Trail branches left while the Cactus Forest Trail branches right. A few hundred yards farther, the Mica View Trail branches right; this can be a short (1.9-mile) loop back to the trailhead or an alternate return from the out-and-back

Saguaro National Park East:
Cactus Forest Trail–Mica View Loop

Cactus Forest Trail. Another 0.2 mile takes you to the Mesquite Trail, branching left, but our trail goes straight (south) another 0.6 mile to the paved Cactus Forest Loop Drive, where there is parking for five cars if you're visiting by car or mountain bike.

A sign indicates that it's another 0.9 mile south to the lime kilns, which will be on the left. The foundations on the right, about halfway to the kilns, are the remains of an early ranger station. At the kilns, there isn't much to see, but a notice board provides interesting history and background.

A hundred yards past the kilns, a sign to the left designates a dead-end trail that goes 0.4 mile southeast to Lime Falls, which are dry most of the year. The trail is not very clear, and following it involves crossing a stream several times, but occasional cairns should get you there if you choose.

Cacti, including saguaros, have been plentiful so far, but for a few hundred yards past the Lime Falls turnoff, there are few cacti and almost no saguaros. Soon the trail begins to climb noticeably for the first time on this hike, reaching a ridge with excellent views back at the Santa Catalinas. Cross a couple more ridges, and old-growth

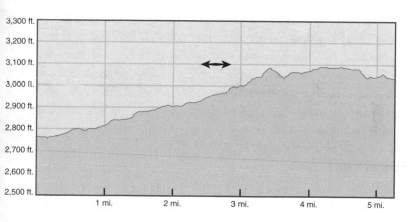

saguaros reappear. This is the most scenic part of the trail. Eventually, the trail crosses the unsigned but substantial Javelina West Wash and continues to the second intersection with the paved Cactus Forest Loop Drive, 1.5 miles from the lime kilns. Here you'll find another small parking area for six cars; this is also the end of the trail section where mountain bikes are permitted.

It's 0.9 mile from here to the end of the trail, heading southwest. This is the rockiest and least-maintained part of the trail, and car noise begins to intrude as you approach the final trailhead. To my mind it's the least attractive section, but there is a pretty stand of teddy bear cholla shortly before the end.

Cactus Forest Trail ends at Old Spanish Trail—a fairly busy road, not a hiking trail. From this road, the ending trailhead is unmarked at the time of this writing; there's simply a dirt shoulder on which a handful of cars can park. So if you were thinking of a car shuttle, you just have to know where this dirt shoulder is. If you have a good city map, you can find it on the left side of Old Spanish Trail, 1.5 miles south of the park exit and 0.2 mile south of Irvington Road. Good luck!

I prefer to make this an out-and-back hike and, when I return to the Mica View Loop turnoff, take Mica View to the left to make an alternate return to the starting trailhead. This trail passes through the Mica View Picnic Area, which can be reached by car from Cactus Forest Loop Drive. It has a dozen mostly unshaded picnic tables with barbecue grills and a pit toilet, but no water. The area is named for views of Mica Mountain, which at 8,666 feet is the highest point in both the Saguaro National Park and the Rincon Mountains. It's about 12 miles east of the picnic area. From here it's an easy and clear 0.7 mile to the trailhead.

Directions

From the northwest, take I-10 to Exit 258 and take Congress Avenue east to Broadway Boulevard. Drive 15 miles on Broadway Boulevard to the trailhead. From the southeast, take I-10 to Exit 275 and drive north on Houghton Road 11 miles to Broadway; then turn right (east) and drive 2.8 miles to the trailhead.

Saguaro National Park East: Douglas Spring and Bridal Wreath Falls Trails

SCENERY: ★ ★ ★ ★

TRAIL CONDITION: ★ ★ ★ ★

CHILDREN: ★ ★ (Douglas Spring)
★ ★ ★ (Bridal Wreath Falls)

DIFFICULTY: ★ ★ ★ ★ (Douglas Spring)
★ ★ ★ (Bridal Wreath Falls)

SOLITUDE: ★ ★ ★ ★ (Douglas Spring)
★ ★ ★ (Bridal Wreath Falls)

A VIEW OF THE SANTA CATALINA MOUNTAINS NORTH OF THE TRAIL

GPS TRAILHEAD COORDINATES: N32° 14.110' W110° 41.215'

DISTANCE & CONFIGURATION: 13-mile out-and-back to Douglas Spring, 5.8-mile out-and-back to Bridal Wreath Falls

HIKING TIME: 7.5 hours to Douglas Spring, 3.5 hours to Bridal Wreath Falls

HIGHLIGHTS: Changing scenery, seasonal waterfall

ELEVATION: 2,750' at trailhead, 3,800' at Bridal Wreath Falls, 4,700' at Douglas Spring

Saguaro National Park East:
Douglas Spring and Bridal Wreath Falls Trails

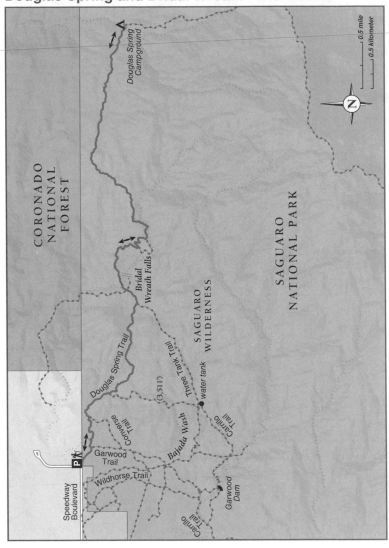

ACCESS: Trailhead open daily, 24/7; park open daily, 7 a.m.–sunset. Admission: $20/$15/$10 per car/motorcycle/ bicycle or pedestrian, payable at the visitor center (7 miles away) and valid for 1 week in both Saguaro National Park (SNP) districts; $40 for 1-year car pass. All National Park Service annual passes accepted. Smartphone users can buy an admission pass through the QR code posted on the information board at the trailhead. Note that entrance fees may increase by $5 each in 2020.

MAPS: National Geographic–Trails Illustrated 237–*Saguaro National Park,* Green Trails Map 2910S–*Saguaro;* free trail map available at visitor center

FACILITIES: Parking for about 20 cars at Douglas Spring Trailhead (horse trailers can park at Wildhorse Gate, 200 yards away); shaded benches but no restrooms; no fee station

WHEELCHAIR ACCESS: None

COMMENTS: Horses permitted; no dogs or mountain bikes allowed. Water sources are seasonal and must be treated.

CONTACTS: Rincon Mountain District Visitor Center, 520-733-5153, nps.gov/sagu

Overview

The Douglas Spring Trail is one of two long routes giving access to the west side of the Rincon Mountains from Tucson (the other is the Tanque Verde Ridge Trail; see Hike 5, page 56). Beginning in lowland mesquite forest thick with cacti and ocotillos, the trail soon climbs up small canyons, through open grasslands, and into mid-elevation

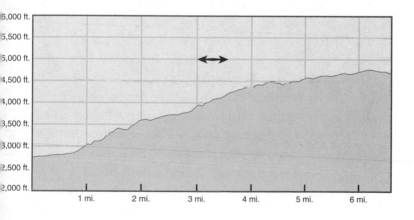

oak–piñon–juniper woodlands, providing a variety of scenery and birdlife. Many hikers visit the seasonal Bridal Wreath Falls, reached by a short side trail and a good destination for an easier family hike. For an all-day hike, go as far as Douglas Spring, where there is a small backcountry campground (see Nearby Attractions). Hardy, fit hikers can go even farther.

Route Details

From the trailhead, the flat, wide, comfortable trail heads east, passing a trail register just before going by a turnoff to your right for the Garwood Dam Loop (see Hike 4, page 49) 0.2 mile from the trailhead. The trail becomes increasingly narrow as it crosses a dry wash and meanders through a mesquite forest. At 0.6 mile, a sign indicates the Converse Trail (shown on some maps as the Wentworth Trail) to your right. Now you start climbing, aided in places by shallow stairs with log or stone risers designed to prevent erosion.

As you climb, glance over your left shoulder for fine views of the salmon-colored buildings of the Tanque Verde Ranch below and the Santa Catalinas on the north horizon. The trail swings southeast, briefly follows the right bank of a steep, rocky little canyon, and comes to a junction at mile 1.5, with the Carrillo Trail bearing right (south). Continue southeast to admire a strangely knobby peak on the horizon at 120° southeast—this is Tanque Verde Peak, reached by its namesake trail (see Hike 5).

About 0.5 mile later, the trail flattens briefly, and another landmark appears on the horizon. Helens Dome, a blocky, oblong peak at 80° east, will frequently appear in front of you for the rest of the ascent. You'll drop across a sandy wash that is usually dry and then continue your ascent up the left side of the increasingly steep and rocky drainage, which may have occasional pools of water in it. You'll top out at a point where a pair of aspen trees have decided to spend their lives together, rooted in the middle of the sand, searching deeply for whatever moisture they can find.

The trail flattens and enters an open area of grasses interspersed with cacti, but with few trees or saguaros. In 1989, most of this area was burned by the Chiva Fire, which raged over 9,500 acres high into the Rincon Mountains beyond Douglas Spring. Three decades later, it's hard to see where the damage was done.

A sign indicates the turnoff to the Three Tank Trail, on the right at the 2.3-mile mark—our trail continues east and fairly flat for another 0.2 mile to the junction with the Bridal Wreath Falls

A MATURE SAGUARO TOWERS OVER A HIKER ON THE DOUGLAS SPRING TRAIL.

Trail. The falls trail goes right, slightly south of east, and the Douglas Spring Trail goes left, slightly north of east. (A third trail heads north to the park boundary.)

If you choose the falls, it's barely 0.25 mile to their base, surrounded by a grove of surprisingly large trees that escaped the devastation of the 1989 fire. The waterfall is seasonal and dry most months of the year, barely dripping at other times. If you hit it lucky, after an early-spring snowmelt or soon after a late-summer monsoon, you could see it in full spate, but this lasts just several days rather than weeks. Still, it makes a good turnaround point for the shorter hike.

Continuing on the Douglas Spring Trail, you'll cross a stream about 100 yards beyond the junction. If it's running, there's water in the falls. The trail is narrow but clear as it climbs gently through open grassland, with grand views of the Rincons ahead and around, and distant vistas of the Tucson valley behind. This section lacks shade and can be tedious on a hot day. Soon you'll pass through a region of shin-stabbing yuccas, often decorated with impressively tall, flowering spikes that persist throughout the winter.

After a series of switchbacks, you'll notice the flora changing again and becoming bushier, with small trees. On the right, a shallow, rocky watercourse may have pools of water or even a trickling stream. The variety of vegetation and splashes of water attract wildlife. When I hiked in March, I met an excited young woman who told me that she had just seen her first mountain lion. All I saw were a pair of deer, some squirrels, and a variety of birds. By April, you should keep your eyes open for lizards and especially rattlesnakes.

For the final almost 2 miles, the trail undulates, cresting false ridges and dropping down, occasionally crossing a damp spot if there has been rain. It finally reaches the high point a few hundred yards before Douglas Spring Campground. A sign indicates an elevation of 4,800 feet, but it's about 100 feet lower on most topographic maps. Water is available for several months of the year from the spring, which is on the right of the trail just before the campground, but it shouldn't be relied on and needs to be treated. The campground has a handful of campsites and an ugly vault toilet—reportedly it was far prettier before the 1989 fire.

Tough, fit hikers can continue south on the Douglas Spring Trail about 2.4 miles to Cow Head Saddle (at about 6,150') and beyond. With a car shuttle, you could take the Tanque Verde Ridge Trail (see page 56) from Cow Head another 11.6 miles—this is a 20.5-mile all-day hike that I did once, 35 years ago. Most hikers will turn around and retrace their steps to the trailhead.

Nearby Attractions

Though this book is a guide for day hikers, it's worth noting that some of Tucson's best backcountry backpacking is found in Saguaro National Park's Rincon Mountain East District. The entire park has only six small backcountry-camping areas, all in this district. Douglas Spring is the closest to a parking area and gives access to trails crossing the high Rincon peaks. A permit is necessary, available from the visitor center for $8 per night, per site. Rangers are on hand to discuss recent reports on the availability of water and possible routes into the high Rincons. No campfires are allowed here.

For more information about the visitor center, see the next hike.

Directions

From Saguaro National Park's eastern visitor center, drive west 0.1 mile to Old Spanish Trail, turn right, and drive north 0.1 mile. Where Old Spanish Trail veers left (northwest), continue north on the minor Freeman Road 3.6 miles to Speedway Boulevard; then turn right (east) on Speedway and drive 3 miles to the trailhead.

From I-10 in northwest Tucson, take Exit 257 and drive east on Speedway Boulevard. Continue 17.5 miles until Speedway dead-ends, and turn right into the parking area for the Douglas Spring Trailhead.

From Vail, southeast of Tucson, take I-10 north to Exit 275 and drive north on Houghton Road 12 miles; then turn right (east) on Speedway and drive 5 miles to the trailhead.

Saguaro National Park
East: Freeman Homestead Trail

SCENERY: ★ ★ ★ ★
TRAIL CONDITION: ★ ★ ★ ★
CHILDREN: ★ ★ ★ ★
DIFFICULTY: ★
SOLITUDE: ★ ★ ★

SAGUAROS—SOME WITH 15–20 ARMS—ARE ABUNDANT ON THIS TRAIL.

GPS TRAILHEAD COORDINATES: N32° 09.916' W110° 43.561'

DISTANCE & CONFIGURATION: 1.1-mile balloon

HIKING TIME: 1 hour

HIGHLIGHTS: Exploratory nature and history trail; saguaros galore

ELEVATION: 3,105' at trailhead, 2,919' at low point

ACCESS: Open daily, 7 a.m.–sunset. Admission: $20/$15/$10 per car/motorcycle/bicycle or pedestrian, payable at the visitor center (almost 2 miles away) and valid for 1 week in both Saguaro National Park districts; $40 for a 1-year car pass. All National Park Service annual passes accepted. Note that entrance fees may increase by $5 each in 2020.

MAPS: National Geographic–Trails Illustrated 237–*Saguaro National Park*, Green Trails Map 2910S–*Saguaro*; free trail map available at visitor center

FACILITIES: Visitor center (see Nearby Attractions); Javelina Picnic Area (with pit toilets and parking) 0.3 mile away; parking at trailhead for 7 cars; no water

WHEELCHAIR ACCESS: None

COMMENTS: No pets, horses, or mountain bikes allowed. Don't return after sunset—the gates close soon after, and you can't drive out.

CONTACTS: Rincon Mountain District Visitor Center, 520-733-5153, nps.gov/sagu

Overview

This is a fun loop for families, with several interpretive stations providing information about the desert for adults, as well as kid-oriented questions or puzzles for the younger members of your group. The stands of saguaros are especially thick and impressive in this area. There are steps and sandy spots in a few places, so strollers aren't recommended. Sure, you could lope around the trail in 20 minutes, but it's worth taking the time and enjoying this introduction to the national park.

Route Details

The trail gets its name from Safford and Viola Freeman, who applied to homestead 640 acres in the area in 1929 and built a three-room adobe house here in 1930, with outbuildings housing a separate kitchen and storage areas. They built an access road that later became Old Spanish Trail, which you may have driven to reach Saguaro National Park. The family lived on the property until 1934, the year after Saguaro National Monument was established. After they left to return to Tucson, Safford's father continued to homestead here. The family sold the house and land to the federal government in 1951, and the acreage became part of the national monument. Apart from remnants of some foundations, nothing is left of the Freeman family's home except an open space in the desert vegetation.

If you can't find a spot in the parking area at the trailhead, you can park at the nearby Javelina Picnic Area (see Hike 5, page 56) and walk back along the road. From the trailhead, the path goes southwest; formed of loose sand and small rocks, it descends imperceptibly through creosote, Mormon tea, prickly pear, and other plants. Just over 0.1 mile along the trail, you reach a fork. Signs indicate that you should take the right fork, taking the loop counterclockwise. This will help you meet and read interpretive trail signs more easily.

As you descend, occasionally down simple steps, you'll see ever more saguaros. Some of them are huge, up to 50 feet in height and carrying 15 or 20 arms. Reportedly, there's a 30-arm saguaro here,

Saguaro National Park East: Freeman Homestead Trail

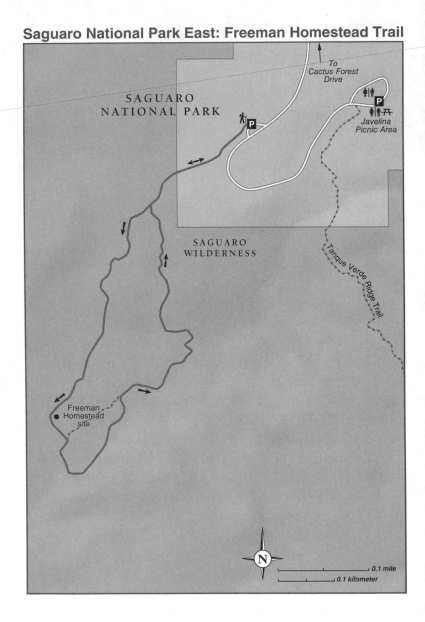

SAGUARO
NATIONAL PARK

To
Cactus Forest
Drive

Javelina
Picnic Area

SAGUARO
WILDERNESS

Tanque Verde Ridge Trail

Freeman
Homestead
site

N

0.1 mile

0.1 kilometer

but I haven't found it. These mature cacti might exceed 150 years in age, and most of their growing is done in the latter half of their lives. It can take 15 years for seedlings to reach more than a foot in height, and 75 years before they start growing their distinctive arms. Nevertheless, they can flower and fruit while still quite young, and a 4-foot-tall, 30-year-old saguaro may boast its first distinctive crown of white flowers in May, followed by red fruits in June.

When you reach the homestead site, you'll find a couple of benches where you can sit down, take in the views, and consider what life must have been like here more than 80 years ago. The homestead itself was behind the benches, and parts of the concrete floor slab remain. A berm near the foundation suggests that a fence once stood here, supposedly made of ocotillo branches.

After you finish looking over the area, continue by skirting widely to the right (west) side of the site and finding the trail, which continues south and reaches a wash and cliff about 0.1 mile south of the homestead. Turn sharply left and follow the wash as it swings east and northeast. There isn't much of a trail here—you simply follow the bottom of the wash, aided by an occasional concrete slab etched with an arrow.

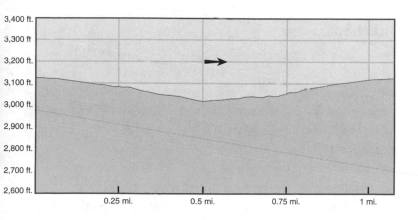

About 0.3 mile along the wash, which, fortunately, is almost always dry, look for the trail breaking away to the north from the left bank.

The trail climbs north a few hundred yards and reaches the fork that you took near the beginning of the hike. Turn right to return to the trailhead.

Nearby Attractions

The **Rincon Mountain District Visitor Center** of Saguaro National Park (the park was upgraded from a national monument in 1994) is also the park headquarters. Located at the park entrance, at 3693 Old Spanish Trail, it's open daily, 9 a.m.–5 p.m., except December 25. Inside you'll find restrooms, a gift shop, exhibits, and rangers on duty who can provide maps, information, and backcountry-camping permits. No food or drink is sold, but water is available so you can fill your own bottle.

Continuing into the park, the 8-mile, one-way Cactus Forest Loop Drive (the only road in the eastern sector of the park) provides excellent views and access to various overlooks and trails. If you haven't been here before, you should certainly experience it before going to the Freeman Homestead Trail.

Directions

Coming from the northwest, take I-10 to Exit 259 in central Tucson. Drive east on 22nd Street 11.3 miles to Old Spanish Trail. Bear right onto Old Spanish Trail, following it southeast 4 miles to the park entrance and visitor center. Shortly past the visitor center, Cactus Forest Loop Drive forks—take the right fork and drive 1.2 miles to the trailhead.

Coming from the southeast, take I-10 to Exit 275 north of Vail and drive north on Houghton Road 8 miles to Escalante Road. Turn right (east) on Escalante and drive 2 miles to Old Spanish Trail, where you turn left and drive north 0.3 mile to the park entrance on the right. Shortly past the visitor center, Cactus Forest Loop Drive forks—take the right fork and drive 1.2 miles to the trailhead.

Saguaro National Park
East: Garwood Dam Loop

SCENERY: ★ ★ ★ ★
TRAIL CONDITION: ★ ★ ★ ★
CHILDREN: ★ ★ ★ ★
DIFFICULTY: ★ ★ ★
SOLITUDE: ★ ★ ★

EXPLORING GARWOOD DAM

GPS TRAILHEAD COORDINATES: N32° 14.110' W110° 41.215'

DISTANCE & CONFIGURATION: 5.6-mile loop

HIKING TIME: 3 hours

HIGHLIGHTS: Superb saguaro forest, historic dam

ELEVATION: 2,750' at trailhead, 3,511' on Carrillo Trail

ACCESS: Trailhead open daily, 24/7; park open daily, 7 a.m.–sunset. Admission: $20/$15/$10 per car/motorcycle/bicycle or pedestrian, payable at the visitor center (7 miles away) and valid for 1 week in both Saguaro National Park districts; $40 for a 1-year car pass. All National Park Service annual passes accepted. Smartphone users can buy an admission pass through the QR code posted on the information board at the trailhead. Note that entrance fees may increase by $5 each in 2020.

MAPS: National Geographic–Trails Illustrated 237–*Saguaro National Park*, Green Trails Map 2910S–*Saguaro;* free trail map available at visitor center

Saguaro National Park East: Garwood Dam Loop

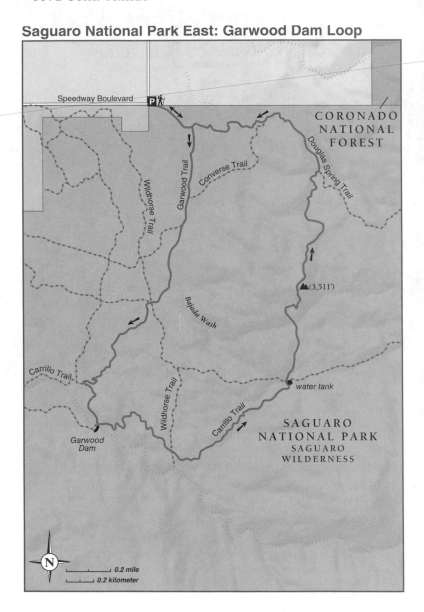

FACILITIES: Parking for about 20 cars at Douglas Spring Trailhead (horse trailers park at Wildhorse Gate, 200 yards away); shaded benches but no restrooms

WHEELCHAIR ACCESS: None

COMMENTS: Horses permitted; no dogs or mountain bikes allowed

CONTACTS: Rincon Mountain District Visitor Center, 520-733-5153, nps.gov/sagu

Overview

This enjoyable loop is one of dozens that can be put together from the dense network of trails lacing the northwestern corner of the national park. Unlike most of the other loops, this one provides 760 feet of elevation gain, allowing much better views than the lower trails immediately to the west. The thick saguaro forest includes the rare cristate form of the cactus, and a small dam and water tank provide insights into Tucson's history three-quarters of a century ago.

Route Details

From the trailhead, the flat, wide, comfortable Douglas Spring Trail (see page 37) heads east, passing a trail register just before the signed Garwood Trail junction, 0.2 mile from the trailhead, where you turn

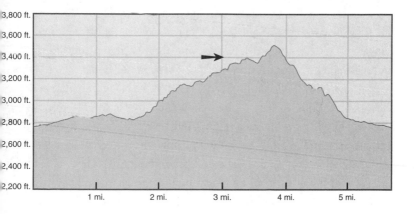

right (south) onto a sandy, narrow trail. The sand is compacted at just the right consistency—hard enough to walk on without slipping yet soft enough to provide cushioning for your feet. Perfect!

The surroundings are lush by desert standards, with mesquite trees, creosote bushes, ocotillos, and many different cacti providing cover for wildlife. This is a wonderful place to hike during the first rains of the monsoon, when the pungent perfumes of the summer-dried plants are released.

Looking straight ahead (south), you'll admire the views of Tanque Verde Ridge that dominate the horizon. Almost 0.5 mile along, a metal sign marks the Converse Trail, which is marked as Wentworth Trail on many maps. Continue south on the Garwood Trail 0.4 mile farther, crossing the signed and usually dry Bajada Wash. In another 0.1 mile you come to a junction where six trails converge. Here there are three signs, so check them all to make sure you continue on the Garwood Trail, which soon swings around to the southwest. After 0.4 mile, cross another dry wash, this one remarkable for the cristate saguaro growing next to it.

Soon the trail follows a couple of gentle switchbacks, taking you to a minor ridge where you intersect the Carrillo Trail, named after Emilio Carrillo, who built his Buena Vista Ranch in 1868 on what later became the Tanque Verde Ranch (see Nearby Attractions). Take this trail left, going briefly east and then swinging south and southeast and climbing around the back of the minor ridge.

About 0.3 mile along the Carrillo Trail, you'll reach the substantial Garwood Dam on your right. It was built by Nelson Garwood, who bought 480 acres in the area in 1945. To reach the property, he constructed a rudimentary road by dragging railroad ties behind his jeep along what is now the Garwood Trail, though it's hard to see signs of that today. In 1948 he began building the dam and a ranch house, although he never brought cattle onto his property. The dam was intended to supply permanent water for the house, and he lived there with his family for some years while selling segments of his property. In 1959 he sold everything, and the house stood empty for

THE TOP OF A CRISTATE SAGUARO

years. Vandals burned it in the early 1970s, and the National Park Service took over the property soon after.

There may be pools of water behind the dam, and you'll enjoy good views from here of the Tucson valley and the Tucson Mountains beyond. It's a good spot for wildflowers in spring, and the smooth rocks behind the dam invite you to sit and have a snack. While the dam looks sturdy, it's dangerous to walk across.

Continue climbing generally east from the dam along the Carrillo Trail, passing the intersection with the north and south arms of the Wildhorse Trail, 0.6 mile away, and continuing up to a round steel tank, 0.8 mile beyond the intersection. Several tanks are marked on park maps. Originally, most of these were natural rock pools that were deep and shaded enough to hold water year-round; they were also important places for the original Native American inhabitants and later for cattle ranchers who leased these lands. Today they are of historical interest—the last grazing lease in the park expired in 1979.

The steel tank is unusual in that it's not a natural formation. It was constructed to hold water from nearby Rock Spring. About 8 feet high and 20 feet across, it's quite an impressive structure, albeit no longer in use. Tanks would often get stagnant and covered with green algae, hence the ubiquitous name Tanque Verde, Spanish for "green tank." To solve the problem, ranchers used to stock the tanks with goldfish to eat the algae.

Four trails converge at the tank, which you need to walk around and behind to find the continuation of the Carrillo Trail, now climbing north. Ahead of you is a gently sloping pyramidal peak, marked simply as 3,511 on topographic maps. This will be the highest point of our loop, 0.5 mile north of the tank.

From the summit, enjoy great views of the Santa Catalinas to the north, the Rincons to the east, Tanque Verde Ridge to the south, and the Tucson valley to the east. You can even pick out your car waiting in the parking lot just over a mile away to the northwest.

Carrillo Trail now descends quite steeply north and, after several hundred yards, flattens and follows a narrow gully that might require wading after heavy rains. The route goes west briefly before swinging north again and reaching the intersection with the Douglas Spring Trail, which takes you to the parking area, 1.5 miles away. Turn left (northwest) and descend along the north side of a hill with expansive views of the Santa Catalinas and Tanque Verde Ranch. In places, the route has been stabilized with wide steps formed with log or stone risers. Soon you'll pass the turnoff to the left for the Converse Trail, cross a sandy wash, and continue past the beginning of the Garwood Trail and to the parking area.

Nearby Attractions

Tanque Verde Ranch (866-413-3833, tanqueverderanch.com) is a high-end dude ranch immediately north of the parking area. With 75 rooms and 180 horses, there's a perfect mount for everyone. While guided horseback riding, sometimes into the national park, is the main focus, the ranch also prides itself on its comfortable rooms and suites, fine dining, and barbecue meals served at the end of a trail ride, sometimes with old-fashioned Western entertainment. Riding lessons are available, as are children's programs. Mountain biking, fishing, and hiking are offered, and guests can use indoor and outdoor pools, a nature center, and a tennis court, as well as avail themselves of spa, yoga, fitness, wellness, and arts-and-crafts programs.

All-inclusive rates run $460–$900 per night (double occupancy); prices include tax, fees, meals, and all activities and are dependent on season and room. Rooms with just breakfast and à la carte activities start around $150.

Directions

From Saguaro National Park's eastern visitor center, drive west 0.1 mile to Old Spanish Trail, turn right, and drive north 0.1 mile. Where Old Spanish Trail veers left (northwest), continue north on the minor Freeman Road 3.6 miles to Speedway Boulevard; then turn right (east) on Speedway and drive 3 miles to the trailhead.

From I-10 in northwest Tucson, take Exit 257 and drive east on Speedway Boulevard. Continue 17.5 miles until Speedway dead-ends, and turn right into the parking area for the Douglas Spring Trailhead.

From Vail, southeast of Tucson, take I-10 north to Exit 275 and drive north on Houghton Road 12 miles; then turn right (east) on Speedway and drive 5 miles to the trailhead.

Saguaro National Park
East: Tanque Verde Ridge Trail

YUCCAS ON THE MIDLEVELS OF THE TANQUE VERDE RIDGE TRAIL

SCENERY: ★ ★ ★ ★
TRAIL CONDITION: ★ ★ ★
CHILDREN: ★ ★ ★
DIFFICULTY: ★ ★ ★ ★
SOLITUDE: ★ ★ ★ ★ ★

GPS TRAILHEAD COORDINATES: N32° 09.938' W110° 43.437'

DISTANCE & CONFIGURATION: 13.8-mile out-and-back

HIKING TIME: 9 hours

HIGHLIGHTS: Views of the Tucson Basin surrounded by the Santa Catalina, Tucson, and Santa Rita Mountains; vegetation changes

ELEVATION: 3,115' at trailhead, 5,983' at Juniper Basin Campground

ACCESS: Open daily, 7 a.m.–sunset. Admission: $20/$15/$10 per car/motorcycle/bicycle or pedestrian, payable at the visitor center (1.6 miles away) and valid for 1 week in both districts; $40 for a 1-year car pass; all National Park Service annual passes accepted. Note that entrance fees may increase by $5 each in 2020.

MAPS: National Geographic–Trails Illustrated 237–*Saguaro National Park,* Green Trails Map 2910S–*Saguaro;* free trail map available at visitor center

FACILITIES: Javelina Picnic Area (with pit toilets and parking) at trailhead; visitor center; no water

WHEELCHAIR ACCESS: None except at Javelina Picnic Area

COMMENTS: Hikers only. Make sure you return before sunset—the gates close soon after, and you can't drive out.

CONTACTS: Rincon Mountain District Visitor Center, 520-733-5153, nps.gov/sagu

Overview

Tanque Verde Ridge is the westernmost mountain finger pointing toward Tucson from the Rincons. As you climb it, views of all the other ranges surrounding the city open, and on clear days you can see into Mexico as well as many of the other minor ranges in southern Arizona. Starting in lush desert vegetation, you'll climb through grasslands and into piñon–juniper vegetation to the small Juniper Basin campsite.

Route Details

The trailhead is on the right side of the entrance of the Javelina Picnic Area and is clearly marked with an information board and map. Looking south from the picnic area, you can see Tanque Verde Ridge, up which you'll be hiking, on the horizon.

The flat, narrow trail heads southwest through thick desert vegetation of cacti and ocotillos. During your first 5 minutes of hiking, you'll swing southeast and drop, crossing a small wash that's usually dry, before reaching a trail register where you're encouraged to sign in. This is the last signpost until you reach the Juniper Basin Campground, almost 7 miles up the ridge.

The trail now climbs southeast toward Tanque Verde Ridge. A few false trails break off to the right, affording better views of Tucson, but you'll keep climbing and dipping a couple of times through almost imperceptible dry streambeds. Views of the Tucson basin will open up. Looking a few miles due west, you'll see an open area dotted with rows of tiny . . . what? With binoculars, you can make out that these are aircraft, wrapped and stored in what locals call The Boneyard. There are more than 4,400 military planes here, of no use at the present but which might fly or be used for parts in the future. See Nearby Attractions for more details.

As you climb toward 4,000 feet elevation, you'll pass through thick stands of ocotillo (*Fouquieria splendens*), one of my favorite desert plants. For much of the year they look like bare, dead, thorny sticks reaching 20 feet tall, but after rains they sprout short-lived,

Saguaro National Park East: Tanque Verde Ridge Trail

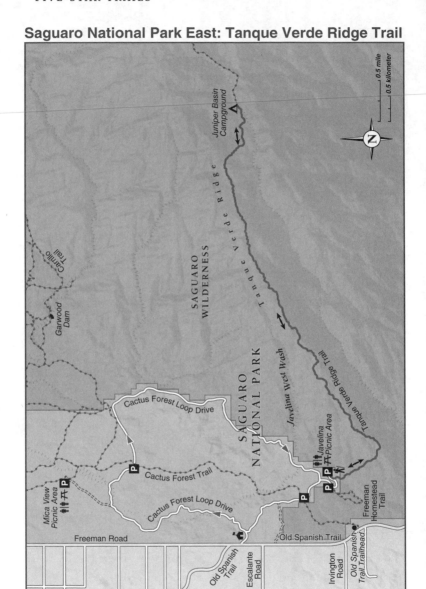

small leaves along the stems. In dry months, the leaves are shed and the cycle can repeat itself during the year. Ocotillos have bright-red clusters of sweet tubular flowers at the tips of the sticks from March through early summer; swaying colorfully in spring breezes, they attract hummingbirds, orioles, and carpenter bees. Traditionally, the stems have been planted to make impenetrable fences and sometimes have been used as support for mud-daubed walls and shade ramadas. Some of the largest specimens can live as long as 100 years.

Just over a mile into the hike, after climbing steadily, the clear trail flattens out for about 100 yards and then climbs through a few rock slabs where the path is not obvious—look for cairns to guide you through the bare spots. As you climb the ridge, you'll find many more sections where you'll need to keep your eyes open for cairns. Meanwhile, you can now admire the views of the Catalinas to the north and the Santa Ritas to the south. Southern Arizona's highest peak, Mount Wrightson, is the uppermost point, roughly in the middle of the Santa Ritas, and if you follow the view of the range to the right, the westernmost peak is Elephant Head. With a tiny dose of imagination, you can see how that peak got its name.

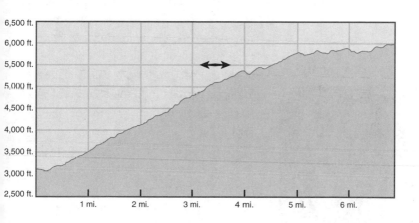

At around 4,300 feet elevation, roughly 2 miles into the hike, you'll notice a sudden change in vegetation: the cacti and ocotillo disappear, and you're walking through open grasslands. The trail is narrow but clear and ascends gently, with a few flattish stretches. Occasional bushes and small trees attract birds, making these grasslands far from monotonous, but the trail lacks obvious landmarks such as creek crossings or signposts.

Roughly 4 miles into the hike, at about 5,300 feet elevation, comes the first of several small but noticeable drops in the trail, and the going gets harder. Bordered by small but viciously sharp agave plants, the path becomes indistinct, though little cairns come through as guides. Bushes and small trees such as oaks, junipers, madrones, and pines start becoming more prominent.

At this point you could decide upon your own trail end and head back, because you'll have seen all the best views. But if you find it somehow unsatisfying to turn around without having reached some kind of destination, you'll certainly enjoy pushing on along the rough trail. Few people hike up here; I saw no one on my last two hikes. As long as you keep your eyes open for cairns where needed, you'll have no problem in reaching the signpost for the Juniper Basin Campground, just a few feet short of the 6,000-foot-elevation mark. There are no views here, except for the surrounding junipers; the three simple campsites (which require $8/night permits from the visitor center) share a couple of metal, bearproof boxes for food storage and have fire rings.

CLARET CUP CACTUS

As you enter the campsite, a small seep provides unreliable water in wetter months but dries out for much of the year. A sign indicates that it's 2.1 miles farther to Tanque Verde Peak, the highest point on the ridge at 7,049 feet. Strong hikers could continue to the peak and return for an 18-mile out-and-back trip. The trail to the peak is no more difficult than it has been thus far. The return along the way you came seems easier, not only because you're descending but also because you can see the trail crossing the bare rocky patches more clearly when looking down than looking up.

Nearby Attractions

The **Pima Air & Space Museum** (6000 E. Valencia Road, Tucson; 520-574-0462; pimaair.org) exhibits more than 300 aircraft in a mainly outdoor setting. Exhibits range from World War II planes to JFK's Air Force One. Open daily, 9 a.m.–5 p.m.; admission is $16.50. Adjoining the museum, Davis-Monthan Air Force Base is home to the 4,400 mothballed military aircraft locally known as The Boneyard. Guided bus tours are offered for $10 Monday–Friday. Reservations are required and must be made at least 10 days in advance at pima air.org/tour-boneyard. Drive along Kolb Road between Escalante and Valencia Roads to appreciate this strange sight for free.

See Freeman Homestead Trail (Hike 3, page 44) for details about the visitor center, 1.6 miles away.

Directions

Coming from the northwest, take I-10 to Exit 259 in central Tucson. Drive east on 22nd Street 11.3 miles to Old Spanish Trail. Bear right onto Old Spanish Trail, following it southeast 4 miles to the park entrance and visitor center. Shortly past the visitor center, Cactus Forest Loop Drive forks—take the right fork and drive 1.6 miles to the trailhead.

Coming from the southeast, take I-10 to Exit 275 north of Vail and drive north on Houghton Road 8 miles to Escalante Road. Turn right (east) on Escalante and drive 2 miles to Old Spanish Trail, where you turn left and drive north 0.3 mile to the park entrance on the right. Shortly past the visitor center, Cactus Forest Loop Drive forks—take the right fork and drive 1.6 miles to the trailhead.

6 Tanque Verde Falls Trails

SCENERY: ★ ★ ★ ★ ★

TRAIL CONDITION:
★ ★ ★ (Main Lower and
Upper Trails)
★ (Scrambling to Falls)

CHILDREN: ★ ★ ★

DIFFICULTY: ★ ★ (Main Lower
and Upper Trails)
★ ★ ★ ★ ★
(Scrambling to Falls)

SOLITUDE: ★ ★ ★

A BEACH AND SWIMMING HOLE ABOVE TANQUE VERDE FALLS

GPS TRAILHEAD COORDINATES: N32° 15.240' W110° 39.919' (Lower Trail);
N32° 15.443' W110° 39.356' (Upper Trail)

DISTANCE & CONFIGURATION: 1.4-mile out-and-back (Lower Trail to lower fall); about
2-mile out-and-back (to main fall); 0.6-mile out-and-back (Upper Trail)

HIKING TIME: Less than an hour to lower fall; 1–2 hours to main fall; less than an hour on
Upper Trail

HIGHLIGHTS: Swimming holes, sandy beaches, waterfalls

ELEVATION: 3,102'–2,880' (Lower Trail), 3,315'–3,150' (Upper Trail)

ACCESS: Open daily, 24/7; free

MAPS: National Geographic–Trails Illustrated 237–*Saguaro National Park*, Green Trails Map
2910S–*Saguaro*

FACILITIES: Parking available on unpaved Redington Road

WHEELCHAIR ACCESS: None

COMMENTS: Short, steep trails descend from the road to Tanque Verde Canyon. Reaching the falls necessitates scrambling over large boulders and possibly wading up the canyon (second set of ratings). Wet rocks can be dangerously slippery, and deadly flash floods can occur during monsoon rains (July–September).

CONTACTS: Sabino Canyon Visitor Center, 520-749-8700; fs.usda.gov/coronado

Overview

Tanque Verde Falls is known throughout the Tucson area as one of the most spectacular but also the most deadly places in Southern Arizona. More than 30 people have died here over the decades, some having been swept away in flash floods and others perishing when they misjudged a daredevil jump from high canyon walls into deceptively inviting pools. So why go?

Below and above the falls are some of Tucson's best beaches and swimming holes. You have to time it just right—they may be bone dry after months with no rain, and you don't want to be there when a heavy rain is forecast.

Route Details

Two short trails lead into the well-vegetated Tanque Verde Canyon. You could hike them both or choose one.

The Lower Trail is signed from Redington Road, and there is a rough parking lot across the road from the trailhead. The trail descends immediately and passes large metal signs warning of death or injury if swimming or diving at the falls. The vegetation is lush with several species of cacti and other desert plants. After a 0.4-mile descent you'll reach Tanque Verde Creek, where there are beaches and swimming holes to enjoy. You could stop here and enjoy the water and sun.

The waterfalls are to your left (east) and are actually a series of falls, with the biggest drop being the final fall, which is around 80 feet. I got as far as the 15-foot-high lowest fall, some 0.3 mile

Tanque Verde Falls Trails

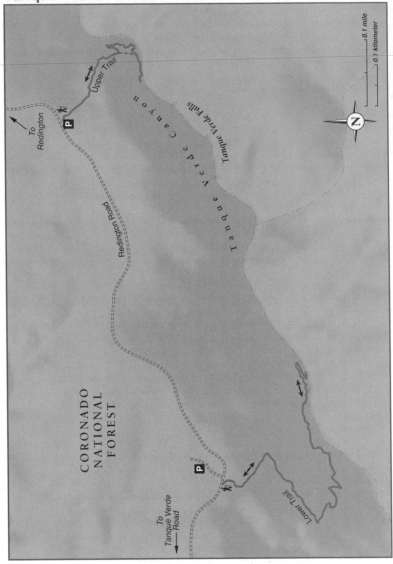

away, and then found that the bouldering and wading needed to continue were a bit too much for this 65-year-old body. Continuing on is a challenge for fit young hikers with route-finding skills (though you can't really get lost; you follow the river up to the final fall.) Googling "hiking to Tanque Verde Falls" will reveal some YouTube videos of folks scrambling up the canyon to the base of the biggest falls.

To reach the trailhead for the Upper Trail, continue along Redington Road 0.7 mile, past the parking area for the Lower Trail. The Upper Trail is not signed at the road, but if you look carefully to your right (south) you'll see metal warning signs set back from the road. There is no designated parking area here, but there are several pullouts on the dirt road where you can park.

The rocky and narrow Upper Trail descends into the canyon steeply and passes through a gate designed to dissuade horses and mountain bikes. A few minutes later there is a sign warning about flash floods in the canyon below. Here the trail forks. The left fork is the easiest way down to the river below. Again, there are sweet little beaches and swimming holes here, and just hanging out is fun. To get to the top of the falls, head right along the river less than 0.2 mile

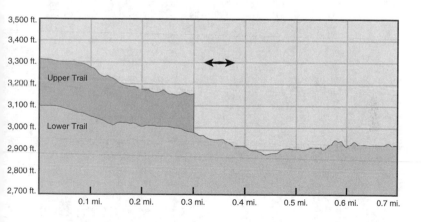

until you reach a bright-yellow sign that reads DANGEROUS AREA: DEADLY WATERFALLS AHEAD. The top of the falls is not far away, but you can't see it unless you ignore the sign and scramble closer. This book does not suggest that you do that. Enjoy the beaches and swimming holes above the falls, and be aware of flash flood warnings.

Directions

From the intersection of Grant Road, Kolb Road, and Tanque Verde Road (locally known as the Dinosaur McDonald's corner) in northeastern Tucson head northeast and then east on Tanque Verde Road 7.9 miles to where it becomes Redington Road. After 3 miles the road becomes unpaved (but suitable for cars). Continue 0.7 mile to the lower trailhead parking area on the left.

THE FIRST SMALL WATERFALL ON THE LOWER TRAIL TO TANQUE VERDE FALLS

Zimmerman Trailhead to Three Bridges

SCENERY: ★ ★ ★ ★
TRAIL CONDITION: ★ ★ ★
CHILDREN: ★ ★ ★ ★
DIFFICULTY: ★ ★
SOLITUDE: ★ ★ ★ ★

UNION PACIFIC TRAINS CROSSING CIENEGA CREEK

GPS TRAILHEAD COORDINATES: N32° 00.831' W110° 38.849'

DISTANCE & CONFIGURATION: 1.8-mile loop

HIKING TIME: 1 hour

HIGHLIGHTS: Trains, bridges, riparian preserve

ELEVATION: 3,435' at trailhead, 3,325' at Cienega Creek

ACCESS: Open daily, sunrise–sunset; no fees or permits required for trail use; permit required for hiking off-trail

MAPS: *Arizona National Scenic Trail Passage 8: Rincon Valley* (aztrail.org/wp-content /uploads/2018/01/08_RinconValley.pdf)

FACILITIES: Parking area with 1 picnic table

WHEELCHAIR ACCESS: From trailhead about 0.1 mile to a memorial view bench

COMMENTS: This is part of the Arizona National Scenic Trail. Horses, mountain bikes, and leashed dogs are allowed.

CONTACTS: Arizona Trail Association, 602-252-4794, aztrail.org; Pima County Natural Resources, Parks and Recreation, 520-724-5000, pima.gov/nrpr

Zimmerman Trailhead to Three Bridges

Arizona National Scenic Trail

Union Pacific Railroad

Marsh Station Road

cable line

Arizona National Scenic Trail

Cienega Creek

Union Pacific Railroad

Cienega Creek

Arizona National Scenic Trail

Marsh Station Road

CIENEGA CREEK NATURAL PRESERVE

To I-10 Exit 281 and Tucson

Arizona National Scenic Trail

N

0.1 mile

0.1 kilometer

Overview

This short loop begins in the desert and drops quickly into Davidson Canyon, which features the lush and protected riparian habitat of Cienega Creek Natural Preserve. Three bridges jostle for space over the creek: two carry Union Pacific Railroad trains, and the third is for Marsh Station Road (called Frontage Road or Pantano Road on older maps). It's an unusual synthesis of technology and nature.

Route Details

The trailhead formerly named for Davidson Canyon was officially renamed in 2012 to honor Gabriel "Gabe" Zimmerman (1980–2011), who was an active user of this part of the Arizona Trail. Zimmerman, an aide to former US Representative Gabrielle Giffords, was one of six people killed on January 8, 2011, when a gunman opened fire while the congresswoman was conducting a meet and greet with Tucson voters. Thirteen people were injured, most seriously Giffords, who resigned from her position and continues to work on her recovery while making appearances in support of issues important to her.

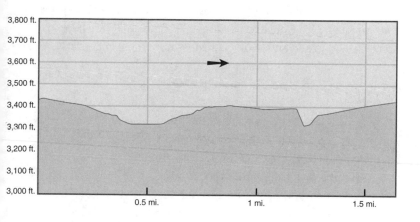

The trailhead features a wheelchair-accessible gate with a life-size plaque of Zimmerman. Walk a few steps south-southeast on a paved trail to the intersection with the Arizona National Scenic Trail (AZT), where you turn sharply left. Before continuing north, check out the plaque just beyond the intersection, which identifies the Rincon Mountains to the north and lists the names of the 19 victims of the 2011 shooting. Nearby is a wheelchair-accessible viewpoint.

The AZT goes north along a straight, wide, rocky path following an underground cable line. After 0.1 mile the trail forks; follow the sign to the right (northeast) for the AZT. The trail descends gently through mixed desert vegetation, with small cacti scattered through ocotillos and creosote bushes. Crush a couple of creosote leaves to appreciate the pungent odor these bushes release after a monsoon.

Within a few hundred yards, you'll see below you a swath of trees that is Davidson Canyon. The trail narrows and drops easily into the wide bed of Cienega Creek, which is dry for much of the year; however, the 15-foot-high packed-earth banks attest to centuries of flow in the past; be prepared for a creek crossing after heavy rains.

The trail follows the creek bottom as it meanders left (west, then north again) through mature stands of Arizona sycamore, aspens, cottonwoods, and other trees. This is an excellent area for bird-watching. Occasional posts with AZT signs indicate the route along Cienega Creek, and hiking here does not require a permit. The rest of the creek is part of a natural preserve, and you'll need a free permit from Pima County to visit it (see "Contacts").

Soon you'll see bridge trestles towering high above the creek. From this angle it's hard to tell why the bridge was built, but if you wait awhile, you'll discover that this is a railroad bridge carrying westbound Union Pacific trains. Most of them are long, colorful freight trains coming through numerous times a day; Amtrak rolls past three times a week on its New Orleans–Los Angeles Sunset Limited route.

The trail dips under the bridge and continues about 100 yards past it to a gap on the right bank of the creek. You might see a pile of rocks or a small AZT sign there. You've hiked just 0.6 mile from the trailhead.

Climb northeast through the gap in the bank, and follow it as it makes a couple of switchbacks to the flatlands above. Two more bridges come into view to the west. The highest and largest is the eastbound Union Pacific railroad bridge; below it is the light-colored bridge carrying Marsh Station Road vehicular traffic over the creek. Look south to glimpse traffic on I-10, almost 2 miles away, and farther south to views of the Santa Rita Mountains and the Whetstone Mountains to the southeast.

The trail reaches the cable line and turns sharply left (southwest), reaching Marsh Station Road after 0.2 mile. At the road you can return the way you came for a 2.7-mile out-and-back, or continue left to the parking lot for the 1.8-mile loop. The AZT crosses the road and continues under the eastbound railroad bridge high on the right side of Cienega Creek. Our trail back to the parking lot necessitates crossing the Marsh Station Road bridge, which does not have a pedestrian walkway. Traffic is sparse, though, and with care you should be able to cross without a problem.

The far end of the bridge crosses over the westbound railway tracks. Immediately past the road bridge, on the right, is a brightly colored sign for the Cienega Creek Natural Preserve and a small parking area for AZT users. This is also an excellent observation point for train aficionados. Opposite the sign, on the left side of the road, a short dirt road leads down to the railway tracks and a trail follows the cable line to the south-southeast. Hike along this trail a few minutes to return to the Gabe Zimmerman Trailhead.

Directions

From Tucson, drive east roughly 20 miles on I-10 to Exit 281 (AZ 83). Immediately after leaving the freeway, turn left over the freeway and follow a sign for Frontage Road to Marsh Station Road. Turn right, then right again, onto Marsh Station Road, and drive 3 miles to the Gabe Zimmerman Trailhead parking area, on your right.

Sabino Canyon

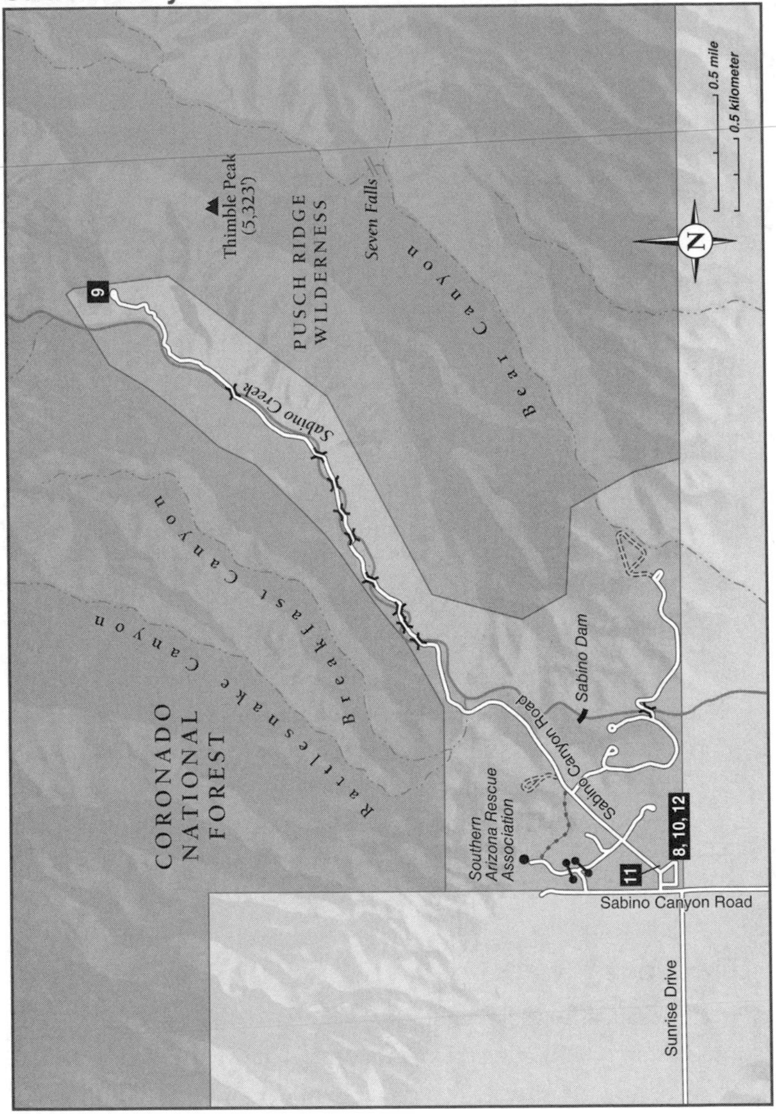

Thimble Peak
(5,323')

PUSCH RIDGE
WILDERNESS

Seven Falls

Bear Canyon

Sabino Creek

Breakfast Canyon

Rattlesnake Canyon

CORONADO
NATIONAL
FOREST

Sabino Dam

Sabino Canyon Road

Southern
Arizona Rescue
Association

Sabino Canyon Road

Sunrise Drive

0.5 mile
0.5 kilometer

N

9

8, 10, 12

11

Sabino Canyon

BLOOMS ON A SAGUARO CACTUS

Blackett's Ridge Trail

SCENERY: ★ ★ ★ ★ ★
TRAIL CONDITION: ★ ★ ★
CHILDREN: ★ ★
DIFFICULTY: ★ ★ ★ ★
SOLITUDE: ★ ★ ★

VIEW OF TUCSON FROM BLACKETT'S RIDGE

GPS TRAILHEAD COORDINATES: N32° 18.560' W110° 49.317'

DISTANCE & CONFIGURATION: 6.2-mile out-and-back

HIKING TIME: 3 hours

HIGHLIGHTS: Splendid views of Sabino Canyon from vertical cliffs; Bear Canyon and city views; bird-watching; a good workout

ELEVATION: 2,725' at parking lot, 4,409' at trail's end

ACCESS: Open daily, 24/7; parking $5/$10/$20 for day/week/year; all National Park Service annual passes accepted

MAPS: Green Trails Map 2886S–*Santa Catalina Mountains*, USFS *Pusch Ridge Wilderness*, USGS *Sabino Canyon;* free map at visitor center

FACILITIES: Visitor center, flush toilets, vending machines

WHEELCHAIR ACCESS: Visitor center, toilets, Sabino Canyon Road (page 90), and the first 0.8 mile of the trail (requires some pushes)

COMMENTS: No pets; no bicycles; horses permitted but rarely encountered. Large parking lot fills as early as 9 a.m. on spring weekends—and if you park on the road outside, you risk a ticket. (From mid-October through April, an overflow parking lot is open at the Southern Arizona Rescue Association, a 0.5-mile drive north. A trail from here makes a 0.3-mile shortcut to Sabino Canyon Road; see map.) The last trail section is signed and mapped as 1.7 miles, but I measured it at about 1.3 miles on my GPS. (It certainly felt like 1.7!)

CONTACTS: Sabino Canyon Visitor Center, 520-749-8700, fs.usda.gov/coronado

Overview

Some Tucsonans take a masochistic pleasure in running up this steep trail and pride themselves on getting from the parking lot to the summit in well under an hour. Others claim to climb it most days of the week to stay in shape. I prefer to take my time to enjoy the best views in Sabino Canyon and keep an eye out for the flora and fauna.

Route Details

From the southeast end of the parking lot, the trail follows the same route as the Phoneline Trail (page 84) for the first 1.4 miles until it reaches a junction signed BLACKETT'S RIDGE TRAIL #48, 1.7 MILES TO END OF TRAIL. From 1937 and into the 1940s, a teacher at the Southern Arizona School for Boys named Don Everett explored this area on foot and horseback, accompanied by some of his students. He would label unnamed landmarks after some of the boys, in this case after a student named Blackett.

At the junction, turn east (right), and within a few yards you'll see a table-size flat boulder shaded by a mesquite tree on the right. You're just 300 feet in elevation above the parking lot, so this rock is a good place to sit and consider whether you have enough water and stamina to climb the steep 1,400 feet from here to the top.

The trail starts climbing moderately for a few hundred yards and then begins a series of steep switchbacks up the western nose of the ridge. Sometimes I've been accompanied by a raven that likes to hang out around these steep rocks. During the summer, lizards abound, and occasional snakes and Gila monsters show up on the sharp, rocky, narrow trail.

Blackett's Ridge Trail

After 15–20 minutes of climbing, watch for a flat area on the left, which gives you a chance to step off the trail and admire the burgeoning view of Tucson to the west and Sabino Canyon to the north and east (your left). Above you are two or three convenient flattish areas to break your hike, all with fine views, so don't feel that you need to stop in the middle of the narrow trail for a drink of water.

Because this trail is short and steep, you'll find that the plant life varies with both elevation and time of year. What you may see at 3,000 feet elevation arrives later in the year at 4,000 feet.

Look for small blue, yellow, white, and orange desert flowers in March; palo verde trees densely blossoming yellow in April; and ocotillos showing off red flowers into May, when saguaros join in with their white blooms. Into the hot months of June and July, many agaves along the trail thrust their 20-foot-high spikes into the air, topped with dozens of tight, bowl-like clusters of yellow and orange flowers. Barrel cacti are among the latest of the cacti to bloom, with a ring of golden flowers forming a striking crown.

After the initial series of switchbacks, the obvious trail includes some shorter, flatter sections, and your first views of Bear Canyon

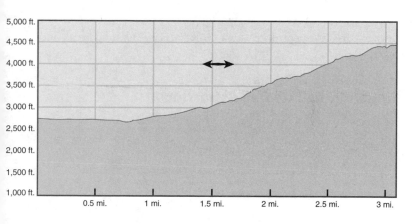

appear to the right (south). About halfway up, the trail climbs through some rocky slabs where the route isn't always obvious, but if you simply keep climbing, you'll find the trail within a minute or two. If you don't, look back and around and you should see the route. You have to keep climbing.

Next comes a clear trail heading to a peak; it's false. There are at least two—some folks say three—false summits. I think it depends on how out of breath you feel after this climb. When you come to a narrow ridge with exciting views of Sabino Canyon and Bear Canyon on either side, you'll know you're near the end of the trail. By now, you will have noticed distinctive Thimble Peak (5,323') on the horizon in front of you, 1.5 miles northeast.

Suddenly, a small marker tells you that you've arrived at the end of the trail. Beyond this sign, you can scramble down a rough path for a couple hundred feet before it peters out in a frighteningly steep saddle; this area is called Saddleback on many maps.

To your left, the sheer cliffs drop hundreds of feet, so watch your step. Most of Sabino Canyon Road is visible, with occasional shuttle vehicles crossing the bridges more than 1,000 feet below. From mid-February to mid-October, swallows are commonly seen swooping along the clifftop as they busily capture insects, and hawks and vultures often patrol the area. Enjoy a bird-watching break and then return the way you came.

Directions and Nearby Attractions

See Hike 11, Sabino Canyon Road, page 90.

Hutch's Pool

SCENERY: ★ ★ ★ ★
TRAIL CONDITION: ★ ★ ★ ★
CHILDREN: ★ ★ ★
DIFFICULTY: ★ ★ ★
SOLITUDE: ★ ★ ★ ★

HUTCH'S POOL

GPS TRAILHEAD COORDINATES: N32° 20.626' W110° 46.831'

DISTANCE & CONFIGURATION: 8.2-mile out-and-back using the trailhead shuttle, 15.8-mile out-and-back from the parking lot

HIKING TIME: 4.5 hours (using trailhead shuttle)

HIGHLIGHTS: Year-round water deep enough to swim in; attractive high-desert scenery

ELEVATION: 3,334' at trailhead, 3,850' at Hutch's Pool

ACCESS: Open daily, 24/7; parking $5/$10/$20 for day/week/year; all National Park Service annual passes accepted

MAPS: Green Trails Map 2886S–*Santa Catalina Mountains*, USFS *Pusch Ridge Wilderness*, USGS *Sabino Canyon*

FACILITIES: Visitor center, flush toilets, vending machines at parking lot; motorized shuttle to trailhead

WHEELCHAIR ACCESS: None on the trail

Hutch's Pool

West Fork Trail

Hutch's
Pool

Sabino Creek

West Fork Trail

CORONADO
NATIONAL
FOREST
PUSCH RIDGE
WILDERNESS

Sabino Creek

Sabino Canyon Trail

Stop
#9

Sabino Canyon Road

Phoneline Trail

Thimble Peak
(5,323')

N

0.2 mile
0.2 kilometer

COMMENTS: No pets. Maps and USFS signs show the distance as 8.2 miles; my GPS showed 7.8 miles. Motorized shuttles run up Sabino Canyon daily except Thanksgiving, December 25, and an occasional maintenance day, leaving the visitor center on the hour and half hour from 9 a.m. to 4 p.m. Fares for the round-trip are $10/adults, $5/children ages 3–12, and free for infants. The 21-passenger enclosed gasoline buses will be replaced by 62-passenger electric shuttles in the second half of 2019; these will feature indoor and out-door seating and audio commentary in various languages via individual headsets. You can reach the trailhead via Sabino Canyon Road (see page 90) and add 7.6 miles out-and-back, or you can join the trail via the Phoneline Trail (see page 84) for longer, all-day hikes.

CONTACTS: Sabino Canyon Visitor Center, 520-749-8700, fs.usda.gov/coronado

Overview

Hutch's Pool comes in a distinct second to Seven Falls as a destination for water-seeking hikers in the Sabino Canyon area, but it ranks first as a year-round water attraction, as it doesn't dry up completely. The first section from the trailhead, the only steep one, rewards you with great views back down Sabino Canyon. Continuing on, you encounter a variety of landscapes, including a steep canyon and high desert grasslands.

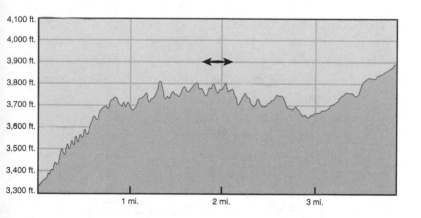

Route Details

Beginning from the last shuttle stop, Sabino Canyon Trail #23 climbs via wide stairs to . . . hey, not so fast. On a recent hike I almost stepped on a rattlesnake curled up on the stairs, less than 100 yards away from the end of the road. I waited awhile and then walked around what I guessed to be the back of the snake—hard to tell when they're coiled up. Keep your eyes open, even if you just got off the shuttle. Of course, I've hiked on these stairs many times without seeing a rattler, so you shouldn't think this particular trail is any more likely to provide you with a snake sighting. That could happen on almost any hike in this book, so be aware.

Climb almost 0.5 mile on well-graded stairs and switchbacks to the intersection with Phoneline Trail #27. This short section is the most heavily used, with shuttle riders experiencing a taste of desert hiking and Phoneline Trail users making a final descent to the road. The views back down Sabino Canyon, with the Phoneline Trail clinging high to the left side, are increasingly impressive as you climb. At the junction, make a hard left to continue northwest along the Sabino Canyon Trail.

The trail continues to climb, but the switchbacks become less frequent. After 0.4 mile the route flattens and follows high up the right side of the canyon, with good views of the canyon below and glimpses of Sabino Creek. After a few hundred flat yards, the trail crosses over the top of a large rock outcrop then diverges away from the canyon to the east, passing through a landscape of grasses, bushes, spring flowers, and occasional yuccas and agaves, but relatively few cacti.

Soon the trail swings back to the north, still mainly flat. About 1 mile from the rock outcrop, it begins to drop toward an intersection of streams coming from several small canyons and flowing into Sabino Creek. A sign indicates West Fork Trail #24, where you turn left (north-northwest) and cross Box Canyon Stream, seeking cairns to guide you. Boulders in the stream may help keep your feet dry if the water is flowing high.

Beyond the stream, the trail heads generally west and, after a few hundred yards, switchbacks suddenly and turns north briefly before continuing west-northwest through golden fields of poppies in March and April, or grasslands and bushes the rest of the year. A few hundred yards farther, you'll pass a football field–size flat area to your left that has stone fire rings where people have camped. Sabino Creek is nearby. Beyond, the trail enters thick riparian woodlands and follows the right bank of the creek. Canyons, streams, grasslands, and now woodlands—this hike certainly offers variety.

Roughly 1.25 miles along the West Fork Trail, cross to the left bank of Sabino Creek, using stepping-stones or possibly wading after monsoons. Cairns show the route. Continue on the left bank for 0.3 mile and look for a 1.5-foot-tall pile of rocks on the right of the trail: this marks the turnoff to Hutch's Pool, barely 100 yards away but not visible from the trail. If you miss the turnoff and start climbing steeply, you'll be on the 5-mile trail to Romero Pass, so go back and look again.

The year-round pool is hidden in a secluded slot canyon, with a tiny beach for wading at the south end and small cliffs and a pretty little waterfall at the north end, where the water is reportedly up to 15 feet deep—check first before plunging in. In winter and spring the water is bracingly cold, but it warms to just right in summer, when the hike is extremely hot (carry plenty of water). At any time, this attractive high-desert pool makes an excellent destination for lunch, after which you return the way you came.

Nearby Attractions

See Hike 11, Sabino Canyon Road, page 90.

Directions

Follow the directions for Hike 11. After you park, either take the shuttle or walk 3.7 miles up Sabino Canyon Road to the trailhead.

Phoneline Trail

APPROACHING THE FLAT ROCK ON THE PHONELINE TRAIL

GPS TRAILHEAD COORDINATES: N32° 18.560' W110° 49.317'

DISTANCE & CONFIGURATION: 4-mile loop, 11-mile out-and-back, or 5.5-mile point-to-point and return on Sabino Canyon Road hike or shuttle

HIKING TIME: 1.75 hours for loop, 5 hours for out-and-back, 4 hours to hike out and return along Sabino Canyon Road

HIGHLIGHTS: Saguaros galore, spring flowers, and soaring canyon views, plus creek and dam views on the loop

ELEVATION: 2,725' at parking lot, 3,190' at high point on short loop, 3,660' at high point on out-and-back

ACCESS: Open daily, 24/7; parking $5/$10/$20 for day/week/year; all National Park Service annual passes accepted

MAPS: Green Trails Map 2886S–*Santa Catalina Mountains,* USFS *Pusch Ridge Wilderness,* USGS *Sabino Canyon;* free map at visitor center

FACILITIES: Visitor center, flush toilets, vending machines

WHEELCHAIR ACCESS: Visitor center, toilets, Sabino Canyon Road (page 90), and the first 0.8 mile of the trail (requires some pushes)

COMMENTS: No pets, no bicycles, horses permitted but rarely encountered. Large parking lot fills by 9 a.m. on spring weekends—and if you park on the road outside, you risk a ticket. (From mid-October through April, an overflow parking lot is open at the Southern Arizona Rescue Association, a 0.5-mile drive north. A trail from here makes a 0.3-mile shortcut to Sabino Canyon Road; see map.)

CONTACTS: Sabino Canyon Visitor Center, 520-749-8700, fs.usda.gov/coronado

Overview

When I have out-of-town guests who want a fun hike where they can see plenty of saguaros and great desert and canyon scenery without taking up too much time and energy, I inevitably take them on the shortened loop of the Phoneline Link Trail. Everyone loves it. With a bit more time on one's hands, the complete Phoneline Trail, which hangs dramatically between clifftop and canyon bottom, makes a hiker feel like an eagle soaring in and out of gullies. Some hikers take the Sabino Canyon shuttle (see page 81) to the end of Sabino Canyon Road and hike the Phoneline Trail in reverse.

Route Details

From the southeast end of the parking lot, the trail begins with a sign for Bear Canyon Trailhead, adjacent to a map and a drinking fountain. Walk east on a flat track wide enough to hike six abreast. After about 100 yards, the optional 0.25-mile Bajada Loop Nature Trail is to the left. It's wheelchair-accessible but unpaved, so helpful pushes may be needed to enjoy this educational experience.

The wide track terminates at Bear Canyon Road, almost 0.5 mile from the parking lot. Follow the road to your right 0.25 mile until you reach a restroom (with flush toilets and drinking water), which you should consider using because the Phoneline Trail is narrow and exposed with no convenient bushes. Stop 2 on the Bear Canyon

Phoneline Trail

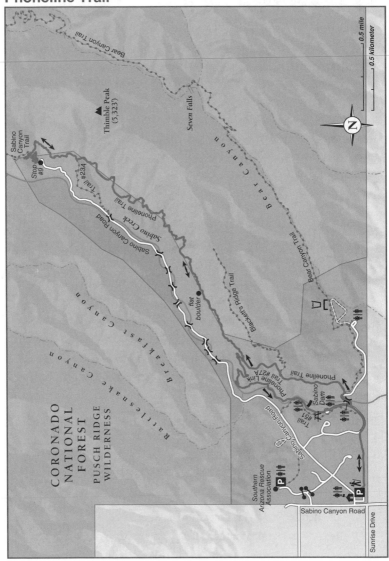

shuttle route is outside the restroom. Turn right (east), following the sign for Sabino Dam East and Bear Canyon. The road crosses a bridge over Sabino Creek—a bridge that can be knee-deep in overflowing water during spring runoffs or autumn monsoons. In that case, take your boots off and wade carefully across. Usually the creek trickles pleasantly under the bridge, but it dries up completely in summer.

Immediately past the bridge, the road comes to a T-junction; cross the junction to find a sign for Phoneline Trail #27. Climb the narrow, rocky trail, and almost immediately find another signed T-junction, where you turn left and start climbing steadily east and swinging quickly north. You are following the route of the historic phone line that used to be the main link between Tucson and the Palisade Ranger Station on Mount Lemmon before the road now known as the Catalina Highway was built.

The climb is gentle—about 500 feet of elevation gain in almost a mile—but provides increasingly open views of the saguaro forest and, in spring, wildflowers. Almost 0.6 mile along the trail, a signed junction to the right (east) indicates the Blackett's Ridge Trail (page 4).

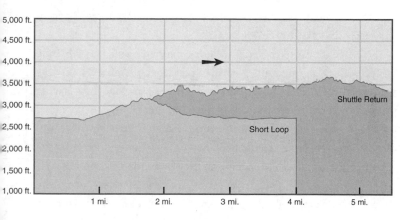

The Phoneline Trail continues northeast and then swings dramatically around to the northwest, hugging the canyon contours.

Views of Sabino Canyon Road below and downtown Tucson, 11 miles to the southwest, become increasingly grand until you reach a trail fork 0.4 mile beyond the Blackett's Ridge junction. Here you have the choice of continuing along the main Phoneline Trail to your right or taking the Phoneline Link Trail #27A to your left—the latter is the shortened loop, described later in this section.

The Phoneline Trail is clear but narrow, with nowhere to step off, climbing gently northeast with increasingly splendid views of the canyon. To the left of the trail, the canyon wall tumbles steeply to the road hundreds of feet below, and to the right it climbs to the canyon top, so finding a place to take a break is exceedingly difficult. Look for a semi trailer–size flat boulder on the left side after about 0.7 mile—it makes a great place to stop for a snack while thinking about how and when this massive piece of rock detached itself from the cliffs above. Onward, the airy route swoops and slants like a hawk, following the contours of the canyon until it reaches the intersection with the Historic Sabino Trail #23A, 2 miles beyond the flat boulder. Here you could descend steeply on a rough and rocky 0.7-mile trail to Sabino Canyon Road (page 90), reaching the road just above Bridge 9 and below Shuttle Stop 8.

Continuing on the main Phoneline Trail another 0.5 mile brings you to the junction with Sabino Canyon Trail #23. At this point, you could turn around and return the way you came, saving yourself the final steep descent, or turn left and zigzag steeply down 0.5 mile to the end of Sabino Canyon Road at Shuttle Stop 9. From Stop 9, you can either continue down Sabino Canyon Road to the visitor center or retrace your hike on the Phoneline Trail.

Phoneline Link Trail #27A makes a convenient descent for the shortened loop, switchbacking toward the road below. After 0.6 mile, you'll reach a trail junction marked CREEK TRAIL #52, where you turn left. (If you turn right, you'll cross Sabino Creek, which can be dry or knee-deep depending on the season, to reach Sabino Canyon Road at Shuttle Stop 1, just 0.1 mile away.)

Creek Trail doesn't have many water views, meandering instead through desert woodland of mesquite and palo verde trees, often accompanied by birdsong. One early morning I surprised a family of javelinas on this section—you never know what you might see. After 0.2 mile, Creek Trail crosses a sandy wash that's almost always dry—look for the brown trail marker on the other side. The trail follows the right side of the wash 0.1 mile and then crosses it again; look for stones marking the way. Another 0.1 mile brings you to an unsigned fork. Going left takes you along the left bank of Sabino Creek, and you arrive at the east side of small Sabino Dam after 0.2 mile. Going right crosses the creek (you might have to wade) and gets you to the west side of the dam. This side also gives access to Bluff Trail #51, leading to Sabino Canyon Road (0.2 mile) and other trails paralleling the main trail.

Above the dam is so-called Sabino Lake, which is dry in summer and a shallow pond in other months. Below the dam, water holes and sliding rocks are popular with kids in spring and fall but dry in summer. Whichever side of the dam you end up on, continue about 0.3 mile to the road bridge that you crossed near the beginning of the hike, and return along the road and wide, flat track to the parking area.

Directions and Nearby Attractions

See next hike.

Sabino Canyon Road

SCENERY: ★ ★ ★ ★
TRAIL CONDITION: ★ ★ ★ ★ ★
CHILDREN: ★ ★ ★ ★ ★
DIFFICULTY: ★
SOLITUDE: ★

SABINO CANYON POOLS BY SHUTTLE STOP 8

GPS TRAILHEAD COORDINATES: N32° 18.600' W110° 49.359'

DISTANCE & CONFIGURATION: 7.6-mile out-and-back

HIKING TIME: 2.5 hours

HIGHLIGHTS: Seasonal swimming holes; canyon views; family-friendly

ELEVATION: 2,725' at visitor center, 3,350' at trail's end

ACCESS: Open daily, 24/7; parking $5/$10/$20 for day/week/year; all National Park Service annual passes accepted

MAPS: Green Trails Map 2886S–*Santa Catalina Mountains,* USFS *Pusch Ridge Wilderness,* USGS *Sabino Canyon;* free map at visitor center. Note, though, that this is one of the few hikes you can do without a map—you can't get lost on the road.

FACILITIES: Visitor center, flush toilets, vending machines, motorized shuttle

WHEELCHAIR ACCESS: The entire road is wheelchair-accessible but will require a helping push on some gentle climbs.

COMMENTS: Best wheelchair hike. Bicycles permitted daily, 5 p.m.–9 a.m., except Wednesday and Saturday. No pets allowed. Motorized shuttles run up Sabino Canyon daily except Thanksgiving, December 25, and an occasional maintenance day, leaving the visitor center on the hour and half hour from 9 a.m. to 4 p.m. Fares for the round-trip are $10/ adults, $5/children ages 3–12, and free for infants. The 21-passenger enclosed gasoline buses will be replaced by 62-passenger electric shuttles in the second half of 2019; these will feature indoor and outdoor seating and audio commentary in various languages via individual headsets. The large parking lot fills by 9 a.m. on spring weekends—if you park on the road outside, you risk a ticket. (From mid-October through April, an overflow parking lot is open at the Southern Arizona Rescue Association, a 0.5-mile drive north. A trail from here makes a 0.3-mile shortcut to Sabino Canyon Road; see map.)

CONTACTS: Sabino Canyon Visitor Center, 520-749-8700, fs.usda.gov/coronado

Overview

This paved road is closed to vehicles (except for limited bicycle and shuttle traffic) and provides walkers, joggers, parents with strollers, and folks in wheelchairs with a gorgeous hiking experience—it's the best place in Tucson to get into the wilderness with a wheelchair. The tour shuttle has a flat fee that allows all-day on-and-off privileges at any of its nine stops and can be used to access the Hutch's Pool Trail (page 79) or to hike the Phoneline Trail (page 84) in reverse.

Route Details

With its nine single-lane bridges crossing Sabino Creek, Sabino Canyon Road was a civil construction project in the 1930s, and some of the blocky bridge architecture echoes that era. Tucson families used to drive up here to take advantage of the cool water holes until the road was closed in the 1970s. Today the road remains in great condition (for the shuttles) and accesses plenty of swimming holes and picnic sites near the bridges and shuttle stops. The best time to go for a dip is spring and fall—the creek dries up in summer (mid-May–August) and is icy-cold in winter.

Begin hiking on the road, heading straight (northeast) from the shuttle-ticket booth. Just past the shade ramada behind the ticket

Sabino Canyon Road

booth on the right side of the road, you'll see a foot trail that parallels the road about 0.5 mile. Most people walk the road, but you can take the parallel trail. Even though you're just a few steps from the parking lot and visitor center, keep your eyes open for wildlife ranging from roadrunners to deer. Mountain lions are seen every year or two. Look up to the right of the road for views of Blackett's Ridge (page 74).

After 0.5 mile, the road to Bear Canyon (page 96) goes to the right—keep going straight (northeast), climbing gently and then dropping slightly. To your right, 0.8 mile along the road, Trail #51 heads to Sabino Dam (see end of previous hike). Enjoy views of the cottonwood trees in Sabino Creek, golden in fall and into the mild winter. Shuttle Stop 1 is between two restrooms on the right, 1.2 miles along the road; there are picnic tables by the second restroom, which has a drinking fountain and wheelchair-accessible flush toilets and picnic tables. Phoneline Link Trail #27A starts from here, climbing to the Phoneline Trail.

By now you're in Sabino Canyon proper, with cliffs rising on both sides. Occasional short trails lead down from the right of the road to picnic areas by Sabino Creek, just a few yards away. Shuttle

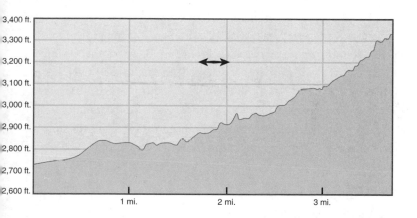

Stop 2 is 1.5 miles along the road; this has the last potable water until Stop 8. Soon after Stop 2, the road crosses the first of nine bridges along Sabino Creek. (Note that the shuttle stops have numbered signs, but you'll have to count the nine bridges for yourself.) Pools and a diminutive waterfall invite kids to play, but don't feel that you need to stop here—plenty of other riparian areas are farther along the road.

After Stop 3 is the second bridge, with a couple of picnic tables nearby. At the end of the bridge, on the right, is a fine example of an Arizona sycamore tree, with its pale, flaky-looking bark. Soon you'll see Thimble Peak—it really does look like a thimble—rising on the horizon, dead ahead as you walk. To your right, Acropolis Wall is the cliff rising more than 400 feet straight up to Blackett's Ridge. You'll continue crossing bridge after bridge, with shuttle stop after shuttle stop; most have no or very basic facilities, but you can explore spots to dip your toes in at every creek crossing.

Soon after Stop 7 (2.9 miles), you'll cross the ninth and last bridge on the road. A few yards farther, on the right, a sign indicates Trail #23A, which climbs rockily and steeply to connect with the Phoneline Trail 0.7 mile away.

Stop 8, at mile 3.2, offers a water fountain and vault toilets. Stairs at the end of a parking area lead down to Sabino Creek, now to your left, and a trail leads upriver to numerous popular swimming holes, tanning rocks, and cascades. From Stop 8, it's another 0.5 mile to the end of the road at Stop 9, which is the trailhead of the hike to Hutch's Pool (page 79) or the Phoneline Trail (page 84) in reverse. The only facilities here are benches; there was a restroom until July 31, 2006, when a massive monsoon caused rockslides in the upper canyon that washed away the entire facility and parts of the road.

Nearby Attractions

The **Sabino Canyon Visitor Center,** open daily, 8 a.m.–4:30 p.m., has information and useful free brochures. It also offers a small but interesting exhibit about the history, geology, and wildlife of the canyon;

a short movie in the theater; and a gift shop with a fine selection of maps, books, and Sabino Canyon paraphernalia. The visitor center is also the Coronado National Forest Ranger Station; the rangers can answer questions about Mount Lemmon and the Catalina Foothills, all of which lie within the forest.

Directions

From I-10 in central Tucson, take Broadway or Speedway Boulevard east about 7 miles to Wilmot Road. Turn left on Wilmot, which veers right at Pima Street and becomes Tanque Verde Road. Travel east on Tanque Verde 1 mile and turn left on Sabino Canyon Road. Follow Sabino Canyon Road 2.1 miles; veer right to continue on Sabino Canyon Road about 2.2 more miles to Sabino Canyon, on your right.

From I-10, coming from the southeast, take Exit 270 (Kolb Road) and follow it north 9.5 miles to Sabino Canyon Road. Turn right on Sabino Canyon Road and follow it about 2.8 miles; veer right to continue on Sabino Canyon Road about 2.2 more miles to Sabino Canyon, on your right.

From I-10, coming from the northwest, take Exit 248 (Ina Road) and head east. After 6.8 miles, Ina becomes Skyline Drive and, almost 2 miles farther, becomes Sunrise Drive. Follow Sunrise about 7 miles until it dead-ends at Sabino Canyon Road. Turn left; Sabino Canyon is the first entrance on your right.

12 # Seven Falls on
Bear Canyon Trail

SCENERY: ★ ★ ★ ★ ★
TRAIL CONDITION: ★ ★ ★
CHILDREN: ★ ★ ★
DIFFICULTY: ★ ★ ★
SOLITUDE: ★ ★

OCOTILLO AND BRITTLEBUSH BLOOM BENEATH SAGUAROS.

GPS TRAILHEAD COORDINATES: N32° 18.560' W110° 49.317'

DISTANCE & CONFIGURATION: 7.8-mile out-and-back, 5-mile out-and-back using the Bear Canyon shuttle

HIKING TIME: 3–5 hours for the whole hike (depending on water levels)

HIGHLIGHTS: Lovely views at Seven Falls with cooling pools below

ELEVATION: 2,725' at parking lot, 3,440' at high point, 3,300' at base of falls

ACCESS: Open 24/7; parking $5/$10/$20 for day/week/year; all National Park Service annual passes accepted

MAPS: Green Trails Map 2886S–*Santa Catalina Mountains*, USFS *Pusch Ridge Wilderness*, USGS *Sabino Canyon;* free map at visitor center

FACILITIES: Visitor center, flush toilets, vending machines; shuttle service to Bear Canyon

WHEELCHAIR ACCESS: Visitor center, toilets, Sabino Canyon Road (page 90), and the first 1.4 miles of the trail (requires some pushes on the unpaved parts)

COMMENTS: No pets; bicycles permitted on paved Bear Canyon Road daily, 5 p.m.–9 a.m., except Wednesday and Saturday; horses permitted but rarely encountered. Motorized shuttles run up Bear Canyon daily except Thanksgiving, December 25, and an occasional maintenance day, leaving the visitor center at 15 and 45 minutes past the hour from 9:15 a.m. to 4.15 p.m. Fares for the round-trip are $8/adults, $4/children ages 3–12, and free for infants. The 21-passenger enclosed gasoline buses will be joined by 62-passenger electric shuttles in the second half of 2019; these will feature indoor and outdoor seating and audio commentary in various languages via individual headsets. The Bear Canyon shuttle takes a different route for most of the way to the Seven Falls trailhead.

CONTACTS: Sabino Canyon Visitor Center, 520-749-8700, fs.usda.gov/coronado

Overview

This trail is a rite of passage for young Tucsonans and University of Arizona students for whom the Seven Falls take on an almost-mythical status. During weekends in spring and fall, flat rocks and shallow pools at the base of the falls are surrounded by scores of semiclad sunbathers, some of whom scramble up unsanctioned routes on either side of the lower falls. The ribbonlike cascades aren't very big, even after rains, but there are seven of them if you count the one below the pools, and they certainly are attractive when in full spate. From mid-May to July, the falls dry out completely.

The trail crosses Bear Creek seven times en route to the falls. When it's dry the crossings are easy, but in high water you may have to wade knee-deep or look for boulders to jump across on, which means that finding the best trail can be time-consuming. Bring a walking stick or trekking pole for greater safety when crossing the water. Ask at the visitor center for current conditions, and beware of flash floods. On August 4, 2007, a monsoonal flood swept through Bear Canyon, forcing dozens of hikers to clamber up the canyon sides to avoid being swept away; lamentably, two young adults drowned, even though they were fit and able to swim.

Seven Falls on Bear Canyon Trail

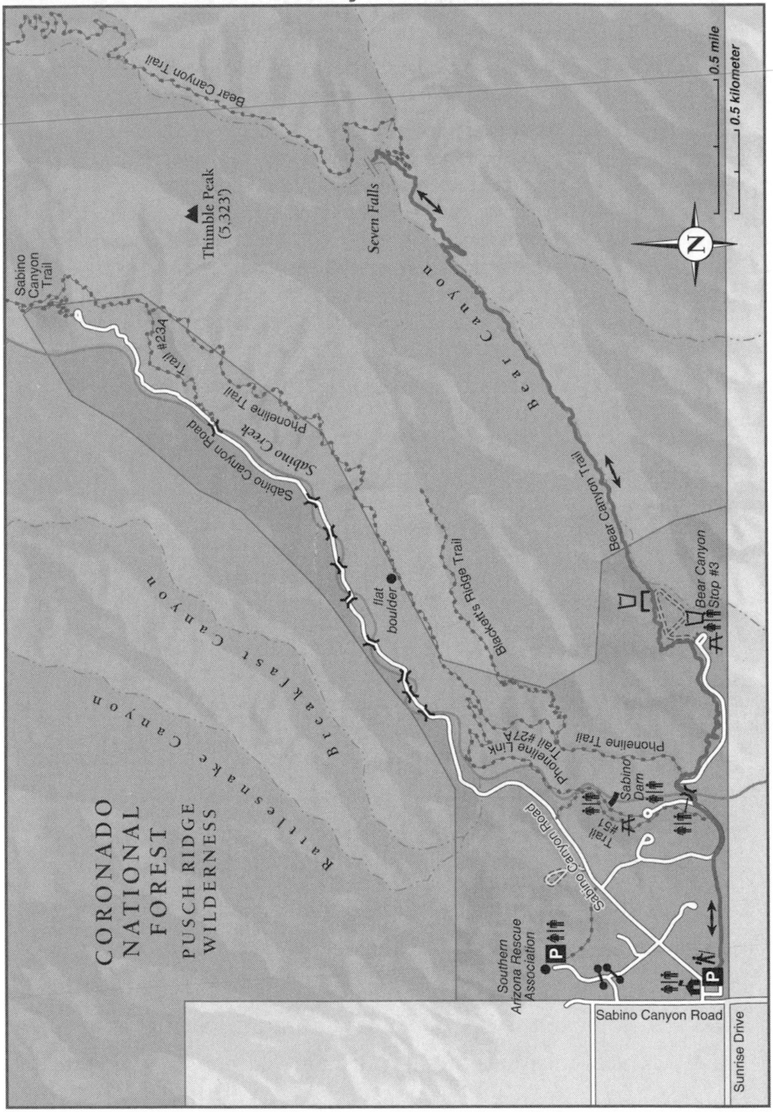

Thimble Peak (5,323')

Seven Falls

Bear Canyon Trail

Bear Canyon

0.5 mile

0.5 kilometer

N

Sabino Canyon Trail

Trail #23A

Sabino Creek Trail

Phoneline Trail

Sabino Canyon Road

flat boulder

Blackett's Ridge Trail

Bear Canyon Stop #3

Breakfast Canyon

Rattlesnake Canyon

CORONADO NATIONAL FOREST

PUSCH RIDGE WILDERNESS

Phoneline Link

Trail #27A

Phoneline Trail

Sabino Dam

Trail #31

Sabino Canyon Road

Southern Arizona Rescue Association

P

P

Sabino Canyon Road

Sunrise Drive

98

Route Details

From the southeast end of the parking lot, the trail follows the same route as the Phoneline Trail (page 84) until after the bridge crossing over Sabino Creek, some 0.75 mile from the parking area. Beyond the bridge, the road hits a T-junction and the right turn is signed SEVEN FALLS. This paved road, which heads briefly south and then east, is the route the Bear Canyon shuttle takes, and many hikers walk out along it. A more natural alternative is to take the trail, which parallels the road on the north side. This trail shares the Phoneline Trail for about 150 feet, and then a small sign indicates Bear Canyon Trail #29; go right (south) about 200 feet before swinging around to the east.

From the almost-flat trail, you catch glimpses of the road to the right and see Blackett's Ridge rearing up a mile to your left, with several ridges of the Santa Catalina Mountains behind. Flowers abound in spring, and saguaros surround you year-round. You'll meet the paved road after about 0.5 mile. This is where the Bear Canyon Shuttle ends at Stop 3, with a restroom, water, and a shadeless picnic table and barbecue grill. If you're riding the shuttle, make sure you know when the last one leaves for the return journey.

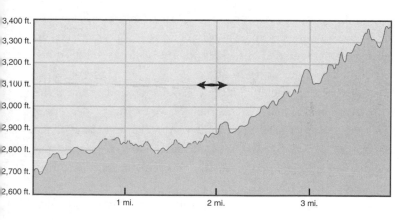

The road continues east but is now unpaved, and the trail continues paralleling it to the north. After 0.4 mile, the unpaved road ends at a ramada with a bench and a water faucet—fill up your water bottles here. From this point, you'll be heading east-northeast on a narrow, rocky, but clear trail following the left side of Bear Creek, which you'll be crossing seven times as you climb gently up the canyon. The first crossing is 0.25 mile from the end of the unpaved road—look for a short flight of rocky steps on the far side of the creek. The crossing is obvious in dry months but can be a challenge during spring runoffs or fall monsoons. If you have any problems wading across in the wet months, you might consider that this is the first of seven crossings!

Most hikers, most of the time, forge on. The first six crossings are clustered together in a 0.6-mile stretch, so if you get your feet wet, you might want to just keep sloshing on rather than drying off every time. The trail is partially shaded by a riparian woodland of willow, ash, and mesquite trees with birds flitting among them, but a glance upward at the walls of Bear Canyon reminds you that you're in the desert.

Half a mile beyond the sixth river crossing, a small sign indicates that the trail drops to the left (north) bank of the creek for a short while. If water levels are high, you might have to scramble over a rough and steep little outcrop. About 300 feet farther you'll come to the seventh crossing, which is the least obvious—hikers often end up missing the right place to cross. Look for a wooden post on the other side of the creek, and aim for that.

This crossing is at about 3,050 feet elevation, and beyond it the trail starts climbing and switchbacking above the right side of Bear Creek. Eventually it flattens and follows the high right side of the canyon, until you reach a trail fork at about 3,440 feet elevation and 0.5 mile beyond the seventh crossing. Take the unsigned left fork, which drops to the base of Seven Falls.

(If you take the right fork, signed BEAR CANYON TRAIL #29, you'll be in for more than 8 more miles of hiking up to 4,720 feet elevation, then down via East Fork Trail #24A and Sabino Canyon Trail #23 to the top end of Sabino Canyon Road. This enables you to climb Bear Canyon and return via Sabino Canyon Road—an approximately 17-mile hike that is doable in one day if you're an experienced hiker with a map.)

The short, steep trail to the base of the falls has excellent views of all seven falls—you can't see them properly from the fork. You'll skirt around the right side of the pools at the bottom, and you can make an eighth creek crossing as you explore. Beware of slippery, algae-covered rocks when the falls are running, and be prepared for dry pools in early summer.

Directions and Nearby Attractions

See previous hike.

CROSSING BEAR CREEK WHEN IT'S DRY IS EASY—BUT SOMETIMES YOU HAVE TO WADE.

Mount Lemmon

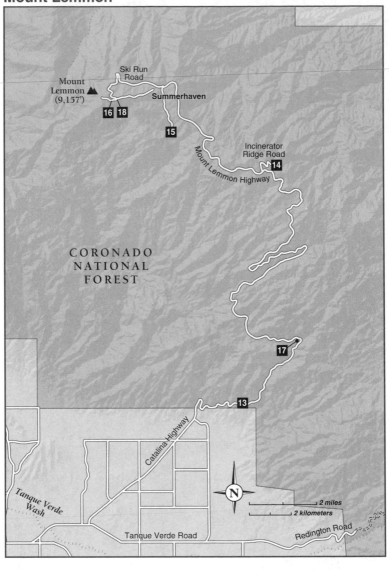

Mount Lemmon

PRICKLY PEAR CACTI, OCOTILLOS, AND MESQUITE TREES SURROUND
SAGUAROS SPREAD OUT ON THE HILLSIDE ALONG THE BABAD DO'AG TRAIL.

Babad Do'ag Trail

SCENERY: ★ ★ ★ ★
TRAIL CONDITION: ★ ★ ★ ★
CHILDREN: ★ ★ ★
DIFFICULTY: ★ ★ ★
SOLITUDE: ★ ★ ★ ★ ★

AS YOU CLIMB TO 4,000 FEET, YOU BEGIN TO SEE SMALL OAK TREES.

GPS TRAILHEAD COORDINATES: N32° 18.555' W110° 43.240'

DISTANCE & CONFIGURATION: 4-mile out-and-back

HIKING TIME: 2.5 hours

HIGHLIGHTS: Pretty waterfall after snowmelt or monsoon rains; changes in flora from saguaros to oaks; surprising view of Catalina Highway from ridge at trail end

ELEVATION: 3,568' at parking lot, 4,656' at trail's end

ACCESS: Open daily, 24/7; free

MAPS: Green Trails Map 2886S–*Santa Catalina Mountains*

FACILITIES: Parking for 17 vehicles. The Palisade Visitor Center is about 17 miles farther up Mount Lemmon.

WHEELCHAIR ACCESS: None

COMMENTS: Horses allowed but rarely encountered. Dogs must be leashed at all times. This elevation gets very hot in summer. Wear decent hiking footwear for traversing the mixed dirt, sand, and rock surface.

CONTACTS: Sabino Canyon Visitor Center, 520-749-8700, fs.usda.gov/coronado

Overview

This trail starts from near the first parking area on General Hitchcock Highway, also known locally as Mount Lemmon Road. The trail climbs steadily but has no very steep sections, and the views of both the vegetation and the mountains are rewarding. The waterfall at the end is dry for most of the year; try to get there early on August mornings after the monsoons or in February and March during snowmelt to see water flowing.

Route Details

Start by driving to the scenic vista and parking area named Babad Do'ag, which means "Frog Mountain" in the Tohono O'odham language. Check out the panels identifying some of the mountains on the horizon before you walk out of the parking area and turn right (northeast). There is no sidewalk, so cross the road with care and walk up about 100 yards to a sign for the trailhead; this is Trail #705. Climb left from the road along an unclear trail for the first 50 yards—it's hard to follow, but cast around and you'll soon find a trail paralleling the road below. After another 200–300 yards, the trail swings sharply left away from the road to the northwest, following a normally dry little streambed, and then becomes quite clear for the rest of the way.

You'll be treading on a mixed dirt, sand, and rock surface for which decent hiking footwear is recommended to avoid a twisted ankle. Around you, prickly pear cacti, ocotillos, and mesquite trees surround saguaros spread out on the hillside. This is almost the

Babad Do'ag Trail

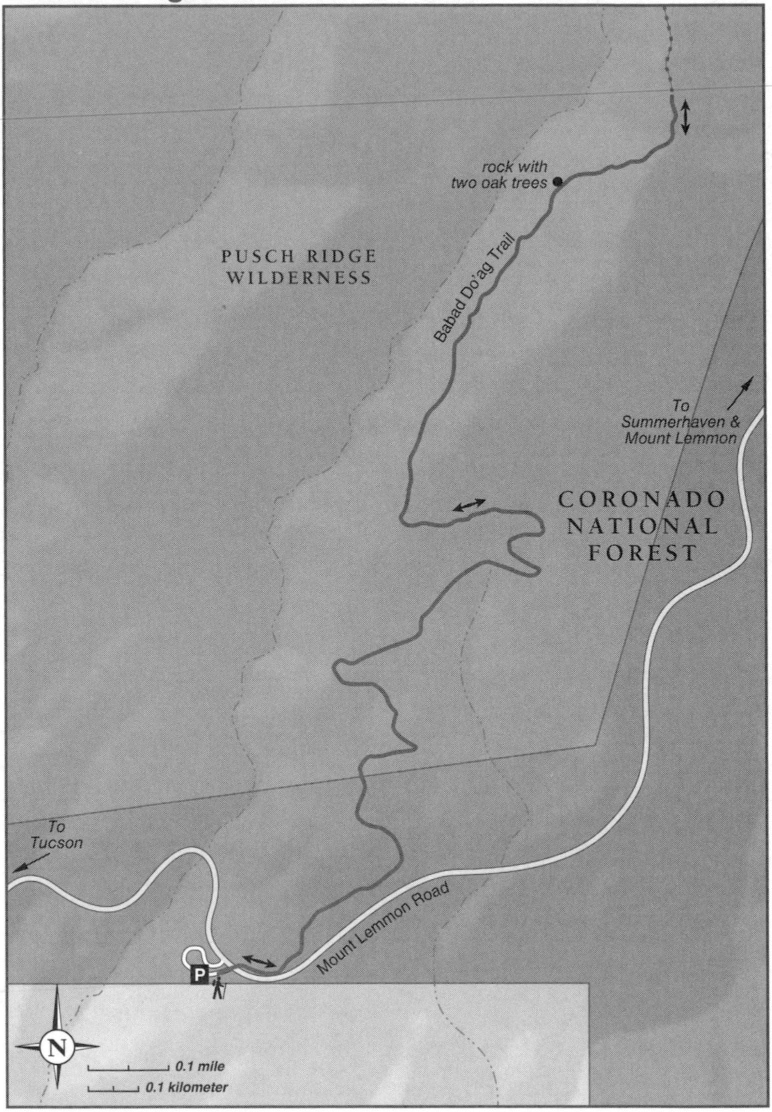

PUSCH RIDGE
WILDERNESS

rock with
two oak trees

Babad Do'ag Trail

To
Summerhaven &
Mount Lemmon

CORONADO
NATIONAL
FOREST

To
Tucson

Mount Lemmon Road

P

N

0.1 mile
0.1 kilometer

highest limit for saguaros, and as you rise above the 4,000-foot-elevation mark, you'll see the vegetation change into thickets of small oak trees surrounded by chaparral and grassland. It's remarkable to see this transition from saguaro forest to oak woodland, and this is one of the best trails from which to observe the transformation.

As you climb, you'll see a valley to your left and a ridge to your right. When you reach a rock where two oaks grow, the trail forks. The left fork is a social trail wandering off to explore the valley; the main trail climbs right (northeast). A few more minutes of hiking brings you to a saddle, where you'll find a sign marking the end of the trail.

There are fine views from here. To the northwest, you'll see the waterfall at about the same elevation as the trail end, and there are unmarked social trails that will get you closer. To the east-northeast, the landscape drops steeply to the curves of Mount Lemmon Road as it hugs the slopes of Molino Canyon, beyond which are Agua Caliente Hill and the Rincon Mountains. To the east-southeast, social trails gain different views of Mount Lemmon Road, and far off to the south are the Santa Rita Mountains. It's a scenic spot to enjoy a snack before returning the way you came.

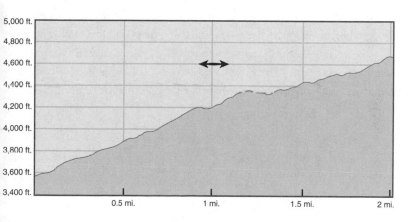

Nearby Attractions

See Hike 17, Molino Basin Trail, for details about Molino Basin Campground, which is reached by a turnoff from Catalina Highway, almost 3 miles beyond the Babad Do'ag parking area.

Directions

From I-10 in central Tucson, take Broadway or Speedway Boulevard about 7 miles east to Wilmot Road. Turn left on Wilmot, which veers right at Pima Street and becomes Tanque Verde Road. Travel east on Tanque Verde about 4 miles, then turn left on Catalina Highway, which veers northeast and goes straight almost 4.5 miles before reaching the Coronado National Forest boundary. This is Milepost 0 on what is locally known as Mount Lemmon Road (but which the U.S. Forest Service calls General Hitchcock Highway), a Sky Island Scenic Byway. Follow the highway almost 3 more miles to the Babad Do'ag scenic vista and parking area, on your right. Note that there are no gas stations on Catalina Highway or Mount Lemmon Road.

From I-10, coming from the southeast, take Exit 270 (Kolb Road) and follow it north 9.5 miles to Sabino Canyon Road. Turn right, drive 0.8 miles, turn right on Tanque Verde Road and continue 2.7 miles to Catalina Highway. Follow the directions above from Catalina Highway.

From I-10, coming from the northwest, take Exit 256 (Grant Road) and head east. After 8.5 miles, turn left on Tanque Verde Road and drive 3.5 miles to Catalina Highway. Follow the directions above from Catalina Highway.

Incinerator Ridge Trail

SCENERY: ★ ★ ★ ★
TRAIL CONDITION: ★ ★ ★ ★
CHILDREN: ★ ★ ★ ★
DIFFICULTY: ★ ★
SOLITUDE: ★ ★ ★

HIKING THROUGH PINE FOREST ON THE INCINERATOR RIDGE TRAIL

GPS TRAILHEAD COORDINATES: N32° 24.700' W110° 42.326'

DISTANCE & CONFIGURATION: 1.3-mile out-and-back

HIKING TIME: 1 hour

HIGHLIGHTS: Excellent views from a minor peak

ELEVATION: 8,000' at trailhead, 8,135' at high point

ACCESS: Open daily, 24/7; free

MAPS: Green Trails Map 2886S–*Santa Catalina Mountains*

FACILITIES: Parking for 6 vehicles at trailhead

WHEELCHAIR ACCESS: None

COMMENTS: Horses and bicycles permitted but rarely seen; no dogs allowed. Make other plans if the parking area is full (see Overview). Mountain bikers consider this one of the most difficult routes on Mount Lemmon.

CONTACTS: Sabino Canyon Visitor Center, 520-749-8700, fs.usda.gov/coronado

Incinerator Ridge Trail

Leopold Point
(8,050')

CORONADO
NATIONAL
FOREST

saddle

Incinerator Ridge Trail

Incinerator
Ridge Peak
(8,135')

To
Tucson

Mount Lemmon Road

Knagge
Trail #18

P

Kellogg
Mountain
(8,401')

Kellogg Trail

Incinerator
Ridge Road

Mount Lemmon Road

To
Summerhaven

0.1 mile

0.1 kilometer

N

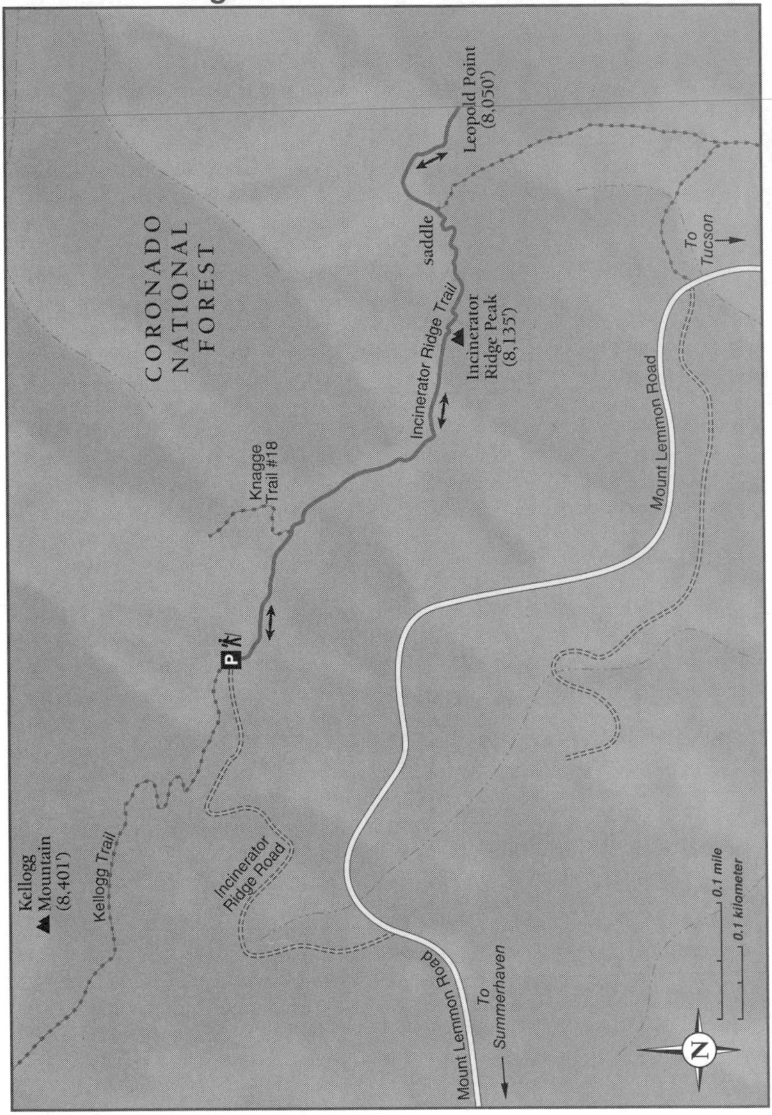

Overview

This short trail gives you a lot of bang for your shoe leather. There are excellent mountain, forest, and valley views all around (though you can't see Tucson), and the rock slabs at the end of the trail are great for resting and picnicking. The main drawback is the dirt access road leading to a diminutive parking area. Cars can get there with care but may find nowhere to park. In that case, if you return along the access road, you'll find a few spots where you can pull over and hike back up the road.

Route Details

Looking out over the north side of the parking area, you'll see a few twisted remains of what was once an incinerator—hence the name of this ridge. The trail leaves from the northeast corner of the parking area, signed INCINERATOR RIDGE TRAIL #18A. It climbs gently 0.1 mile to the junction with Knagge Trail #18, which drops steeply to the left into the lowlands north of the Catalina Mountains. This trail is named after a family who mined in the area in the early 20th

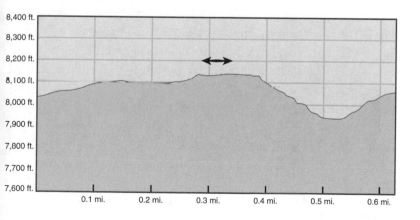

century and also provided pack-train services to the Summerhaven area before roads were available.

Stay on the Incinerator Ridge Trail as it continues flatly southeast. Looking to your right (south) through the pine trees, you'll catch glimpses of Catalina Highway below you. Soon you'll see a helicopter-landing pad to the south and, beyond it, Rose Canyon Lake, which at about 0.25 mile long is the largest lake in the Santa Catalina Mountains. Stocked with trout in summer, the lake has a campground nearby. Where the trail reaches the ridge, you can see the small communities of San Manuel and Mammoth in the San Pedro River valley to the northeast.

The trail begins to climb again and swings east as it reaches Incinerator Ridge Peak (8,135') almost 0.4 mile from the trailhead. This is the highest point on the trail, but the best views are farther away, on the slightly lower peak directly east. The trail drops clearly into a saddle at about 7,960 feet elevation between these two peaks. Here you'll find two trails, unsigned as of this writing. The one that drops to the right (southeast), completed in late 2012, goes to the San Pedro Vista lookout on Catalina Highway.

Our trail climbs left (north-northeast) into an area of large boulders. You'll round the left (north) side of Leopold Point, making your way through the boulders as you climb to the top of the peak. The high point is marked by a log stuck vertically into the summit rocks. Continue east about 100 feet to an inviting ledge with views in all directions, pull out a snack, and relax.

Leopold Point (8,050') isn't marked on most maps—I found it on an obscure USGS map. It's probably named after writer, environmentalist, and forester Aldo Leopold (1887–1948), who worked for the U.S. Forest Service in the Southwestern states, including two years stationed in Arizona.

The views here are superb in all directions. To the south is a precipitous cliff, Barnum Rock, about 0.4 mile away, and beyond to the southeast is Tucson, backed by the Santa Rita Mountains. East-northeast, back the way you came, has views of the radio towers on

Mount Bigelow. To the north are views into the San Pedro River valley. Bring a map and compass and enjoy picking out landmarks, then return the way you came.

Nearby Attractions

The **Palisade Visitor Center,** 0.4 mile farther along Catalina Highway, has information, maps, books, and a gift shop. It's usually open Thursday–Monday, 8 a.m.–4.30 p.m.

Rose Canyon Campground (877-444-6777, recreation.gov) is the largest campground on the mountain, with 73 sites. It is reached by a turnoff from Catalina Highway, 2.2 miles before Incinerator Ridge Road. It has drinking water and vault toilets but no hookups. Some sites can be reserved. **Spencer Canyon Campground** (520-749-8700, fs.usda.gov/coronado) is reached by a turnoff 2.1 miles above Incinerator Ridge Road. It has 68 sites and similar facilities but is on a first-come, first-served basis. Both allow RVs or trailers up to 22 feet, charge $22 per night, and are open mid-April–late October. For camping in winter, see Nearby Attractions for Hike 17, Molino Basin Trail (page 126).

Directions

Follow the directions for Hike 13, Babad Do'ag Trail (page 104), to reach Milepost 0 on Mount Lemmon Road (Catalina Highway). From Milepost 0, drive 19.3 miles to the poorly marked Incinerator Ridge Road, on your right. (If you reach the Palisade Visitor Center, you've driven 0.4 mile too far.) Incinerator Ridge Road, unpaved but passable for cars if you drive carefully, reaches the tiny parking turnaround after 0.5 mile. The road may be closed from mid-December to March.

15 # Marshall Gulch Loop

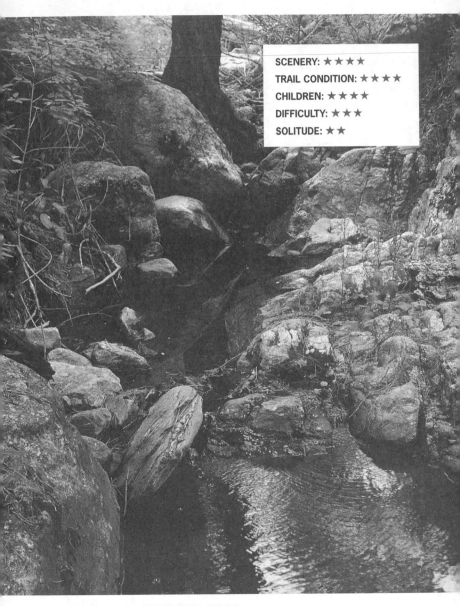

SCENERY: ★★★★
TRAIL CONDITION: ★★★★
CHILDREN: ★★★★
DIFFICULTY: ★★
SOLITUDE: ★★

MINI-WATERFALL IN MARSHALL GULCH

GPS TRAILHEAD COORDINATES: N32° 25.695' W110°45.342'

DISTANCE & CONFIGURATION: 3.6-mile loop, 2.4-mile out-and-back to Marshall Saddle

HIKING TIME: 2.25 hours for loop, 1.5 miles for out-and-back to saddle

HIGHLIGHTS: Exploring one of Sabino Creek's highest tributaries; pine, oak, and aspen forests; cliff views; summer flowers; fall colors

ELEVATION: 7,460' at trailhead, 8,160' at high point

ACCESS: Open daily, 24/7; parking $5/$10/$20 for day/week/year; all National Park Service annual passes accepted

MAPS: Green Trails Map 2886S–*Santa Catalina Mountains,* USFS *Pusch Ridge Wilderness*

FACILITIES: Pit toilets at trailhead; parking for about 18 cars (no trailers or RVs)

WHEELCHAIR ACCESS: Toilets only

COMMENTS: Horses allowed but rarely encountered. Dogs must be leashed at all times. If the parking area is full (most summer weekends), look for spaces along the road to the trailhead or in several small lots adjoining picnic areas along the last 0.5 mile of the road. The trail may be closed by snow in the winter, and the last 0.2 mile of the access road is closed December–March.

CONTACTS: Sabino Canyon Visitor Center, 520-749-8700, fs.usda.gov/coronado

Overview

This is a very popular loop hike for Tucsonans looking to beat the summer heat. Combined with a picnic lunch or a visit to a Summerhaven restaurant (see Nearby Attractions), this hike completes a relaxing day in the mountains. Going counterclockwise, as described here, the trail follows an evergreen-forested stream and later emerges to yield rocky vistas, followed by a saddle and aspen groves. Other hikers may prefer the clockwise route, which starts off more steeply.

Route Details

At the north end of the parking area, to the right of the toilets, look for a sign indicating Marshall Gulch Trail #3 and a narrow trail zigzagging right and up into the trees. After a couple of brief switchbacks, the trail straightens and climbs west through an evergreen forest of ponderosa pine and Douglas-fir, mixed with oaks and madrones. Down below to your left, the terrain drops to Marshall Gulch, a tributary of Sabino Creek (which ends up in Sabino Canyon). The trail stays high less than 0.5 mile before dropping and easily crossing the narrow stream.

Marshall Gulch Loop

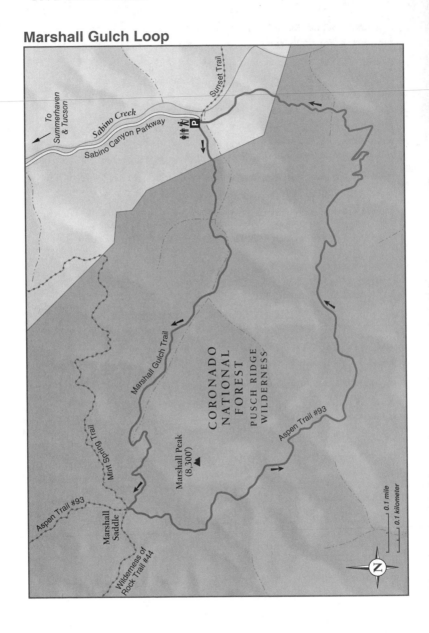

Almost immediately after you make your way across the stream, you'll reach a T-junction, where you turn right. (Left takes you back to the parking lot, following the streambed and easily crossing it again for a loop of less than a mile.)

The trail climbs gently, with the stream teasing you to your right. There's water in it almost all year long. Take your time, enjoy the sounds of nature, and maybe cool your feet. Before you know it, you'll be crossing the stream again, from left to right, climbing west-northwest into the forest. After several hundred yards of hiking, you might notice a small weather station on the right side of the trail with rain gauges measuring rainfall variability in the Santa Catalina Mountains. About 100 yards farther, the trail crosses the stream a final time, from right to left.

Continue climbing steadily through ferns surrounding a mix of burned and living pines. High to the northwest on the aptly named Radio Ridge, which leads up to Mount Lemmon, you'll see several communication towers. A final push up a rocky trail with views of granite cliffs and outcrops brings you to Marshall Saddle (7,920'), where signs point out the five trails that meet at this point. (If you

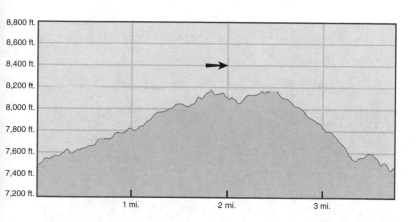

hike the Wilderness of Rock Loop, page 131, you'll again reach this significant hiking crossroads.)

While resting at the saddle, look a few degrees north of west to spy Lemmon Rock Lookout, a U.S. Forest Service fire lookout perched atop a cliff; you can visit it on the Meadow Trail (see next hike). Hikers on the Arizona National Scenic Trail will discover that Marshall Gulch is a tiny section of the 800-mile trail that crosses the entire state, from Mexico to the Utah state line.

From Marshall Saddle, you can return the way you came, making an out-and-back hike of 2.4 miles, or turn left, heading south on signed Aspen Trail #93, to make the full loop. This is the area in which the devastating 2003 Aspen Fire started, and you can see remnants of the destruction mixed in with years of recovery. During late summer, in July and August, alpine wildflowers proliferate in this section. October is an excellent month to enjoy fall foliage.

The Aspen Trail climbs gently, then flattens after it leaves Marshall Saddle. After several hundred yards, the trail swings southeast and then east as it contours around Marshall Peak (about 8,300') to the left of the trail. There is no path to the elongated, wooded summit. Most hikers look toward the right of the trail, where they can glimpse Tucson to the south and southwest through the trees. Look for unsigned side trails leaving the Aspen Trail to the right to gain better views of Tucson.

HIKERS ON THE MARSHALL GULCH TRAIL

Continuing east on the Aspen Trail, you'll climb to the high point of the loop, although it's hard to tell which is the highest point as the trail undulates through the forest. The last mile swings around to the north and drops, sometimes steeply, with views of the cliffs of the uppermost reaches of Sabino Canyon to the right; again, unsigned short side trails will give better views. As you hike through this last section, look around for quartz and mica specks, which glisten on a sunny day.

The trail tumbles down to the Marshall Gulch parking area. If you prefer hiking the trail clockwise, in reverse of this description, you'll find a sign for Aspen Trail #93 at the south end of the parking area, from which it climbs steeply south before swinging around to the west.

Nearby Attractions

About a mile before the trailhead, Sabino Canyon Parkway, the approach road, passes through the village of **Summerhaven.** Almost half of the village was destroyed in the summer of 2003, when about 340 homes and businesses burned during the Aspen Fire. Summerhaven continues to recover and offers a couple of eateries and a village store–cum–gift shop, but no gas station.

South of the village, several parking lots adjoin the uppermost reaches of Sabino Creek and provide access to many cool, shady picnic areas with tables and barbecue grills. These lots serve as overflow parking for the nearby Marshall Gulch/Aspen trailhead. The road and parking areas close during winter snows.

Directions

Follow the directions for Hike 13, Babad Do'ag Trail (page 104), to reach Milepost 0 on Mount Lemmon Road (Catalina Highway). From Milepost 0, drive about 25 miles to the village of Summerhaven and continue another mile to the Marshall Gulch trailhead. Note that there is no gas in Summerhaven, so make sure you've left Tucson with several gallons in your tank.

16 # Meadow Trail Loop

SCENERY: ★ ★ ★ ★ ★
TRAIL CONDITION: ★ ★ ★ ★
CHILDREN: ★ ★ ★ ★
DIFFICULTY: ★ ★
SOLITUDE: ★ ★

RAPPEL ROCK

GPS TRAILHEAD COORDINATES: N32° 26.416' W110° 47.151'

DISTANCE & CONFIGURATION: 1.6-mile loop, 2.1 miles with side trip to lookout

HIKING TIME: 1-hour loop, 1.5 hours with side trip

HIGHLIGHTS: Fine views of Tucson; exceptional views from lookout; pretty meadows surrounded by coniferous forest

ELEVATION: 9,100' at trailhead, 8,800' at low point

ACCESS: Open daily, 24/7; parking $5/$10/$20 for day/week/year; all National Park Service annual passes accepted

MAPS: Green Trails Map 2886S–*Santa Catalina Mountains,* USFS *Pusch Ridge Wilderness*

FACILITIES: Pit toilets at trailhead; parking for about 20 cars (no trailers or RVs)

WHEELCHAIR ACCESS: Toilets only

COMMENTS: Horses allowed but rarely encountered. Dogs must be leashed at all times. If the parking area is full, look for spaces along the road to the trailhead or in the unmarked parking area near the top of the ski area, about 0.2 mile back along the road on the south side. The trail and road may be closed by snow in the winter—but it's a short winter in southern Arizona!

CONTACTS: Sabino Canyon Visitor Center, 520-749-8700, fs.usda.gov/coronado

Overview

This lovely loop takes you through alpine meadows and coniferous forests before reaching views of Tucson. The first section is flat and suitable for introducing pre-kindergarten youngsters to the high country. A gentle 300-foot descent loops around to a side trail that heads to a fire lookout with extensive views of southern Arizona—this view is the only reason the hike gets five stars for scenery. The final return is a slightly steep challenge for the young ones.

Route Details

At the parking area, you'll find a map board and a sign for Mount Lemmon Trail #5. Take this trail, which skirts around the chain-link fence surrounding electrical power equipment before striking out west-southwest through the pines. After about 0.2 mile you'll reach a signed trail fork where you take the right (west-northwest) branch, labeled MEADOW TRAIL #5A. This short side trail, which will return to the Mount Lemmon Trail after 0.8 mile, gives this hike its name.

Through the trees to your right, you'll glimpse buildings belonging to the University of Arizona astronomy observatory (see Nearby Attractions). The trail traverses a mix of ferns, bracken, and living and dead conifers—a legacy of the Aspen Fire of 2003. As the trail's name suggests, meadows are crossed, and you have intermittent views of Tucson to the south. The trail is clear and rather rocky.

About 0.5 mile from the parking lot, the trail swings left (southwest), away from the university buildings, and continues fairly flatly a few hundred yards through meadows and pine forests. Then it eases into a gentle descent, which steepens into an easy zigzag on an earthen trail through continuing pines.

Meadow Trail Loop

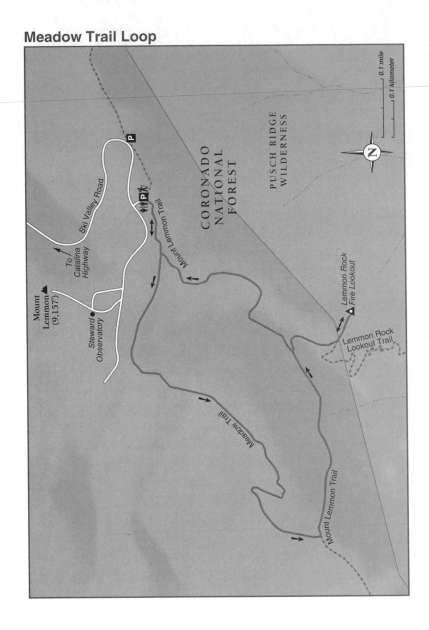

You reach the halfway point of the loop when the Meadow Trail rejoins the Mount Lemmon Trail at a signed intersection. There are good views to the south, with Thimble Peak and Sabino Canyon's Phoneline Trail clearly visible at 162° to the southeast. At this junction, near the low point of the trail, turn left (east-northeast, then east) along the Mount Lemmon Trail, which roughly follows the 8,800-foot contour line.

You'll enjoy views of the Tucson valley to your right and begin to climb gently until you reach a signed turn for the Lemmon Rock Lookout Trail #12 to the right (south-southeast). Here, you can continue on Mount Lemmon Trail to the northeast and back to the parking area, or you can head south on the recommended side trip to the Lemmon Rock Lookout.

The Lemmon Rock Lookout Trail descends through the pine forest and continues down to the Wilderness of Rock (see page 131). Wander down just a few hundred yards to the turnoff to the lookout on your left, and then climb to the lookout tower itself. There has been a lookout here since 1913, and the current tower is open to visitors during the dry summer fire season, when it is occupied

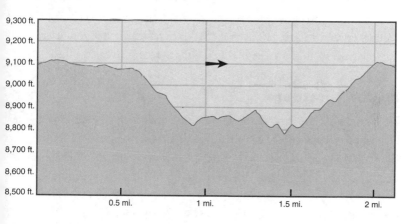

around the clock by a U.S. Forest Service firefighter who spends the entire summer in the cramped but totally scenic quarters. The first year Audrey and I visited the tower, we were warmly welcomed by firefighter Dave Medford and his dog, Gus (the following year, the firefighter on duty did not invite visitors).

Dave pointed out all the landmarks and mountain ranges visible from his lookout, explaining the southern Arizona weather patterns that he can see unfolding above, below, and around him. Gus enjoyed getting a head rub until he was back on duty, with a friendly bark to alert us to the arrival of the next visitors.

If you're here outside of the fire season, the views from the rock upon which the lookout tower is built are almost as great as from the tower itself. Looking west, you'll see three nearby outcrops that are favored by rock climbers. The one on the left is Rappel Rock, the middle one is Fortress Rock, and the series of slabs to the right are The Ravens. Way off to the south and southwest, the Tucson valley spreads out before you, surrounded in the distance by the Tucson, Santa Rita, and Rincon Mountains. It's a splendid survey of almost everywhere in this book.

Back on the Mount Lemmon Trail, you'll climb northeast on the steepest part of the loop. This is where the youngest members of your group might want a piggyback ride. It's wide and rocky until you reach the fork with the Meadow Trail. Turn right to return to the trailhead.

Nearby Attractions

To the right of the entrance to the parking area is a sign for the **Mount Lemmon Sky Center** (520-626-8122, skycenter.arizona.edu). Part of the University of Arizona's Steward Observatory, it can be visited most Thursday, Friday, Saturday, and Sunday nights on 5-hour guided tours, with opportunities for using large telescopes to view celestial objects. Guided by enthusiastic professional astronomers, tours are limited to 34 people and cost $75 (discounts available). Reservations are recommended.

VIEW OF A STORM FROM THE FIRE LOOKOUT TOWER, WITH RAPPEL ROCK IN THE FOREGROUND

Directions

Follow the directions for Hike 13, Babad Do'ag Trail (page 104), to reach Milepost 0 on Mount Lemmon Road (Catalina Highway). From Milepost 0, drive 24.6 miles to the Ski Valley turnoff (Ski Run Road), to the right just before the village of Summerhaven. After about 2 miles, you'll pass through Mt. Lemmon Ski Valley and continue about 1.8 steep, curving miles to the trailhead. This last section is usually closed in winter.

SCENERY: ★ ★ ★ ★
TRAIL CONDITION: ★ ★ ★ ★
CHILDREN: ★ ★ ★ ★
DIFFICULTY: ★ ★
SOLITUDE: ★ ★ ★ ★

GRASSLANDS ALONG THE MOLINO BASIN TRAIL

GPS TRAILHEAD COORDINATES: N32° 20.255' W110° 41.474'

DISTANCE & CONFIGURATION: 5-mile out-and-back, 2.5-mile point-to-point with shuttle

HIKING TIME: 2 hours for out-and-back

HIGHLIGHTS: Campgrounds at either end of trail; historic site; unusual oak woodland–mesquite grassland; hiking part of the Arizona Trail

ELEVATION: 4,359' at trailhead, 4,919' at high point, 4,859' at trail's end

ACCESS: Parking 6 a.m.–10 p.m.; $5/$10/$20 for day/week/year; all National Park Service annual passes accepted

MAPS: Green Trails Map 2886S–*Santa Catalina Mountains;* free map at visitor center

FACILITIES: Restrooms at trailhead; picnic table; campgrounds; no drinking water

WHEELCHAIR ACCESS: In developed areas; none on trail

COMMENTS: Multiuse trail for hikers, equestrians, mountain bikers, and leashed dogs; no fee for 7 Arizona Trail parking slots. A 2-car shuttle can make this a 2.5-mile one-way trail.

CONTACTS: Sabino Canyon Visitor Center, 520-749-8700, fs.usda.gov/coronado

Overview

This trail links two campgrounds and makes an ideal short hike for campers as well as day users. It is just high enough to be above the saguaro zone and gives the opportunity to hike through a transition zone of grasslands studded with sharp-leaved yuccas, evergreen oaks, and mesquite trees.

Route Details

The trailhead is at the southwest corner of the parking area, marked by a small metal sign for Molino Basin Trail #11. The trail goes southwest in the direction of two Arizona Trail signs clearly visible ahead and enters Molino Basin Campground, passing two tent-camping sites before crossing the paved entrance road into the campground. Continuing generally southwest, the trail swings around the southeast side of the campground, which generally remains out of sight, though you do see the Catalina Highway in the distance to your left.

After 0.5 mile the trail begins climbing steadily in a generally western direction, and the Catalina Highway now becomes visible to your right—it has done a complete hairpin around the campground. At 0.8 mile there is a signed side trail to the right leading 0.1 mile north to the Upper Molino Campground.

The Molino Basin Trail continues climbing west with good views of the basin behind you and mountain walls rising almost 1,000 feet on either side. The trail is clear and yuccas punctuate the landscape. The high point is reached 2.2 miles from the trailhead where a sign indicates the short side trail to the Gordon Hirabayashi Recreation Area, which drops to the right, continuing west and then swinging north to the entrance of the Gordon Hirabayashi Campground about 200 yards away. An additional 200 yards brings you to a small parking area near the Catalina Highway where you could have left a car for a shuttle (but the mostly downhill return the way you came is easy).

Gordon Hirabayashi was a young Japanese American man who legally challenged the forced relocation and internment of 117,000

Molino Basin Trail

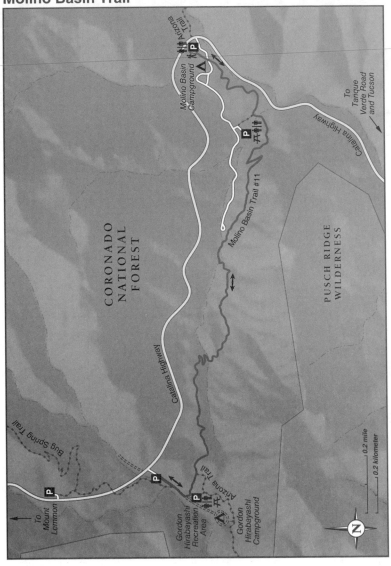

Japanese Americans during World War II and who refused to be interned. He was convicted of violating the relocation order and served a sentence at the Catalina Federal Honor Camp, a prison without bars that stood on this site from 1939 to 1973. Today you can explore the foundations of some of the prison buildings and learn about both the Japanese American internment and the history of the camp in a series of well-illustrated panels near the end of this hike.

Nearby Attractions

Molino Basin Campground (520-749-8700, recreation.gov) has 37 tent or RV sites with picnic benches and barbecue grills. It has vault toilets but no hookups or drinking water (bring your own). Some sites are wheelchair accessible. It allows RVs or trailers up to 22 feet, charges $10 per night, and is open November–April. Most sites are first come, first served. **Gordon Hirabayashi Campground** (877-444-6777, recreation.gov) has 12 similar sites. Other campgrounds on the mountain are higher and are open in summer; these two are closed in summer because of the heat.

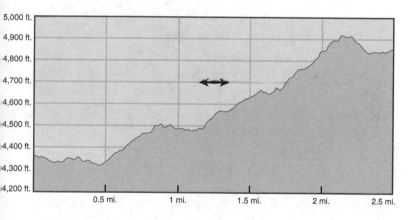

Directions

Follow the directions for Hike 13, Babad Do'ag Trail (page 104), to reach Milepost 0 on Mount Lemmon Road (Catalina Highway). From Milepost 0, drive 5.7 miles up the Catalina Highway to the campground and trailhead entrance on your left.

AN OAK TREE CATCHES SOME AFTERNOON SUN ON A WINTRY DAY ALONG THE MOLINO BASIN TRAIL.

Wilderness of Rock Loop

SCENERY: ★ ★ ★ ★ ★
TRAIL CONDITION: ★ ★ ★
CHILDREN: ★ ★
DIFFICULTY: ★ ★ ★ ★ ★
SOLITUDE: ★ ★ ★

ONE OF THE MANY ROCK FORMATIONS IN THE WILDERNESS

GPS TRAILHEAD COORDINATES: N32° 26.452' W110° 47.023'

DISTANCE & CONFIGURATION: 5.9-mile downward loop

HIKING TIME: 4.25 hours

HIGHLIGHTS: Mount Lemmon Rock Lookout, views of precipices (sometimes with rock climbers), rock formations, late-summer flowers

ELEVATION: 9,040' at trailhead, 7,200' at low point

ACCESS: Open daily, 24/7, but limited access or closed in winter depending on weather or snow conditions; parking $5/$10/$20 for day/week/year; all National Park Service annual passes accepted

MAPS: Green Trails Map 2886S–*Santa Catalina Mountains*, USFS *Pusch Ridge Wilderness*

FACILITIES: Pit toilets about 0.2 mile from trailhead; parking for about 15 cars (no trailers or RVs)

WHEELCHAIR ACCESS: None

COMMENTS: Horses allowed but rarely encountered. Dogs must be leashed at all times. If the parking area is full, look for spaces along the road beyond the parking area or in the second parking area, about 0.2 mile farther down the road.

CONTACTS: Sabino Canyon Visitor Center, 520-749-8700, fs.usda.gov/coronado

Wilderness of Rock Loop

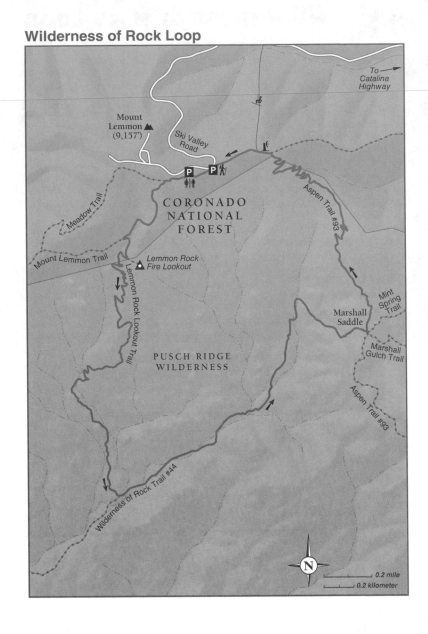

Overview

This cool, high hike is a great way to spend a summer day away from Tucson's heat. You'll start just below the summit of Mount Lemmon and descend steeply almost 2,000 feet, past rock formations and through pine forests. The Wilderness of Rock is an area of mainly granite boulders and cliffs forming a wide band around the south side of the higher sections of Mount Lemmon. This loop enters the eastern part of the wilderness and exits via the popular Marshall Gulch saddle and up to the top of Mt. Lemmon Ski Valley, Tucson's backyard ski area.

Route Details

From the unsigned, unpaved parking area on the left side of the road, at the top of the ski area, look for a trail paralleling the left side of the road, going west-southwest and offering great views of the Tucson valley to your left. In just under 0.2 mile you'll arrive at the parking area for the Meadow Trail (see page 120), where you can also park, though this lot is often full in summer.

Find a map board and a sign for Mount Lemmon Trail #5. Take this trail, which skirts around the chain-link fence surrounding

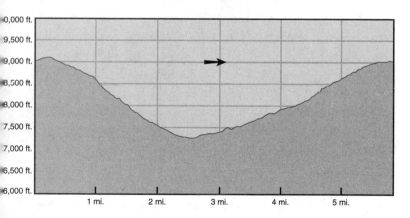

electrical power equipment, before striking out west-southwest through the pines. After about 0.2 mile you'll reach a signed trail fork; take the left branch, heading generally southwest and downhill 0.4 mile to the beginning of Lemmon Rock Lookout Trail #12. A sign indicates it to your left.

Descend south on the Lemmon Rock Lookout Trail about 0.2 mile to where the trail makes a sharp right hairpin turn. (At this point, if you continue straight for about 100 yards, you can visit the fire lookout described in Hike 16, Meadow Trail Loop, page 120.) The Lemmon Rock Lookout Trail now starts descending in earnest, and a sign informs you that you're entering the Santa Catalina Natural Area. If you're here in August—which is late spring at these elevations— you'll see many wildflowers along the trail. To the west are fine views of the huge slabs of Ravens Rock and, below them, the popular rock-climbing outcrop appropriately named Rappel Rock. If you're lucky, you'll catch sight of ant-size climbers silhouetted against the sky.

The trail does nothing but switchback down past these sights, and after about a mile of descent it crosses a small creekbed, which may have water in it during all but the driest months of early summer. Beyond, the rough, loose, rocky trail continues its inexorable descent with more switchbacks. You'll have been walking through mixed pine–oak woodland, with both living and burned trees—it's amazing how some survived and others were destroyed by the Aspen Fire. As you get lower, you'll start seeing some of the oddly shaped boulders that give the Wilderness of Rock its name.

Eventually, some 2.6 miles from the trailhead, you'll reach a T-junction that's the lowest point of the trail. Take a hard left onto Wilderness of Rock Trail #44. There is a place to camp, but you'll find better spots with rough fire rings 100 yards up the trail. A small stream paralleling this trail might have water in spring after snow-melt and in late summer after the monsoons, and trickles in other months. The creek usually dries out in midsummer.

Now the trail climbs steadily to the east and northeast, crossing the stream numerous times in the first mile of the fairly gentle climb. As you get higher, keep your eyes open to the left for views of the Lemmon Rock Lookout and the towers of Radio Ridge. About 1.7 miles and 700 feet above the Wilderness of Rock trail junction, you reach the busy Marshall Saddle, also reached via the Marshall Gulch Loop (see page 114) from the other side.

Turn left (north) onto the signed Aspen Trail #93. This becomes a ridge trail, with views to the right (east) of burned trees and views to the left of surviving forest. Also to the right, on the skyline, you'll see the University of Arizona observatories. Aspen Trail becomes increasingly steep as it climbs north and then northwest toward Radio Ridge. It's a 1.3-mile climb to the intersection with Aspen Draw Trail #423, where you turn left onto a dirt road, passing the top of the Ski Valley chairlift, electric pylons, and radio towers, until you reach the road and your car, 0.2 mile past the ski area.

Nearby Attractions

In midwinter, you might find the trail closed or impassable because of snow. Instead, take the opportunity of a few runs at **Mt. Lemmon Ski Valley** (520-576-1321, skithelemmon.com), the southernmost ski area in the United States. Admittedly, the one good chairlift provides access to just 22 shortish runs, but it's fun and, by skiing standards, not expensive ($45 all-day admission for adults; various discounts available). The season, limited by snowfall, varies from a couple of weeks to a couple of months—check the website. Operational for over half a century, the ski area failed to open in the winters of 2013–14 and 2017–18 because of lack of snow—climate change in action. During the summer, the lift becomes a Sky Ride ($15 for adults; various discounts available), with round-trip views in all directions. In October, Ski Valley holds an Oktoberfest, with oompah music, German food and beer, and golden fall views.

Directions

See Hike 16, Meadow Trail Loop, page 120.

Santa Catalina Foothills

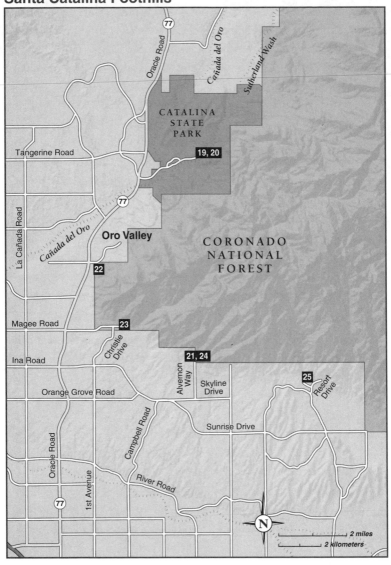

Santa Catalina Foothills

TEDDY BEAR CHOLLAS ON THE PONTATOC RIDGE TRAIL

137

19 Catalina State Park:
Nature and Birding Loops

SCENERY: ★ ★ ★ ★
TRAIL CONDITION: ★ ★ ★ ★ ★
CHILDREN: ★ ★ ★ ★
DIFFICULTY: ★ ★
SOLITUDE: ★ ★

HORSES ARE PROHIBITED ON THE BIRDING TRAIL, BUT LIZARDS ARE WELCOME.

GPS TRAILHEAD COORDINATES: N32° 25.581' W110° 54.454'

DISTANCE & CONFIGURATION: 2-mile figure-eight

HIKING TIME: 1 hour or, for birders, as long as you want

HIGHLIGHTS: Great views of Pusch Ridge, interpretive signs, fun introduction to the Arizona–Sonora desert

ELEVATION: 2,720' at trailhead, 2,805' at high point

ACCESS: Trail open 5 a.m.–10 p.m.; $7/carload (1–4 passengers), $3/pedestrian or bicyclist

MAPS: Green Trails Map 2886S–*Santa Catalina Mountains,* USFS *Pusch Ridge Wilderness;* free sketch map at visitor center

FACILITIES: Ranger station and gift shop, open 8 a.m.–5 p.m.; campground with showers and flush toilets; drinking water; picnic areas; equestrian center; large parking area at trail-head with seasonal gift shop and pit toilets

WHEELCHAIR ACCESS: For developed areas; none for trails

COMMENTS: Leashed pets and mountain bikes allowed

CONTACTS: Catalina State Park, 520-628-5798, azstateparks.com/catalina

Overview

This figure-eight trail combines two 1-mile loop trails that both leave from Catalina State Park's main trailhead, so you can do just one if you're pressed for time. Both are trails for slow hiking, reading the interpretive signs, and perhaps introducing small children to the wonders of the Arizona–Sonora desert. There are a few steepish sections, but they don't last long. The mountain views are a bonus!

Route Details

From the north end of the parking area, to your left as you face the road, walk about 100 yards to a small traffic circle that is the end of the road and has three trailheads. Ignoring the main Romero Canyon Trailhead, go to the northernmost part of the traffic circle and a Nature Trail sign. Within 100 yards, another sign shows six possible trails—again, follow the Nature Trail sign.

Now you'll climb steeply but briefly up a wide trail of mixed rocks and sand to the first of numerous interpretive signs. Looking right (south and southeast), you'll enjoy views of Sutherland Wash below and the mountains of Pusch Ridge on the close horizon above. The sheer-sided, flat-topped, blocky peak to the south is the unimaginatively named Table Mountain. Roughly east, you'll see Romero Canyon (see page 144).

After another 5 minutes of easy climbing, you'll reach a fork for the Nature Trail Loop. It doesn't much matter which way you walk it; I describe it going left (west). There are frequent informative signs—I

Catalina State Park: Nature and Birding Loops

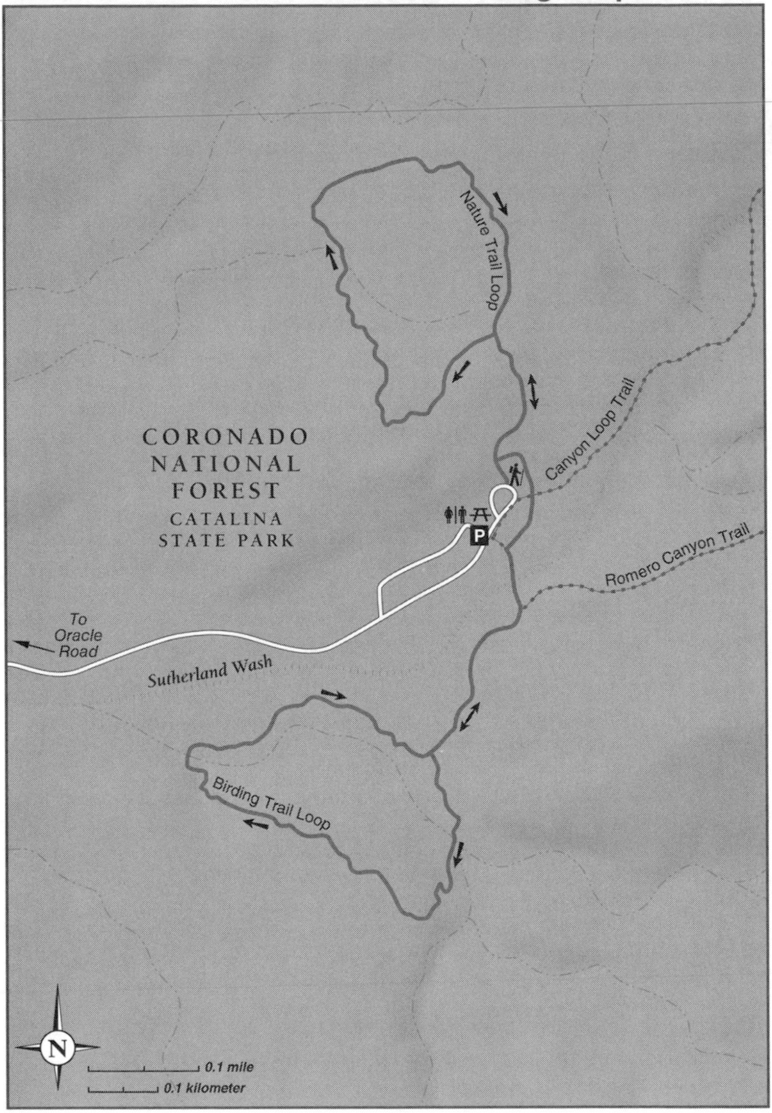

Nature Trail Loop

Canyon Loop Trail

Romero Canyon Trail

CORONADO
NATIONAL
FOREST
CATALINA
STATE PARK

To
Oracle
Road

Sutherland Wash

Birding Trail Loop

N

0.1 mile

0.1 kilometer

like the cement slabs with animal footprints, which remind me of movie stars' handprints on the Hollywood Walk of Fame. Javelinas, coyotes, and roadrunners are certainly the stars of the Southwestern deserts.

Benches are intermittently placed for hikers to rest and enjoy the view. One of the benches is dedicated to Gale W. Monson (1912–2012) and his wife, Sarah. Considered a father of Arizonan field ornithology, Monson was one of the authors of the first annotated checklist of Arizona birds. This is as good a place as any to identify your first cactus wren.

Continue around this 1-mile loop and return to the Nature Trail Loop sign; then descend to the sign showing six trails, mentioned earlier. Turn left (east) toward the Birding Trail. You'll soon have a couple of choices, either skirting around the side of the road to the southeast or taking a trail to the southeast, but either way you'll quickly get to the Romero Canyon Trail and turn south, crossing Sutherland Wash. This is normally dry or has an easily negotiated shallow flow of water. Rarely, a minor wade may be necessary.

South of Sutherland Wash, you'll almost immediately see a sign for the Birding Trail to the right. The wide trail, like most of the

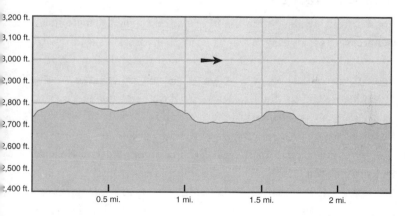

lower trails in this area, meanders through a mesquite bosque (woodland), and you can appreciate how thorny the mesquite tree is. Its beanlike pods bear seeds that were once ground into flour to provide Southwestern Native Americans with sustenance. Nowadays, you're most likely to encounter the gastronomy of mesquite as a natural flavor of bee honey or smoked meat.

After about 0.2 mile the trail reaches the Birding Trail Loop, described here going left (south), though you can go either way. Barely 0.1 mile beyond, the trail crosses the usually dry Montrose Wash and begins to climb steps fashioned from railroad ties to the top of a small mesa. Frequent signs describe the natural history of the area; there are also benches and fine Pusch Ridge views.

The best time for photographs of sunlight on Pusch Ridge is in the 2 hours before sunset, which coincides with one of the two best times for birding and animal-watching (the other is the hours after sunrise). After strolling around the small mesa, walk down another set of stairs, recross Montrose Wash, and rejoin the trail, heading left (north) back to the parking area.

Nearby Attractions

Another worthwhile loop is the informatively signed **Romero Ruins Interpretive Trail,** an easy 0.75-mile walk that passes a saguaro with more than 30 arms and that loops through the indistinct foundations of a small Hohokam village and the more obvious remnants of the Romero ranch. The trail leaves from the right side of the park road, about halfway between the entrance and the trailhead described earlier. A picnic area across the road provides parking.

Two miles north of the park, the nonprofit **Western National Parks Association** (12880 N. Vistoso Village Drive, Oro Valley; 520-622-6014; wnpa.org) sells Tucson's widest variety of outdoors books, along with field guides, maps, music, hiking equipment, and authentic Native American crafts and jewelry. Hours are daily, 10 a.m.–5 p.m. They also offer workshops, tours, and free lectures. Reach the store by turning north from Catalina State Park on Oracle Road, driving 1.7 miles to Rancho Vistoso Boulevard, turning left (west), and driving 0.3 mile to Innovation Park Drive. Turn left and drive 0.25 mile; the store is on your left.

See the next hike for more nearby attractions.

Directions

Take Oracle Road (AZ 77), Tucson's major road going north from the west side of town, to Catalina State Park: From the intersection of Oracle and Grant Roads, drive north on Oracle to enter the town of Oro Valley and reach the entrance to Catalina State Park, on the right about 12.3 miles north of Grant Road. Turn right into the park, passing the ranger station after 0.4 mile (if the station is closed, use the self-pay ticket booth). Continue northeast about 2 more miles on a paved road to the trailhead, at the end of the road. There is ample parking and a restroom.

AMONG SAGUAROS, THIS ONE IS A CHAMPION.

20

Catalina State Park:
Romero Canyon Trail to Romero Pools

SCENERY: ★ ★ ★ ★ ★
TRAIL CONDITION: ★ ★ ★
CHILDREN: ★ ★ ★
DIFFICULTY: ★ ★ ★ ★
SOLITUDE: ★ ★ ★

HEDGEHOG CACTI BLOOM BRILLIANTLY IN APRIL AND MAY.

GPS TRAILHEAD COORDINATES: N32° 25.532' W110° 54.465'

DISTANCE & CONFIGURATION: 5.6-mile out-and-back, 6.7-mile loop via Canyon Loop Trail

HIKING TIME: 4 hours

HIGHLIGHTS: Gorgeous high-desert flora; mountain and desert views; pools to cool your feet

ELEVATION: 2,720' at trailhead, 3,680' at high point, 3,600' at pools

ACCESS: Open daily, 5 a.m.–10 p.m.; $7/carload (1–4 passengers); $3/pedestrian or bicyclist

MAPS: Green Trails Map 2886S–*Santa Catalina Mountains*, USFS *Pusch Ridge Wilderness*; free sketch map at visitor center

FACILITIES: Ranger station and gift shop, open 8 a.m.–5 p.m.; campground with showers and flush toilets; drinking water; picnic areas; equestrian center; large parking area at trailhead with seasonal gift shop and pit toilets

WHEELCHAIR ACCESS: In developed areas; none on trails

COMMENTS: The first 1.25 miles of the trail are in Catalina State Park, where leashed pets, horses, and mountain bikes are allowed. The rest of the trail is in Coronado National Forest, where pets and bikes are prohibited.

CONTACTS: Catalina State Park, 520-628-5798, azstateparks.com/catalina; Coronado National Forest, 520-749-8700, fs.usda.gov/coronado

Overview

This rocky trail follows yet another of the many gorgeous canyons climbing into the Catalinas. Great mountain views and high desert flora characterize the hike, and wildlife ranging from skunks to deer has been reported, although most people will see only lizards and birds. The seasonal Romero Pools invite exploration and are a good turnaround point, although the trail continues high into the Catalinas, connecting with trails that lead to Mount Lemmon, Sabino Canyon, and other landmarks.

Route Details

The canyon is named after the Romero family, who were ranchers in the area in the mid- to late 19th century. Records vary, but Francisco Romero seems to have been the first settler here, and ruins of his house can be seen on the 0.75-mile Romero Ruins Interpretive Trail, elsewhere in the park.

The Romero Canyon Trail leaves south from the trailhead at the northeast end of the main park road. (There are three trailheads within 100 yards of one another—this is the main one, and well signed.) Almost immediately you'll cross the wide and usually sandy Sutherland Wash, although you may need to negotiate some water after heavy rain. Beyond the wash, at a trail signpost, turn left (northeast) to climb a sandy trail that soon swings east and reaches another signed junction, 0.6 mile from the trailhead; take the right fork. (To the left is the Canyon Loop Trail, a 2.3-mile loop back to the trailhead and an alternate return from the Romero Pools.)

Catalina State Park: Romero Canyon Trail to Romero Pools

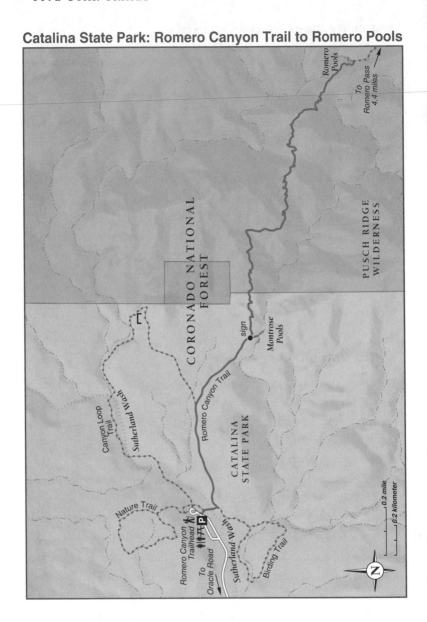

The trail continues through a mesquite bosque and, 0.5 mile from the previous junction, reaches the signed turnoff to Montrose Pools. (You can take a brief side trip south, right, to a bench overlooking the seasonal pools in a steep canyon below. A rough trail switchbacks down to the pools.) The Romero Canyon Trail turns left (east) and becomes much narrower as it climbs steps made with railroad ties to prevent erosion. Soon after the Montrose Pools junction, a sign indicates that you are entering Coronado National Forest.

This area has gorgeously varied high-desert flora: In April and May, ocotillos bloom reddish orange, prickly pears boast yellow flowers, and hedgehog cacti present lilac-colored bouquets. Agaves, yuccas, and saguaros wait to enter the display in late May and June, and barrel cacti add golden blooms throughout the summer.

Eventually the trail flattens, and on your left you'll see some strange rocks that look like large chunks of dirt with fist-size rocks embedded in them. The trail contours south a few hundred yards and then climbs east again, through occasional narrow, rocky passages and past ocotillos. You'll eventually catch sight of Romero Canyon to your left, but don't be tempted to descend if you see water. Follow the

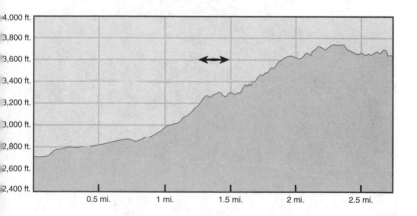

clear main trail until it reaches a minor saddle and then drops a few hundred yards to the pools.

Here the trail crosses the water (except in dry months) and continues climbing 4.4 miles to Romero Pass, 2,400 feet above you. Most hikers stop to explore the pools, which stretch out for several hundred yards north and east of the crossing. Flattish areas to the northeast can make adequate wilderness campsites. The pools are seasonal, although some of the deeper, more sheltered ones almost always have a little water. After heavy rains you'll see waterfalls. At all times step carefully, because the rocks are slick with algae and you can easily take a tumble.

Return the way you came until you reach the signed right turn for the Canyon Loop Trail. Here you can either continue 0.6 mile to return to the trailhead or turn right and hike 1.7 miles to enjoy the

THE LOWER SECTION OF THE ROMERO CANYON TRAIL

longer (but easy and scenic) return route. This heads east and northeast through the mesquite bosque until a hairpin bend takes you suddenly north and west to two benches, where you can rest and enjoy superb views of the western Catalinas. Just beyond the benches, the trail forks—the left fork is for horses, and the right fork takes hikers down a curving flight of stairs into the canyon bottom.

Head west, then swing north, following the left bank of a seasonal creek several hundred yards until a crossing, 0.9 mile from where you entered the Canyon Loop Trail. By this point the creek is more likely to be dry, depending on the season. Immediately past the crossing, a sign indicates the Sutherland Trail to the right, while the Canyon Loop Trail goes straight. The well-signed trail swings west and then south, crossing the increasingly dry creek a few times. To the south and southwest are impressive views of the blocky mountains forming Pusch Ridge, the most obvious of which are the massive cliffs of Table Mountain.

Near the end of the route, the trail intersects the Birding and Nature Trails. The road is 20 yards beyond, and the parking area and Romero Canyon Trailhead are another 100 yards along the road.

Nearby Attractions

Catalina State Park has a comfortable campground with flush toilets and hot showers. All sites have picnic tables and barbecue grills, but ground fires are prohibited. Drinking-water faucets are scattered throughout. Nightly rates during the high season (January 1–March 31) are $30 for the 120 campsites with electricity. During the hotter months, the rates are $5 less. Reservations, recommended in the high season, can be made online at azstateparks.com/catalina or by calling 520-586-2283. A nonrefundable $5 reservation fee applies.

See previous hike for other nearby attractions.

Directions

See previous hike.

21

Finger Rock Trail to Mount Kimball

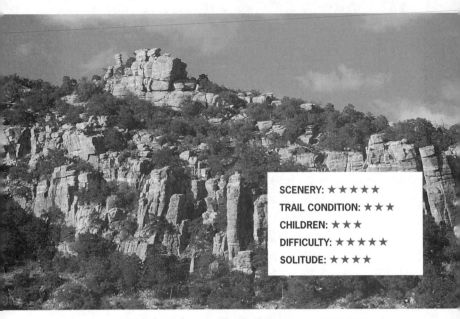

SCENERY: ★ ★ ★ ★ ★
TRAIL CONDITION: ★ ★ ★
CHILDREN: ★ ★
DIFFICULTY: ★ ★ ★ ★ ★
SOLITUDE: ★ ★ ★

ROCK FORMATIONS IN THE UPPER REACHES OF FINGER ROCK TRAIL

GPS TRAILHEAD COORDINATES: N32° 20.215' W110° 54.600'

DISTANCE & CONFIGURATION: 10.2-mile out-and-back

HIKING TIME: 8.5 hours

HIGHLIGHTS: Fabulous views of iconic Finger Rock; saguaro forest; bagging a peak with superb vistas

ELEVATION: 3,100' at trailhead, 7,258' at Mount Kimball

ACCESS: Trail open daily, 24/7; parking lot open during daylight hours; free

MAPS: Green Trails Map 2886S–*Santa Catalina Mountains*, USFS *Pusch Ridge Wilderness*, USGS *Tucson North*

FACILITIES: The parking lot for 35 cars (no large vehicles) fills early on weekends; if it's full, overflow parking is available 0.25 mile back along Alvernon Way on gravel roadsides.

WHEELCHAIR ACCESS: None

COMMENTS: Dogs prohibited; no water available

CONTACTS: Coronado National Forest, 520-749-8700, fs.usda.gov/coronado

Overview

Finger Rock is a major landmark on Tucson's mountainous northern horizon. This steep, difficult, but clear trail climbs Finger Rock Canyon almost a vertical mile up into the Catalinas, never getting close to the pinnacle it's named after. Instead, it continues much higher, reaching a satisfying but uncomplicated summit from which you can see everything north of Tucson (but not the city itself). You'll enjoy climbing through changing ecosystems, from stands of saguaro to a pine forest.

Route Details

Start from the Richard "Dick" McKee Trailhead, at the north end of Alvernon Way about 100 yards from the parking lot. The trailhead's name honors McKee, a conservationist and member of the Pima County Attorney's Environmental Enforcement Unit who died in 1999 at age 43 of complications from leukemia. The Finger Rock Trail was one of his favorite hikes in the Catalinas.

The trailhead, shared with the Pontatoc Ridge Trail (see page 168), features informative notices about the bighorn mountain sheep that roam the area. They had died out in the 1990s, but a herd of 30 bighorns from Yuma was reintroduced here in November 2013. Two very short, fairly steep switchbacks bring you to a signed trail fork where Finger Rock Trail #42 goes north. The trail, nearly flat to begin with, provides great views of the saguaro-forested lowlands, the digit-in-the-air Finger Rock, and the pine-forested mound of Mount Kimball to the right of the rock.

After about a mile of easy hiking with a gentle ascent, you'll notice a couple of large, green aspen trees to your left, indicating that there is indeed some water, some of the time, in Finger Rock Canyon. Maps mark a spring here. In this greener area, an unsigned trail, blocked with a row of stones, goes down to the left to explore the water, but the Finger Rock Trail begins to climb steeply to the right.

As you climb, you'll enjoy watching the canyon open to your left into a gorgeous bowl full of saguaros, with a lovely tan-colored

Finger Rock Trail to Mount Kimball

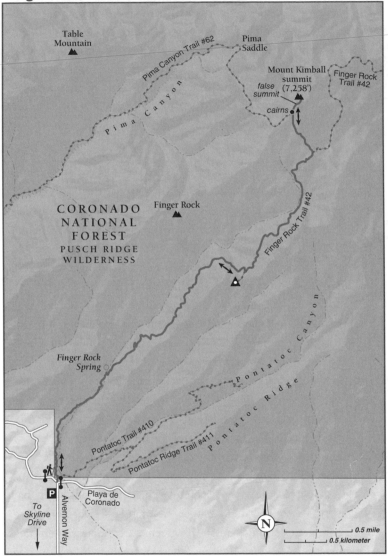

Table
Mountain

Pima Canyon Trail #62

Pima
Saddle

Mount Kimball
summit
false
summit
(7,258')

Finger Rock
Trail #42

cairns

Pima Canyon

CORONADO
NATIONAL
FOREST
PUSCH RIDGE
WILDERNESS

Finger Rock

Finger Rock Trail #42

Pontatoc Canyon

Finger Rock
Spring

Pontatoc Ridge

Pontatoc Trail #410

Pontatoc Ridge Trail #411

Pontatoc Ridge

Playa de
Coronado

Alvernon Way

P

To
Skyline
Drive

N

0.5 mile
0.5 kilometer

wall rising vertically for about 500 feet on the opposite side of your trail. If you're here in spring, you'll see plenty of wildflowers. The trail is clear but quite difficult, with some leg-stretching steps, loose rocks, and awkwardly placed spiny plants of all kinds—often in rather exposed areas, so pay attention.

Eventually, you start climbing above the highest saguaros and lose sight of Finger Rock. The flora changes into pine–oak woodlands and—yay!—the trail actually becomes flat for a relaxing 200 yards before climbing up through the trees. In a couple of places, minor unmarked trails drop to your left—continue on the main trail, heading generally northeast.

Almost 3 miles into the hike, the route turns east then southeast as it contours up through the trees. You'll come to a sharp hairpin bend with a side trail heading due south (right), barred from the main trail by a row of stones. If you take this fairly flat side trail due south about 0.2 mile, you'll reach a saddle, at about 5,600 feet elevation, with stunning views of Tucson. In fact, for many hikers this is a destination in itself, and they'll retrace their steps to the trailhead for an out-and-back hike of about 6 miles.

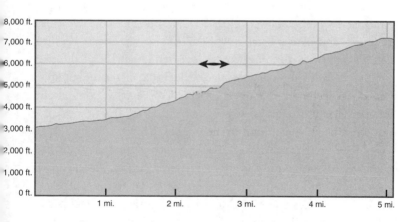

Back at the hairpin bend, you find yourself swinging north and then northeast, and as you climb you'll start noticing some strange assemblies of plants—I saw ferns growing around prickly pears and yuccas, shadowed by pine and oak trees with mistletoe growing on them. The trail continues to be quite clear, but there are some sections of loose rocks. Vistas of cliffs and spires dominate the view to the north, while Tucson can be seen to the south.

About 4.5 miles into your hike, you'll reach the first trail sign since you began—you are almost at your goal. The sign indicates Finger Rock Trail #42 going right (east) another 2 miles to its intersection with the Ventana Trail, and Pima Canyon Trail #62 going left (north). If you're really pooped, you could take Finger Rock Trail about 50 yards to a drop-off with good views of Romero Canyon and Mount Lemmon. To reach Mount Kimball, however, you need to take the Pima Canyon Trail, which is actually a little less steep than the hike has been thus far. The trail sign is at 6,850 feet elevation, so you have only another 400 feet to gain.

As you set out on the Pima Canyon Trail, you'll immediately see views of the rounded peak of Mount Kimball to the northwest. After about 0.5 mile, the trail reaches a saddle with two small rock cairns on either side of the path (pranksters occasionally remove one). Turn right (north) onto a short trail that follows the pine-forested crest of Mount Kimball to a viewpoint—don't stop here, though, because there's a better view to come. Continue right another 100 yards or so until you come to a dining table–size boulder that marks the summit. Immediately behind it is a lovely rocky outcrop upon which you can rest and take in the expansive views, which stretch from the southwest to the north and around to the southeast.

Major landmarks include Picacho Peak, sitting alone in the desert at 290° northwest; the white domes of the Biosphere, almost due north; Mount Lemmon, to the northeast; and, to the southeast, Tanque Verde Ridge and Mica Mountain, which at 8,666 feet is the highest peak in the Rincons. Don't forget to look straight down over the northern edge of the rocky outcrop to catch sight of an elegantly thin rock spire rising 100 feet up out of the forest.

Mount Kimball was named after Frederick Kimball, an Arizona state senator who helped develop Summerhaven as a summer getaway for Tucsonans during the first three decades of the 20th century. He was also a supporter of preservation and conservation in the Catalinas.

Most hikers return the way they came, though alternatively you can continue on the Pima Canyon Trail to the Pima Canyon Trailhead, 7.1 miles away, for a tough 12.2-mile trip that requires a car shuttle.

Nearby Attractions

The **DeGrazia Gallery in the Sun** (6300 N. Swan Road; 520-299-9191; degrazia.org) is 2 miles from the trailhead, near the intersection of Swan Road and Skyline Drive. This 10-acre National Historic District was the home and workplace of local artist Ted DeGrazia. The grounds include a museum of the painter's work, an adobe chapel, and other Southwestern architecture. A gift shop sells art books, posters, and knickknacks, and original pieces are available for purchase. Open daily, 10 a.m.–4 p.m., except January 1, Easter, Thanksgiving, and December 25; admission is $8, with discounts for children.

Directions

From central-east Tucson, head north on Swan Road to Skyline Drive, passing the DeGrazia Gallery to your right; turn left (west) on Skyline and drive 1 mile, then turn right (north) on Alvernon Way and drive 1 mile to the parking area. Alternatively, head north on Campbell Avenue to Skyline Drive, turn right (east), and drive 0.4 mile to where Skyline forks and becomes Sunrise Drive. Take the left fork to continue on Skyline another 0.7 mile to Alvernon Way, and turn left (north) to reach the parking area.

From I-10, take Exit 250 (Orange Grove Road) and drive 7 miles to Skyline Drive; then drive 1.1 miles to the fork with Sunrise Drive, continuing on Skyline to Alvernon.

Note: Alvernon Way, a main street crossing most of central Tucson, does not have a bridge across the Rillito River. Therefore, the trailhead must be approached from Skyline Drive, as described above.

SCENERY: ★ ★ ★ ★
TRAIL CONDITION: ★ ★ ★ ★
CHILDREN: ★ ★ ★ ★
DIFFICULTY: ★ ★
SOLITUDE: ★ ★ ★

FLOWERS, TREES, BUSHES, AND SAGUAROS ON THE LINDA VISTA LOOP

GPS TRAILHEAD COORDINATES: N32° 22.834' W110° 57.665'

DISTANCE & CONFIGURATION: 3-mile loop

HIKING TIME: 1.5 hours

HIGHLIGHTS: Palo verde and cactus forest, views of Pusch Peak

ELEVATION: 2,675' at trailhead, 3,070' at high point

ACCESS: Parking area open 5 a.m.–9 p.m.; overnight parking permit available from Oro Valley Parks and Recreation, 520-229-5050; no fee

MAPS: Green Trails Map 2886S–*Santa Catalina Mountains*

FACILITIES: Parking for about 10 cars

WHEELCHAIR ACCESS: None

COMMENTS: No dogs or bikes allowed; horses permitted but infrequently seen

CONTACTS: Coronado National Forest, 520-749-8700, fs.usda.gov/coronado

Overview

Linda Vista (Spanish for "lovely view") is a fun, easy loop with attractive views of Pusch Peak at the western end of the Santa Catalina mountain range. The desert vegetation is thick, beautiful, and varied. Folks living in Tucson's northwest sector will find this an easily reached backyard hike. Late afternoon provides photographers with the best light for the mountains. The trail is narrow, and children need to be careful of prickly plants that grow up to the trail's edge.

Route Details

The trailhead has a map board and a choice of two routes going either east (left) or south (straight); both come back to this trailhead. I describe the loop going east, making the longest possible hike. (Don't get confused by the map board at the trailhead, which has north pointing down instead of the more usual up.)

Immediately, superb views of Pusch Peak open in front of you, and you'll climb gently about 0.1 mile to an unsigned Y-junction. Go left—if you take the right fork, you'll cut almost a mile off the loop.

The trail approximately follows the boundary of Coronado National Forest, and you'll see some upscale houses to your left, one of which is covered with solar panels. (It never ceases to surprise me

Linda Vista Loop

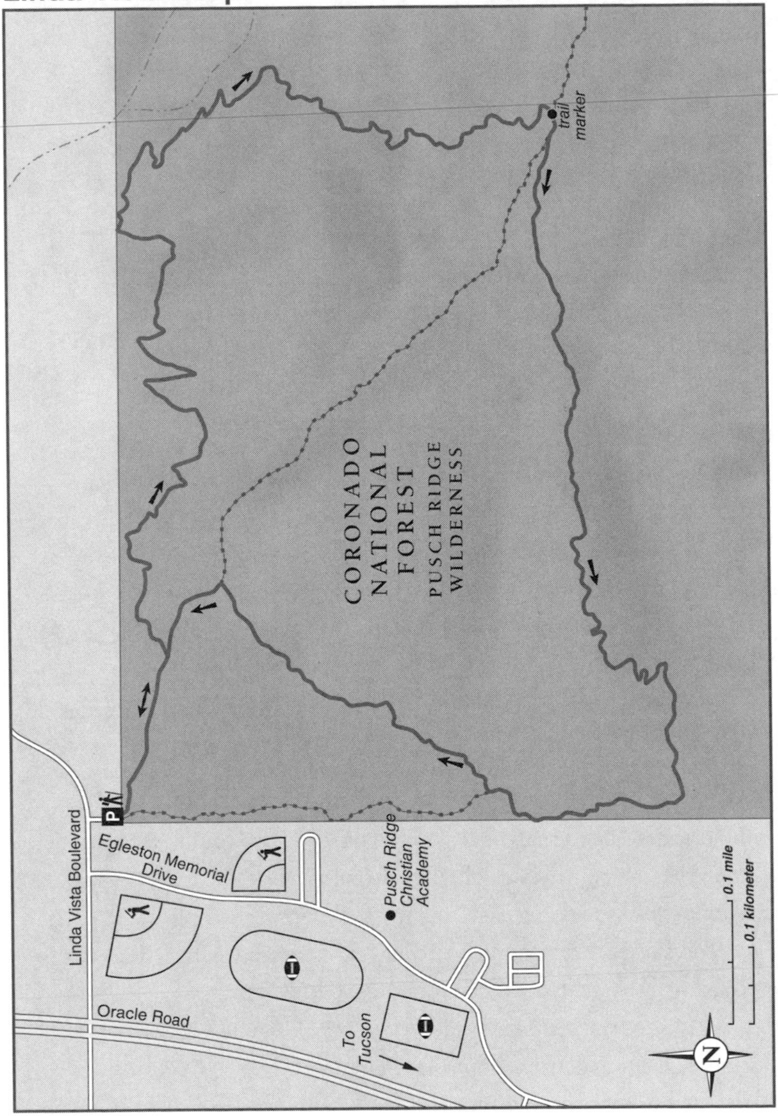

CORONADO
NATIONAL
FOREST

PUSCH RIDGE
WILDERNESS

trail
marker

Linda Vista Boulevard

P

Egleston Memorial
Drive

Pusch Ridge
Christian
Academy

Oracle Road

To
Tucson

0.1 mile

0.1 kilometer

N

that so few houses in the Tucson area have solar panels—after all, this is one of the sunniest places in the country.)

The trail traverses lush vegetation with many mature saguaro cacti, including one that has more than 25 arms—I lost count trying to get an accurate number. Keep your eyes open for it about 0.3 mile along the trail. You'll also see several kinds of cholla cacti, along with prickly pears, ocotillos, and many palo verde trees.

Palo verde is Spanish for "green stick," and these trees are unusual in having a green bark that can photosynthesize. Most trees have green leaves for photosynthesis, but palo verdes, found only in the desert Southwest, bear the tiniest of leaflets and rely on their green bark to compensate. It's a wonderful example of a tree adapting to its environment. In 1954, Arizona proclaimed the palo verde its state tree.

During April and into May at higher elevations, palo verdes have a colorful blooming season, with thousands of small yellow flowers changing the bare green branches into lovely golden boughs. If you look carefully enough, you might see a small yellow crab spider camouflaged to look like a flower; these spiders don't make webs but instead lie in wait for insects feeding on nectar. Once the bloom

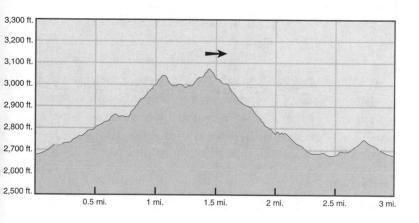

is over, pollinated flowers develop into dangling seedpods that were once an important food source for the local Tohono O'odham people, who ground the seeds in stone mortars to make flour.

Occasionally and briefly descending on its zigzagging eastward leg, the trail makes one noticeable descent before it eventually turns right and heads south. On this southbound leg, a few false trails to your right (west) look as if they might head back to the trailhead, but they come to a viewpoint just a few yards away before petering out quickly. Meanwhile, the main trail meanders south and passes a rusty trail sign on the left. It's so rusted that nothing on it can be read, but you're now more than halfway around the loop.

Behind the rusty sign, a narrow trail climbs east to Pusch Peak—the Linda Vista Loop Trail continues west. (The trail to the mountain is not marked on any maps and is not described here.) Barely 0.1 mile beyond the rusty trail marker, the trail reaches an unsigned Y. Take the left fork to complete the loop. (The right fork goes straight back to the parking lot, if you're in a hurry.)

The westward leg of the loop yields views of Oro Valley, a burgeoning suburban town. (With no offense to its 44,000 residents, you'll probably be casting a look over your shoulder for the prettier mountain views.) Descend toward a school as the trail heads north, almost reaching the boundaries of the school property. At a trail fork behind the school, you can either go straight (north) 0.3 mile to the trailhead or take the right (northeast) fork to complete the longest loop through the cactus–palo verde forest. A few hundred yards farther is an unsigned T-junction. The right (east) trail goes up to the rusty trail sign. The left (west) trail leads to the parking lot, about 0.2 mile away.

Directions

From the Oracle Road–Grant Road intersection in Tucson, take Oracle Road (AZ 77) 9.2 miles to Linda Vista Boulevard in the community of Oro Valley. Turn right onto Linda Vista, and drive 0.1 mile to the parking area and trailhead.

23 Pima Canyon Trail to Mount Kimball

SCENERY: ★ ★ ★ ★ ★
TRAIL CONDITION: ★ ★
CHILDREN: ★ ★ ★
DIFFICULTY: ★ ★ ★ ★ ★
SOLITUDE: ★ ★ ★ ★

VIEW OF PUSCH PEAK FROM LOWER PIMA CANYON

GPS TRAILHEAD COORDINATES: N32° 21.205' W110° 56.871'

DISTANCE & CONFIGURATION: 14-mile out-and-back

HIKING TIME: 10 hours

HIGHLIGHTS: Superb views; 2 small dams attracting wildlife; summiting a peak

ELEVATION: 2,920' at trailhead, 7,258' at Mount Kimball

ACCESS: Trailhead parking open sunrise–sunset. Trail open daily, 24/7, for pedestrian access; no fee

MAPS: Green Trails Map 2886S–*Santa Catalina Mountains,* USFS *Pusch Ridge Wilderness,* USGS *Tucson North*

FACILITIES: Parking for about 50 vehicles (may fill up on spring weekends); water fountain at trailhead; no restrooms

Pima Canyon Trail to Mount Kimball

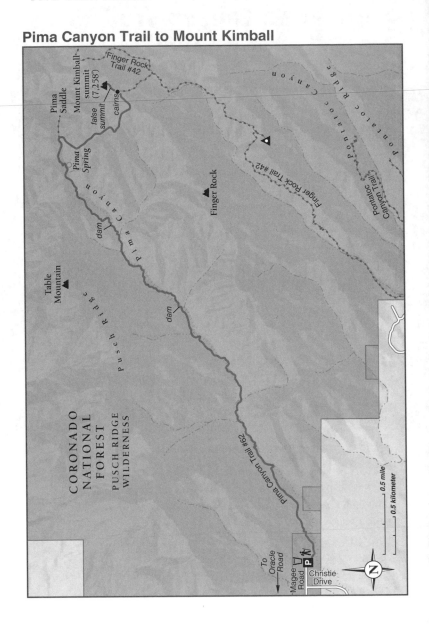

WHEELCHAIR ACCESS: None

COMMENTS: Horses permitted but rarely seen; dogs not allowed. Older maps predating late-20th-century housing developments show the trailhead farther east. Avid, fit hikers with two cars can climb up Finger Rock Trail and descend via Pima Canyon. The parking area and first 0.3 mile of the trail are owned by Pima County. The remainder is in the Coronado National Forest.

CONTACTS: Pima County Natural Resources, Parks and Recreation, 520-724-5000, pima.gov/nrpr; Coronado National Forest, 520-749-8700, fs.usda.gov/coronado

Overview

This trail attracts many hikers on its lower part, but in its difficult higher reaches it draws fewer hikers than the more iconic Finger Rock Trail or the ever-popular Sabino Canyon. Those who go high enjoy superb views, including the rarely seen back side of Finger Rock, before bagging the summit of Mount Kimball. Two small dams built to attract wildlife provide splashes of water, riparian plants, butterflies, and birds. I almost rated this hike two stars for kids until I encountered a tough family group that included a 10-year-old boy who told me it was "really, really hard, and we got lost, but Dad found the way."

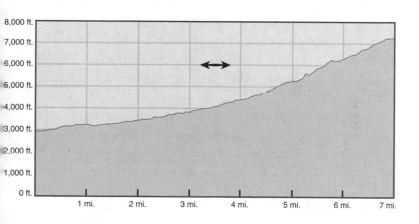

Route Details

The attractive trailhead at the east end of the parking lot features two simple monuments, one honoring former Pima County Supervisor Iris O. Dewhirst, after whom the trailhead is named and who helped maintain public access to Pima Canyon during housing development in the 1980s, and the other honoring Tom Bingham, who was also involved in preserving canyon access and who died in 1992 while rock climbing alone in the canyon he loved.

The trail goes generally east, passing informative signs and scattered upscale homes, and soon dips under a bridge that carries Barrell Cactus Court above hikers. Then it begins to climb steadily but not steeply, with views of most of Tucson to your right and saguaro forest to your left. Enter Pima Canyon fairly high on the left side as the trail swings northeast and away from the city.

After about a mile, the trail drops quite suddenly to cross the usually dry creekbed—this is about as far as many casual walkers go, and you'll see fewer people continuing. To your left are photogenic views of the mountains of Pusch Ridge, which form the northern edge of Pima Canyon.

Hike along the right side of the creekbed a few hundred yards, and then cross again to the left side before returning to the right side. This third crossing may have trickles of water (not in late spring and summer) and has a few short false trails. One of the middle trails continues to climb along the right side of the creekbed and above a lush area of mesquites.

Over the next mile you'll recross the creek, usually dry but sometimes flowing shallowly, another half-dozen times. Lovely riparian woodlands of mesquite and cottonwoods indicate that there is water underfoot, even if it is infrequently seen. As you climb higher, the canyon walls close in around you for a stretch before they open into a shallow basin.

About 2.5 miles from the trailhead, at around 3,800 feet elevation, the woodlands give way to gorgeous high-desert vegetation dominated by sticklike ocotillos and staghorn chollas, spiky yuccas

VIEW DOWN PIMA CANYON FROM ABOVE THE SECOND DAM

and agaves, and a variety of cacti. Soon the trail crosses some rocky slabs with cairns helping you find the way and then threads its way between two grapefruit-size depressions in the rock. These are mortars, used centuries ago by Native American women to grind mesquite beans and other local plants.

A couple hundred yards beyond the mortars, on a short side trail to the left, is a rock-and-mortar dam, some 5 feet high and 15 feet across, built more than half a century ago by Arizona Game and Fish to provide water for wildlife. Behind it there's almost always a small pool of water, which attracts butterflies, birds, amphibians, occasional deer, and who knows what else. This is a frequent turnaround spot for hikers looking for a shorter scenic trip; it's about 6 miles out-and-back.

Cairns show the main trail continuing northeast up Pima Canyon and gradually merging into oak woodlands. About a mile above the dam, the trail becomes thin, loose in places, and rather exposed. It's not very difficult, but a novice hiker with a fear of heights might want to turn back here because it does get steeper and looser.

The trail drops suddenly and begins to cross the canyon for the umpteenth time, but this time it climbs a central buttress that splits the canyon before crossing the second arm. When you're all the way across, look for a second dam to your right—it blends into the rock and is easily missed. This one is a little bigger than the first, but it tends to get silted up more.

Above the second dam, the clear trail climbs steeply, with great views back down the canyon. The trail becomes a little overgrown in places but can be clearly followed to Pima Spring, about a mile beyond the dam. There's a small concrete holding tank below you to the left of the trail and, about 20 yards farther, another tank above you on the right.

Above the spring, the trail gets steeper and looser. This is the most difficult section but is fairly clear, so most hikers have few problems as long as they concentrate on their footing. As you climb out of the canyon, you'll start to catch sight of Tucson again. Roughly half a steep mile beyond the spring, you'll reach a battered sign for Pima Saddle. If you have the energy, you can either continue climbing straight (east) 0.25 mile to the saddle or turn right on the trail to Mount Kimball, another 1.5 miles away.

The route, now contouring fairly flatly to the southwest, is moderately exposed. There are a couple of slightly washed-out spots where the trail is not immediately obvious, but you'll find it quickly enough a few yards on. Then swing around to the southeast, climbing up occasional cairned rocky slabs. Looking south (right), you'll get dramatic views of the back side of Finger Rock below you, with Tucson behind. Finally the trail turns northeast, passes a false summit, and reaches the spectacular top. See Hike 21 (page 150) for descriptions of views from Mount Kimball.

Directions

From east-central Tucson, head north on Swan Road to Sunrise Drive and turn west (left) on Sunrise, which becomes Skyline Drive and then Ina Road. Almost 5 miles from Swan, you'll reach the intersection of Ina Road and First Avenue to the south and Christie Drive to the north. Turn right on Christie and follow it about 1.4 miles to Magee Road, where you turn right to reach the trailhead.

Alternatively, from I-10 take Exit 256 (Grant Road). Follow Grant Road east 1.8 miles to First Avenue; turn left and drive north 6 miles to Ina Road, and cross Ina onto Christie Drive. Continue as described above.

From downtown, take Broadway east 1 mile to Euclid Avenue, and turn left (north). After 2 miles, at Grant Road, Euclid becomes First Avenue; continue as described above.

From I-10, take Exit 248 (Ina Road), and drive east on Ina Road 6.1 miles to Christie Drive; turn left to reach the trailhead.

FINGER ROCK AS SEEN FROM THE PONTATOC TRAIL

SCENERY: ★ ★ ★ ★ ★
TRAIL CONDITION: ★ ★
CHILDREN: ★ ★ ★
DIFFICULTY: ★ ★ ★
SOLITUDE: ★ ★ ★

GPS TRAILHEAD COORDINATES: N32° 20.215' W110° 54.600'

DISTANCE & CONFIGURATION: 5.2-mile out-and-back

HIKING TIME: 3.25 hours

HIGHLIGHTS: Views of Tucson and Finger Rock; teddy bear cholla thicket; old mine

ELEVATION: 3,100' at trailhead, 4,390' at trail's end

ACCESS: Trail open daily, 24/7; parking lot open during daylight hours; no fee

MAPS: Green Trails Map 2886S–*Santa Catalina Mountains,* USFS *Pusch Ridge Wilderness,* USGS *Tucson North*

FACILITIES: Parking lot for 35 cars (no large vehicles) fills early on weekends; if it's full, overflow parking is available 0.25 mile back along Alvernon Way on gravel roadsides.

WHEELCHAIR ACCESS: None

COMMENTS: No dogs allowed. USFS trail signs and maps indicate that the trail is 2.6 miles one-way; my GPS reading was just under 2 miles.

CONTACTS: Coronado National Forest, 520-749-8700, fs.usda.gov/coronado

Overview

This trail affords excellent views of Tucson and its surrounding mountains from different angles—bring a city map and binoculars to pick out the streets and landmarks. Looking away from Tucson, you'll have vistas of Finger Rock (see Hike 21, page 150) and Pontatoc Canyon in the front ranges of the Santa Catalina Mountains. The hike ends at an old mine that gives the trail its name.

Route Details

The trailhead, at the north end of Alvernon Way, about 100 yards from the parking lot, is shared with the Finger Rock Trail (see page 150) and features informative notices about the bighorn mountain sheep that roam the area. Two very short, fairly steep switchbacks bring you to the signed trail fork where Finger Rock Trail #42 heads north and Pontatoc Trail #410 heads east (right).

Pick your way down a little drop-off where the trail isn't obvious; look for it below you as it goes east, past a row of several upscale residences to the right of the trail. Within a few minutes the trail veers northeast, away from those nice-looking homes and into even-nicer-looking wilderness scenery, dominated by Finger Rock views to the north and Pontatoc Ridge, a roughly triangular, blocky-looking outcrop, to the east. Near the top of the ridge, you can see black caves that are the entrances to old mines.

About 0.6 mile from the trailhead, you'll cross a tiny wash (almost always dry) and start climbing along the right side of the wash until you reach a signed fork 0.75 mile from the trailhead. Here you could continue following the Pontatoc Trail—which goes straight (east) into Pontatoc Canyon for about 3 miles—or turn right (southwest) onto Pontatoc Ridge Trail #411, the hike described here.

The narrow trail flattens and looks down on the route you've just walked up. Almost 0.25 mile from the fork, you'll see large, flat, rocky areas to the right that are a perfect place to stretch out on while you have a snack and admire the view of Tucson's west side.

Pontatoc Ridge Trail

Downtown is about 8 miles southwest, with the Tucson Mountains overlooking it from the west.

The trail continues southwest, past the flat rocks, approximately 100 yards before it swings east and starts climbing, with ever-wider views of central Tucson. Another 0.2 mile brings you to an unusually dense thicket of teddy bear cholla (*Cylindropuntia bigelovii*), a cactus with a thick covering of golden spines that look teddy-bear soft from a distance but are finely barbed and very sharp. They will attach themselves to you with the merest touch, giving the plant the nickname "jumping cactus." Other closely related species are also known to jump . . . so beware!

Beyond the cholla thicket, the trail becomes indistinct in areas where it climbs rocky slabs. Watch for cairns to guide you, and ignore side trails that are crossed with a line of small rocks to indicate that they aren't the best way. Within a few minutes you should be on a distinct trail again, still climbing gently. To your left you'll see the Pontatoc Trail far below, wending its way up the canyon.

About 0.6 mile beyond the teddy bear chollas, the trail crosses a narrow saddle. Due south of the saddle, you'll have a great view of

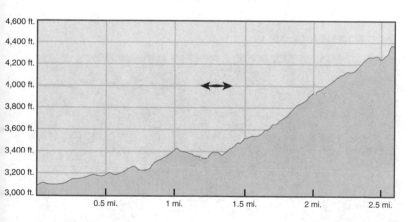

ruler-straight Swan Road traversing the east side of Tucson to Davis-Monthan Air Force Base, 10 miles away, and the Santa Rita Mountains beyond.

The narrow trail continues climbing Pontatoc Ridge several hundred yards to a sign that oddly proclaims DOGS PROHIBITED BEYOND THIS POINT. (Dogs weren't allowed in the first place.) Above you are three cavelike openings to mine shafts that are not maintained and may be dangerous. The trail ends here, but you can scramble up short, steep, loose paths to the mine openings and look inside—a flashlight is useful. The mines, worked from 1906 to 1917, yielded small amounts of copper and silver.

Any exploration beyond the end of the trail is entirely at your own risk.

Nearby Attractions

See Hike 21, Finger Rock Trail to Mount Kimball, page 150.

Directions

See Hike 21—the same parking area is used.

EASTERN COLLARED LIZARD

Ventana Canyon to Maiden Pools and The Window

SCENERY: ★ ★ ★ ★ ★

TRAIL CONDITION: ★ ★ ★

CHILDREN: ★ ★ ★ (Maiden Pools)
★ ★ (The Window)

DIFFICULTY: ★ ★ ★ ★ (Maiden Pools)
★ ★ ★ ★ ★ (The Window)

SOLITUDE: ★ ★ ★ (Maiden Pools
★ ★ ★ ★ ★ (The Window)

THE SPIRES OF WINDOW PEAK, FRAMED BY THE WINDOW

Ventana Canyon to Maiden Pools and The Window

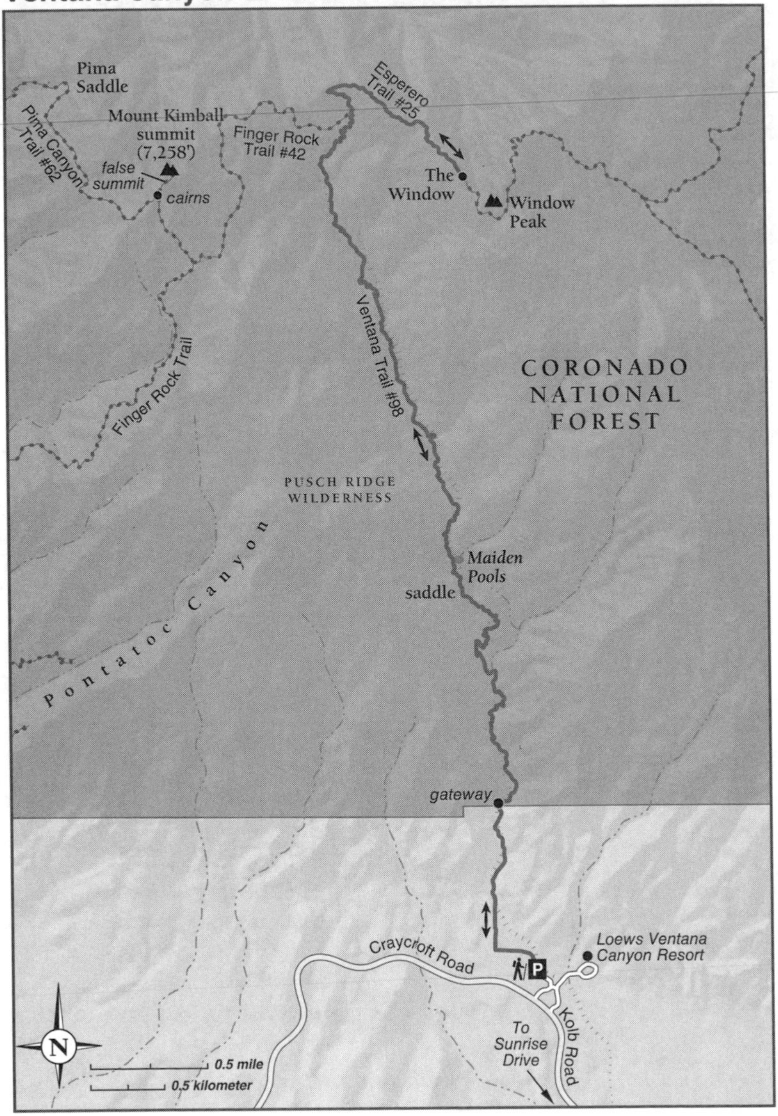

Pima
Saddle

Pima Canyon
Trail #62

Mount Kimball
summit
(7,258')

false
summit

cairns

Finger Rock
Trail #42

Esperero
Trail #25

The
Window

Window
Peak

Finger Rock Trail

Ventana Trail #98

CORONADO
NATIONAL
FOREST

PUSCH RIDGE
WILDERNESS

Maiden
Pools

saddle

Pontatoc Canyon

gateway

Craycroft Road

Loews Ventana
Canyon Resort

To
Sunrise
Drive

Kolb Road

N

0.5 mile

0.5 kilometer

GPS TRAILHEAD COORDINATES: N32° 19.674' W110° 51.184'

DISTANCE & CONFIGURATION: 4.6-mile out-and-back to Maiden Pools, 12.8-mile out-and-back to The Window

HIKING TIME: 3.5 hours to Maiden Pools, 10.5 hours to The Window

HIGHLIGHTS: Gorgeous canyon, pools, lush vegetation, birding, and an impressive geological formation

ELEVATION: 3,025' at trailhead, 4,300' at Maiden Pools, 7,000' at The Window

ACCESS: Trailhead open daily, dawn–dusk; no fee

MAPS: Green Trails Map 2886S–*Santa Catalina Mountains,* USFS *Pusch Ridge Wilderness,* USGS *Tucson North*

FACILITIES: Trailhead parking for about 25 cars; no large RVs

WHEELCHAIR ACCESS: None

COMMENTS: Hikers only. The Coronado National Forest trailhead map indicates 12.8 miles out-and-back to The Window, other maps show 13.2 miles, and previous guidebooks vary. My GPS showed 12.1 miles.

CONTACTS: Coronado National Forest, 520-749-8700, fs.usda.gov/coronado

Overview

The hike to Maiden Pools offers exceptional views of Ventana Canyon and is a fairly popular picnic destination. Above the pools, a less traveled trail ascends through thriving woodlands to a ridge with views

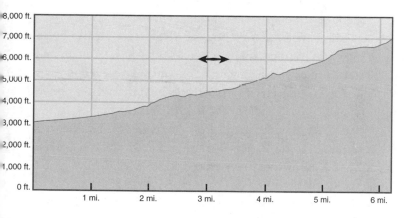

of Mount Lemmon and other landmarks. Keep going to a natural rock window, which makes for a satisfying destination and provides unusual photo ops.

Route Details

From the trailhead, you're forced to follow a narrow path almost a mile, with chain-link fences on either side and NO TRESPASSING signs. This is not as bad as it sounds: thick vegetation and boisterous birdsong provide a good introduction to the trail, and hikers are happy that landowners were able to provide a corridor to the canyon. Even within this 15-foot-wide corridor, you'll cross a stream a few times as you ascend almost unnoticeably.

A switchback gateway, marking the border between private properties in Pima County and Coronado National Forest, is designed so that horses cannot pass. You come to a sign for Ventana Trail #98, beyond which the trail continues its gentle ascent with a few more creek crossings. These are usually straightforward, with rock slabs conveniently placed to keep your feet dry. In summer and late fall, the crossings are often dry, and they rarely fill to where you'll have to wade. In spring, you'll see butterflies along the creek.

Soon the canyon narrows, and dramatic rock cliffs and towers dominate the view. At times it feels as if you're surrounded by an Asian-mountain painting. About 1.5 miles into the hike, at around 3,400 feet elevation, you'll hit a series of switchbacks and find yourself climbing quite steeply. The trail is rocky but firm and clear, eventually topping out at a saddle at about 4,250 feet elevation.

Here you're rewarded with a great view to the south of the eastern reaches of growing Tucson. The flat area in the middle distance is the Davis-Monthan Air Force Base, with Mount Wrightson and the Santa Ritas dominating the horizon. A couple of flat places on the saddle are good spots for a picnic. Beyond, the trail drops a few hundred yards to the Maiden Pools.

The pools are on the right side of the trail and extend for several hundred yards. Some are linked by pretty little waterfalls, and social side trails give access to a few of the pools. After extended dry periods, such as June–July before the monsoons and November–December before the winter snowmelt, the pools are mainly dry.

Above the pools, the thick vegetation attests that there's water in the canyon for most of the year. Oak trees are common, with occasional aspens, sycamores, and cottonwoods livening up the mix and many smaller bushes grabbing at your legs. The trail ascends in fits and starts, with a switchback here and a step-up there, interspersed with unexpected flat areas or descents to the creek, which you cross several times. The underbrush occasionally makes the trail a little unclear, but helpfully placed cairns will guide you.

Eventually there are more steep sections than flat ones, and you encounter loose trail underfoot. If you pay attention to your surroundings, you'll see a jagged cliff on the northeastern horizon, and for a few hundred yards you can make out the natural rock window that gives the canyon its name— *ventana* is Spanish for "window." From this angle, ascending to The Window looks like an epic rock climb, but you will not need ropes because hikers approach The Window from the far side. Later on the trail, the view of The Window is hidden.

As you climb higher, pine trees begin to introduce themselves in the oak woodland. To your left, just south of west, you can appreciate the cliffs of the north face of Mount Kimball (see pages 150 and 161). You reach a trail junction about 5 miles from the trailhead, with a metal marker indicating the Finger Rock Trail going left (west) and the Esperero Trail going right (northeast).

This is actually the end of the Ventana Trail—continue on the Esperero Trail about another mile. It's steep enough that rock steps have been built into it at several points, and at one point the trail heads west about 0.1 mile, which might make you think you're heading the wrong way. Fear not: it switches back and reaches a wonderful, almost flat ridge that you follow east, with views of Tucson to your right and Mount Lemmon to your left. This in itself is a great end to a hike, but the best is yet to come.

The final push is a few hundred yards of climbing, generally southeast, toward and then behind the rock buttress that houses

The Window. You can't see this natural rock arch until you've almost passed it, so as you ascend the steep, loose trail behind the buttress, make sure to keep looking to your right.

The Window itself is about 15 feet high and 25 feet wide. Every time I go up there, it's really windy, so hold on to your hat. Views to the west include Mount Kimball, Ventana Canyon, and much of Tucson; as you look the other way, the spires of Window Peak dominate the view. Just remember that the west side of The Window is a vertical cliff, so explore with care.

Directions

From I-10 coming from the northwest, take Exit 248 (Ina Road), and head east. After 6.8 miles Ina becomes Skyline Drive and, almost 2 miles farther, becomes Sunrise Drive. Follow Sunrise about 6 miles to Kolb Road and turn left (north). Follow Kolb Road about 1.25 miles, passing the entrance to Loews Ventana Canyon Resort on your right and then taking the next right onto Resort Drive. Drive 0.1 mile to the employee parking lot on your left, and then drive through this lot to the fenced-off area designated for trailhead parking.

From I-10 coming from the southeast, take Exit 270 (Kolb Road), and head north 9.6 miles to Sabino Canyon Road. Turn right (northeast) and go 2.9 miles on Sabino Canyon Road until it again becomes Kolb Road. Continue north on Kolb Road 3.3 miles to the entrance to Loews Ventana Canyon Resort on your right, and continue as described above.

From most parts of Tucson on Speedway Boulevard and roads south of Speedway, drive east to Kolb Road and turn left (north) on Kolb to its intersection with Sabino Canyon Road, and continue as described above.

THE WINDOW OVERLOOKS THE UPPER END OF VENTANA CANYON.

Saguaro National Park West, Tucson Mountains, and Tortolita Mountains

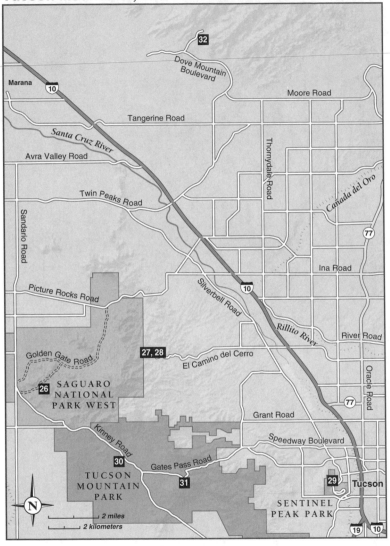

Saguaro National Park West, Tucson Mountains, and Tortolita Mountains

FLOWERING SAGUARO ON THE HUGH NORRIS TRAIL (PAGE 182)

SCENERY: ★ ★ ★ ★ ★
TRAIL CONDITION: ★ ★ ★ ★
CHILDREN: ★ ★ ★
DIFFICULTY: ★ ★ ★ ★
SOLITUDE: ★ ★ ★ ★

SAGUAROS FOLLOW THE TRAIL TO THE RIDGE.

GPS TRAILHEAD COORDINATES: N32° 16.286' W111° 12.182'

DISTANCE & CONFIGURATION: 9.8-mile out-and-back

HIKING TIME: 5 hours

HIGHLIGHTS: Ridge views, desert flora, great 360-degree vistas from Wasson Peak

ELEVATION: 2,575' at trailhead, 4,687' at Wasson Peak

ACCESS: Trailhead open daily, sunrise–sunset. Admission: $20/$15/$10 per car/ motorcycle/bicycle or pedestrian, payable at the visitor center (2.5 miles away) and valid for 1 week in both Saguaro National Park districts; $40 for a 1-year car pass. All National Park Service annual passes accepted. Note that all fees may go up by $5 in 2020.

MAPS: National Geographic–Trails Illustrated 237–*Saguaro National Park*, Green Trails Map 2910S–*Saguaro*; free trail map available at visitor center

FACILITIES: Parking for 8 vehicles (no RVs or trailers) at trailhead and across the road; visitor center. See Nearby Attractions for an alternate trailhead.

WHEELCHAIR ACCESS: None

COMMENTS: The unpaved access loop closes at sunset, so don't get caught! This is a hiker-only trail.

CONTACTS: Red Hills Visitor Center, 520-733-5158, nps.gov/sagu

Overview

This is the longest trail in the Tucson Mountain (West) District of Saguaro National Park. Much of the beginning of the route involves hiking up shallow steps, but once you reach the long ridge, superb views unfold in all directions. The trail is clear, and it's almost impossible to get lost. Wasson Peak is the highest peak in the Tucson Mountains.

Route Details

The trail, named after a Tohono O'odham police chief who worked in the San Xavier Reservation in the 1930s, goes east from the tiny parking lot and, with minor exceptions, continues roughly east the whole way. If you leave in the morning to avoid the afternoon heat, you'll be facing the sun, so don't forget your sunglasses.

Climbing up long but shallow steps with stone risers, you'll pass a trail register on your left after 150 yards where you're encouraged to sign in. Almost immediately, if the sky is clear, there are views of the white domes of the Kitt Peak observatories on the horizon about

Saguaro National Park West: Hugh Norris Trail to Wasson Peak

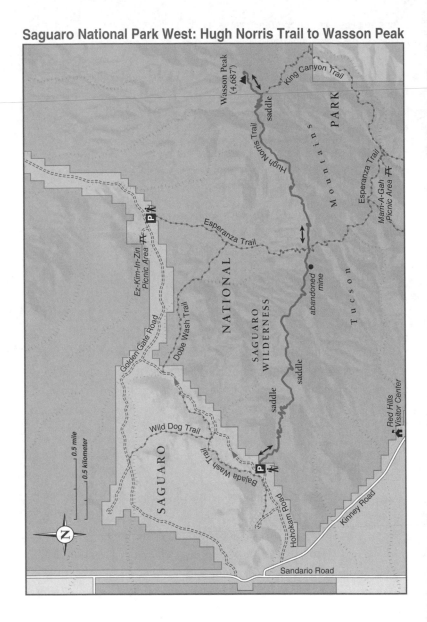

32 miles southwest and, farther south, the distinctive triangular Baboquivari Peak, a sacred mountain for the Tohono O'odham people.

About 0.3 mile from the trailhead, the trail drops briefly south, crosses a sandy wash, and then continues east, still climbing the easy, loping steps up a valley. You're surrounded by as thick a stand of saguaros as you'll see anywhere. The trail climbs gradually, with occasional switchbacks, to a saddle at about 3,150 feet and 0.6 mile from the sandy wash. If you've been counting, you'll have climbed more than 700 steps from the trailhead to the saddle, and there will be far fewer steps ahead.

From this first saddle, you catch sight of the trail curving around fairly flatly to the right and several hundred yards in front of you. Behind you, to the west, you can see the farmlands of the Avra Valley. The rectangular water ponds in the valley are a ground-water-recharging facility run by Tucson Water, using CAP (Central Arizona Project) water channeled from the Colorado River via canals and pipelines. The trail swings briefly south as it continues with more steps through a gardenlike area of truck-size granite boulders scattered around, inviting exploration.

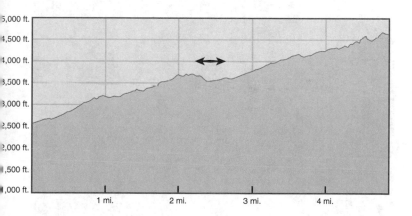

Soon you're heading back east, finally walking along a trail without steps; this is the trail you could see from the first saddle. To the north, beyond the well-defined boundary of the protected area of the national park, are views of the houses and trailers of the Picture Rocks area of the Avra Valley, along with various mountains rising out of the flat desert floor. Two conical formations near a mining area are named Twin Peaks; to their right lies the double-ended mountain of Panther Peak and Safford Peak, and to the far distant northwest is the steep profile of Picacho Peak.

The trail rises almost imperceptibly for a while and then makes a few quick switchbacks to arrive at a second saddle, at about 3,350 feet elevation and 0.7 mile from the first saddle. Suddenly you get a view over the ridge to the south: the building with the curved front and parking lot, just over a mile away and 800 feet below you, is Saguaro National Park's Red Hills Visitor Center.

SAGUAROS, PRICKLY PEAR, AND OCOTILLOS ALONG THE HUGH NORRIS TRAIL

Now, the rocky but clear and well-graded trail tends to stay on or near the top of the ridge, with changing views to the south and north. After climbing about 0.7 mile, the trail descends and, as you go down, you'll see the grounds of the Arizona-Sonora Desert Museum in the valley to the southeast and, behind it on the horizon, Mount Wrightson, the highest peak in southern Arizona. Just past the point where the trail starts to climb again, you'll see a fenced-in abandoned mine on the right. As with the many other old mines in the Tucson Mountains, entering is dangerous and strongly discouraged.

The trail continues about 0.2 mile beyond the mine to a well-signed intersection with the Esperanza Trail. Beyond, the trail climbs steadily but easily, with rocky and sandy footing, some flattish stretches, occasional dips, and sporadic steps. During April and May much of the area is accented by the red flowers of ocotillo, mixed in with agaves and cholla cacti.

The mountain ahead of you looks steep but is easily climbed, with 10 well-graded switchbacks leading to a high saddle that throws open views of all of Tucson below you. The distance from the Esperanza Trail intersection to this saddle is almost 2 miles. Barely 25 yards beyond is a marker for the King Canyon Trail, where you turn left and continue an easy 0.3 mile to the summit of Wasson Peak, with views of the Tucson basin to the east, surrounded by the Catalina, Rincon, and Santa Rita mountain ranges. (The King Canyon Trail heads right and descends to the pass, where it joins the Sweetwater Trail, covered in the next hike.) There is a trail register 100 yards before the summit of Wasson Peak.

The peak was named after John A. Wasson, a co-founder and controversial early editor of the *Arizona Citizen* newspaper, which later became the *Tucson Citizen* daily, which ceased printing in 2009.

Nearby Attractions

The **Arizona-Sonora Desert Museum** (2021 N. Kinney Road, 520-883-2702, desertmuseum.org) is justifiably the best "museum" in southern Arizona. Most of it is outdoors, with exhibits showing off the plants and animals of the Sonoran Desert. There's much to see here: two walk-in aviaries bring you close to hummingbirds and orioles; winding trails separate you from javelinas with almost-invisible electronic fences; caves have secret passages that kids can squirm through; and aquariums and terrariums surprise you with desert creatures. The museum has snack bars and an upscale restaurant as well. Admission: $21.95/day for adults, various discounts available.

The **Esperanza Trailhead** is 2.75 miles north and then east of the Hugh Norris Trailhead. The parking area here accommodates horse trailers and about 20 cars and has an accessible restroom. The Ez-Kim-In-Zin Picnic Area is across the road. The Esperanza Trail climbs 1.7 miles to the intersection with the Hugh Norris Trail, then drops 1.4 miles to the Mam-A-Gah Picnic Area on the King Canyon Trail. If you've had the bad luck of not getting a parking spot at the Hugh Norris Trailhead, you'll almost certainly get one here, and you can hike to Wasson Peak on this shorter, steeper trail.

Directions

From I-10, take Exit 257 (Speedway Boulevard), and drive 4.8 miles west to Camino de Oeste, where Speedway becomes Gates Pass Road. Continue 4.6 miles on Gates Pass Road, over Gates Pass (no trailers or RVs allowed), to Kinney Road. Turn right on Kinney, passing the Arizona-Sonora Desert Museum to reach the Red Hills Visitor Center after almost 5 miles. From the visitor center, it's another 1.6 miles to Hohokam Road, where you turn right onto an unpaved loop road and drive 0.8 mile to the trailhead. *Note:* Beyond the trailhead, Hohokam Road is one-way northeast for a couple of miles, so don't try to arrive at the trailhead from the north.

If you have an RV or trailer, take Ajo Way (AZ 86) from south Tucson to reach Kinney Road. Ajo Way intersects I-10 at Exit 263 or I-19 at Exit 99. Drive west from these exits, turn right onto Kinney, and proceed as described above.

27 Saguaro National Park West:
Sweetwater Trail to Wasson Peak

SCENERY: ★ ★ ★ ★ ★
TRAIL CONDITION: ★ ★ ★
CHILDREN: ★ ★ ★
DIFFICULTY: ★ ★ ★
SOLITUDE: ★ ★ ★

VIEW FROM THE PASS TOWARD KING CANYON TRAIL

GPS TRAILHEAD COORDINATES: N32° 17.326' W111° 07.259'

DISTANCE & CONFIGURATION: 6.4-mile out-and-back to pass at end of Sweetwater Trail, 8.8-mile out-and-back to Wasson Peak

HIKING TIME: 3.25 hours to pass, 4.5 hours to Wasson Peak

HIGHLIGHTS: Classic Sonoran Desert flora and scenery in the lower part; views of Tucson in the distance; nice vistas from the pass and fabulous 360-degree views from Wasson Peak

ELEVATION: 2,810' at trailhead, 3,870' at pass, 4,687' at Wasson Peak

ACCESS: Camino del Cerro Trailhead parking area, open sunrise–sunset, gives access to Saguaro National Park West; admission is $20/$15/$10 per car/motorcycle/bicycle or pedestrian and is valid for 1 week in both Saguaro National Park districts; $40 for a 1-year

Saguaro National Park West: Sweetwater Trail to Wasson Peak

car pass; all National Park Service annual passes accepted. Smartphone users can buy admission using a QR code displayed on a map board 100 yards from the parking lot. Otherwise, the visitor center (2700 N. Kinney Road) is an hour's drive away. Note that fees may increase by $5 each in 2020.

MAPS: National Geographic–Trails Illustrated 237–*Saguaro National Park*, Green Trails Map 2910S–*Saguaro;* free trail map available at visitor center

FACILITIES: None except for parking (about 20 cars and a couple of horse trailers)

WHEELCHAIR ACCESS: None

COMMENTS: Horses are permitted as far as the pass but rarely encountered; no dogs, pets, camping, or mountain bikes allowed. This route is waterless and extremely hot in summer.

CONTACTS: Red Hills Visitor Center, 520-733-5158, nps.gov/sagu

Overview

Of the four main routes to Wasson Peak, the Sweetwater Trail is the least crowded and the second longest. The hike is relatively gentle to the pass, which marks the end of the Sweetwater Trail and has fine views to the north and south. It's a satisfying destination for hikers with younger children or those with limited time. If you can continue on the steeper section to Wasson Peak, the panorama is definitely rewarding.

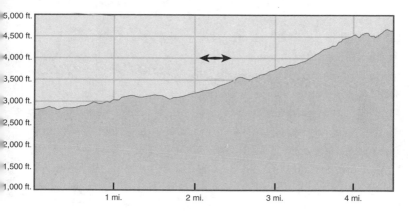

Route Details

At the west end of the parking area, the trailhead has a sign for trails to Wasson Peak. Walk west on a flat, rocky trail, soon passing a Saguaro National Park sign and map indicating the park boundary (where smartphone users can buy admission via a QR code). At a trail register and signed T-junction 0.2 mile from the parking area, turn left (south) onto the wide and obvious Sweetwater Trail.

The trail soon swings southeast and crosses a dry wash, with plenty of loose rocks and pebbles, and generally continues climbing slightly to the south, with a couple of minor descents crossing washes taking you southwest or southeast. Occasionally, stairs are built into the trail, as much to control erosion as to help the hiker. The desert vegetation is thick with saguaros and other cacti, intermingled with a cornucopia of low trees and bushes. After an adequately moist winter, you can expect spring wildflowers, though if the winter has been dry, there won't be much of a bloom.

A little over a mile from the trailhead, you'll catch distant but notable views of Tucson, including downtown, to your left (east). These views last a short while as the trail flattens and then begins a gentle descent, at times paralleling the wire fence of the national-park boundary.

You'll cross a small but steep wash, which may have water flowing in it briefly after a monsoon. Stone stairs guide you up the southern side of the wash, which I'm guessing is the "sweetwater" that the trail is named after; it's the largest watercourse on the trail. (About 2 miles east of here, Pima County has protected more than 700 acres as the Sweetwater Preserve, where you can access mountain biking and hiking trails from the southern end of Tortolita Road.)

Now the trail climbs steadily southwest, with the "sweetwater" valley below and to the right. Views open toward the north, with Wasson Peak on the western horizon. The Sweetwater Trail ends at the 3,870-foot-high pass, where it enters the King Canyon Trail. From the pass, the King Canyon Trail (see Nearby Attractions) winds down

ONLY HIKERS ARE PERMITTED ON THE UPPER PART OF THE TRAIL TO WASSON PEAK.

to the southwest, with the grounds of the Arizona-Sonora Desert Museum visible more than 2 miles away and more than 1,000 feet lower in the valley.

The pass provides good views but isn't much of a picnic spot if you're planning to stop here and return. There are no convenient rocks to sit on, and you'll have to picnic sitting on the dirt or standing up.

If you're ready to proceed to Wasson Peak, 1.2 steeper miles farther, continue west and then northwest along the King Canyon Trail, which climbs narrowly and rockily from the pass. A sign indicates that this is a FOOT TRAIL ONLY—NO STOCK. As the inclination increases, the trail starts switchbacking and passes a closed-off mine shaft about 0.7 mile above the pass. In another 0.2 mile, the King Canyon Trail intersects the Hugh Norris Trail and turns right (northeast).

The final 0.3 mile is an easy ridge walk along the ending section of the Hugh Norris Trail (see previous hike) to the summit of Wasson Peak (4,687'). This is the highest point in the Tucson Mountains, and while it's low compared to the other ranges surrounding the city, it affords exceptional views looking up and around the horizon. A map and compass will help you identify some of the more prominent peaks.

Nearby Attractions

The **King Canyon Trail** also reaches the 3,870-foot-high pass described above. The trailhead is on the right (north) side of Kinney Road, 100 yards past the entrance to the Arizona-Sonora Desert Museum coming from Tucson. There is a dirt parking area for about 15 cars, but no other facilities. Follow signs for the Mam-A-Gah Picnic Area, which is accessible along a rocky road for hikers and equestrians only. Mam-A-Gah, with a pit toilet and a half-dozen picnic tables, will be on your left 0.9 mile from the trailhead; it's another 1.4 miles on a good, clear, rocky trail to the pass. At 7 miles out-and-back, this is the shortest route to Wasson Peak.

Directions

From central Tucson, take I-10 north to Exit 252 (Ruthrauff Road/ El Camino del Cerro). Turn left (under the interstate) and drive west on El Camino del Cerro 5.6 miles to the parking area. The last 2.6 miles are twisty, but you'll see signs for either El Camino del Cerro or Sweetwater Trail.

From the Foothills north of Tucson, take Orange Grove Road west to La Cholla Boulevard. Turn left (south) and drive 2 miles to Ruthrauff Road; then turn right (west), drive 1 mile to I-10, and continue straight (west) on El Camino del Cerro as described above.

28 **Saguaro National Park West:**
Thunderbird Loop

SCENERY: ★★★★
TRAIL CONDITION: ★★★
CHILDREN: ★★★
DIFFICULTY: ★★★
SOLITUDE: ★★★★

A SAGUARO ARM TOUCHES TWIN PEAKS AND POINTS TO PANTHER AND SAFFORD PEAKS.

GPS TRAILHEAD COORDINATES: N32° 17.326' W111° 07.259'
DISTANCE & CONFIGURATION: 7-mile balloon loop
HIKING TIME: 3.25 hours
HIGHLIGHTS: Thick Sonoran Desert flora and scenery at its best; old mines
ELEVATION: 2,810' at trailhead, 2,900' at high point, 2,450' at low point

Saguaro National Park West: Thunderbird Loop

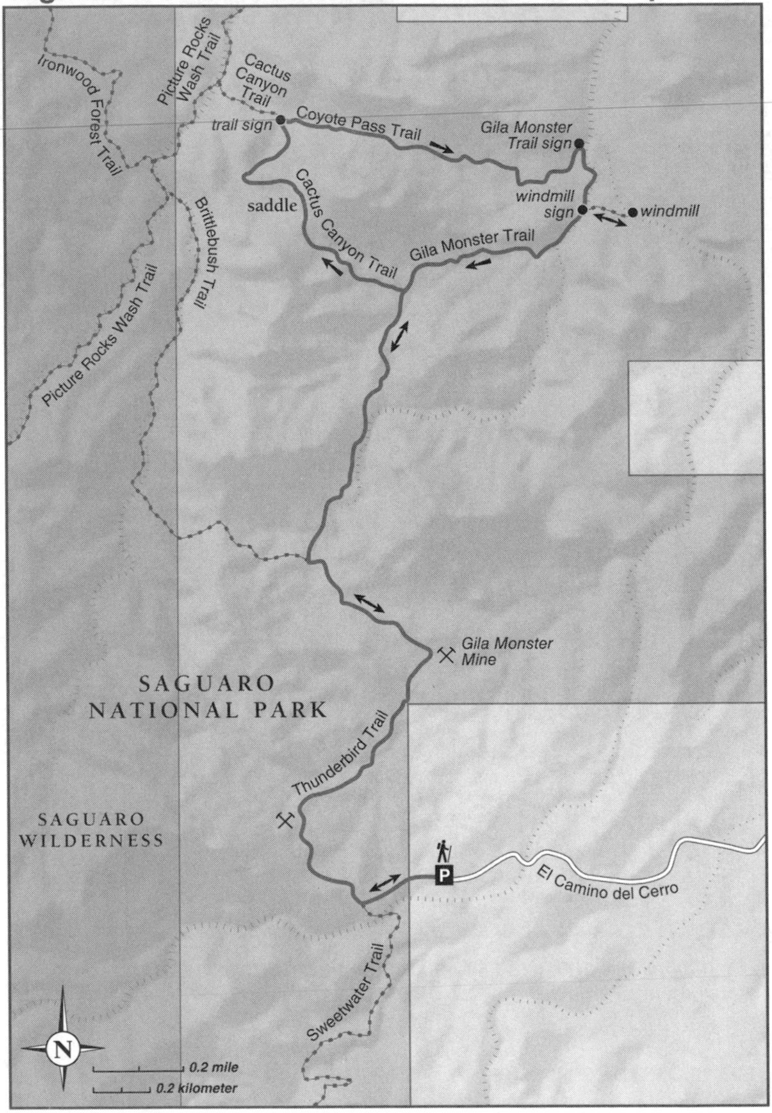

Ironwood Forest Trail

Picture Rocks Wash Trail

Cactus Canyon Trail

trail sign

Coyote Pass Trail

Gila Monster Trail sign

saddle

windmill sign

windmill

Cactus Canyon Trail

Gila Monster Trail

Brittlebush Trail

Picture Rocks Wash Trail

Gila Monster Mine

SAGUARO NATIONAL PARK

Thunderbird Trail

SAGUARO WILDERNESS

El Camino del Cerro

Sweetwater Trail

N

0.2 mile

0.2 kilometer

ACCESS: El Camino del Cerro Trailhead parking area, open sunrise–sunset, gives access to Saguaro National Park West; admission is $20/$15/$10 per car/motorcycle/bicycle or pedestrian and is valid for 1 week in both Saguaro National Park districts; $40 for a 1-year car pass; all National Park Service annual passes accepted. Smartphone users can buy admission using a QR code displayed on a map board 100 yards from the parking lot. Otherwise, the visitor center (2700 N. Kinney Road) is an hour's drive away. Note that fees may increase by $5 each in 2020.

MAPS: National Geographic–Trails Illustrated 237–*Saguaro National Park,* Green Trails Map 2910S–*Saguaro;* free trail map available at visitor center

FACILITIES: None except for parking (about 20 cars and a couple of horse trailers)

WHEELCHAIR ACCESS: None

COMMENTS: Horses are permitted but rarely encountered; no dogs, pets, camping, or mountain bikes allowed. Hiking distance is 7 miles on local maps, 6.2 miles according to my GPS.

CONTACTS: Red Hills Visitor Center, 520-733-5158, nps.gov/sagu

Overview

The Thunderbird Trail is the handle of this lollipop-shaped route, and at its end you'll do a loop along the attractively named Cactus Canyon, Coyote Pass, and Gila Monster Trails, which wind along valleys passing minor but scenic peaks. Along the way are several closed historic mines—it's illegal and dangerous to enter them, but

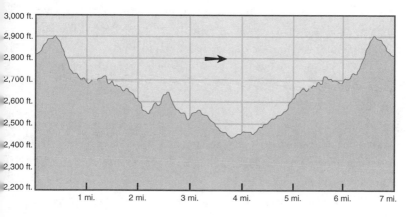

it's thought-provoking to consider this part of the Southwest's heritage and wonder about what life must have been like for pioneering miners attempting to make a living without the conveniences of air-conditioning and bottled water. Other sights to look for are cristate saguaros, spring flowers, and a windmill.

Route Details

At the west end of the parking area, the trailhead has a sign for trails to Wasson Peak. Walk west on a flat, rocky trail, soon passing a Saguaro National Park sign and a map indicating the park boundary (where smartphone users can buy admission via a QR code). At a trail register and signed T-junction 0.2 mile from the parking area, turn right (northwest) onto the Thunderbird Trail.

The trail, rocky and wide enough for two, rises briefly, soon coming to its unexciting high point, and descends gently to a fork marked with a plain metal post. Perhaps it was once a trail sign. (A very short side trail rises to your left and comes to the first of many small mine shafts riddling the area.) The main trail continues, descending very rockily north then northeast, soon passing another mine shaft on the left. You're now about 0.5 mile from the trailhead. Roughly 0.25 mile farther, you'll pass a rare cristate saguaro on your left—it's about 50 yards from the trail, so keep your eyes open to see it.

Still going gently downhill, you'll briefly intersect the national-park boundary, marked with a wire fence and a sign telling you it's 0.9 mile back to El Camino del Cerro. A few hundred yards beyond, you'll reach the Gila Monster Mine, one of the biggest in the area and marked on some maps. Copper, lead, and zinc were the major minerals extracted here from two shafts roughly 10 yards apart. It's closed, as are all the mines in the area.

Several trails converge on this mine; you'll need to turn sharply left (northwest) just before the mine entrance and hike on a narrow, ascending trail. Soon the trail undulates up and down, one person wide, crossing minor washes, with saguaros of all sizes everywhere.

About 0.5 mile from the Gila Monster Mine, the Brittlebush Trail diverges to the left (west) but is easy to miss. There is no sign, though there might be a pink plastic ribbon tied to a branch or a tiny pile of rocks marking the turn.

Our trail continues north then north-northeast to a clear junction marked with a small pile of rocks. This is the unheralded end of the Thunderbird Trail, and if you look left (west) you'll see a sign less than a hundred yards away. It indicates the beginning of the Cactus Canyon Trail, your route to the Coyote Pass Trail 0.7 mile away.

The Cactus Canyon Trail soon crests a small saddle, and as it does you get lovely views of Panther and Safford Peaks (to the left and right) on the horizon about 3 miles northwest, with Picture Rocks Road in the valley below. Dropping from the saddle, you'll note more signs of mining activity and then reach a sign pointing out the beginning of Coyote Pass Trail, with Gila Monster Trail 0.8 mile away to the northeast and Picture Rocks Wash Trail 0.2 mile to the northwest. Turn right.

The Coyote Pass Trail is fairly flat, following and occasionally crossing an almost-always-dry streambed—to my mind, the least

TYPICAL VEGETATION ON THE THUNDERBIRD LOOP

enjoyable part of the hike. Toward the end of this trail are several TRAIL CLOSED signs; stay on the sandy creekbed until the intersection with the signed Gila Monster Trail. This is the lowest part of the hike, and you'll be gently climbing most of the rest of the way.

Turn right (roughly south) on the Gila Monster Trail, following a dry wash about 15 feet wide. After 0.1 mile, a sign on the left of the wash says WINDMILL. Tulips abound. A short side trail, maybe 300 yards or less, leads to a small, forgotten windmill perched over a concrete tank. One of the windmill blades reads "Aermotor USA." This Texas-based company has sold windmills since 1888 and continues to provide ranchers and homesteaders with windmills designed to pump groundwater.

Returning from the windmill side trip, you'll continue southwest along the wash bottom 0.1 mile to a fork in the streambed; take the right (west) fork. A bit over 100 yards along, the streambed narrows and the left (south) bank becomes a 15-foot-high earthen cliff. Look for the trail leaving the streambed on the right bank, heading northwest. There is no sign. Soon the Gila Monster Trail swings west, and you continue about 0.3 mile, looking for the pile of rocks marking the north end of the Thunderbird Trail. (If you reach the sign for the Cactus Canyon Trail, you missed it.) Turn left (south) on the Thunderbird Trail and retrace your steps along it to the parking area.

Nearby Attractions

The northern end of Saguaro National Park West has several more trails, including the Brittlebush, Ringtail, Mule Deer, Picture Rocks Wash, and Ironwood Forest Trails, which can be added to the loop described above to make a longer day hike. Using a compass and one of the maps listed in the Key Information will give you opportunities to explore further.

Directions

See previous hike.

SCENERY: ★ ★ ★
TRAIL CONDITION: ★ ★ ★ ★ ★
CHILDREN: ★ ★ ★
DIFFICULTY: ★ ★
SOLITUDE: ★ ★

LOCALS CALL SENTINEL PEAK "A" MOUNTAIN.

GPS TRAILHEAD COORDINATES: N32° 12.826' W110° 59.9755'

DISTANCE & CONFIGURATION: 4-mile balloon from lower parking lot; much shorter from upper parking lot

HIKING TIME: 1.75 hours from lower parking lot

HIGHLIGHTS: Surrounding mountain vistas and great views of downtown Tucson

ELEVATION: 2,499' at lower parking lot, 2,766' at upper parking lot, 2,898' at Sentinel Peak

ACCESS: Daily, 9 a.m.–8 p.m. (closes at 6 p.m. on Sunday); no fee

MAPS: None besides the trail map provided here

FACILITIES: 2 free parking lots, picnic bench; no restrooms

WHEELCHAIR ACCESS: 0.1 mile of trail from east end of upper parking lot to 2 signed overlooks

COMMENTS: Sentinel Peak is known locally as "A" Mountain. Leashed dogs permitted.

CONTACTS: Tucson Parks and Recreation, 520-791-4873, tucsonaz.gov/parks

Sentinel Peak

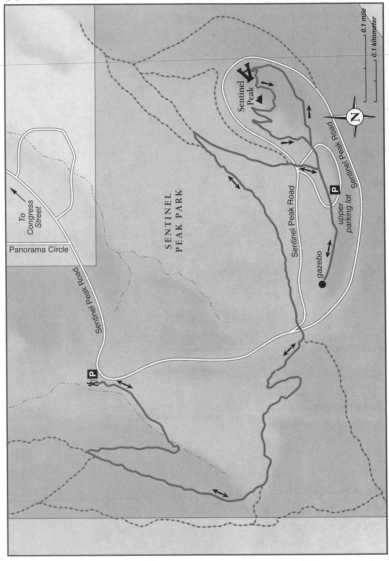

Overview

Sentinel Peak, a small, outlying summit at the southeastern end of the Tucson Mountains, overlooks the city and gives great views of downtown and the whole city spreading out beyond, backed by the Santa Catalina and Rincon Mountains. Many visitors simply drive to the upper parking lot and walk a few hundred yards to the best city views. My description starts from the lower parking lot and follows an easy, scenic trail through the upper parking lot to the summit.

Route Details

The huge letter *A* on the east side of Sentinel Peak, visible from much of Tucson, stands for the University of Arizona, whose students constructed and then whitewashed it on the mountain in 1915, following a football victory. Since then, students have whitewashed it annually, with a patriotic change to red, white, and blue after 9/11. It's even been colored green for St. Patrick's Day! In recent years, Tucson Parks and Recreation has maintained and whitewashed the logo.

The trail leaves the southwest corner of the lower parking lot at a sign for the Gilbert Escandón Jiménez Trail, named in 2012 for

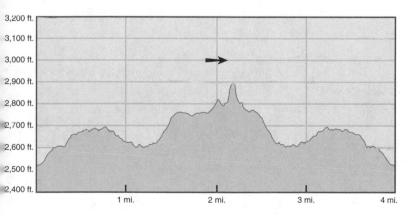

a local resident and hiker who had been climbing the route for more than 70 years before his death in 2015 at age 89. The thin, rocky trail goes south and starts by paralleling the road to the upper parking lot. Look over your left shoulder for views of downtown. Very soon, the trail veers away from the road, and 0.1 mile later it hairpins, crossing a small gully.

As you climb the hairpins, the Santa Catalina Mountains come into view to the north. About 0.25 mile from the trailhead, you reach a T-junction where you turn left (south). An additional 0.3 mile takes you to a ridge from which you can see the southern end of the Tucson Mountains to the southwest and the Santa Ritas to the southeast. The trail follows this scenic ridge to the east and soon comes to a view of a hill topped with a stone gazebo, or ramada. This is the western end of Sentinel Peak, which is circumnavigated by a one-way road going past the A and the upper parking lot, though neither can be seen from this point.

The trail switchbacks down to the road, and you cross it at the point where the one-way loop around Sentinel Peak begins. Hiking along the road is not recommended because it is narrow and curving, and it has no pedestrian path. Instead, pick up the trail on the other side of the road and continue east on the left side of the lower part of the road. Very soon you'll pass a rustic memorial stone and cross for a man nicknamed Gibby who presumably loved the outdoors.

The trail is flat and rocky until about 0.3 mile from the road crossing, where it suddenly climbs steeply and briefly to the right and encounters a T-junction; turn right, roughly southwest and in the direction of the stone gazebo, climbing a rocky path to the road around Sentinel Peak. Cross the road and you'll see the entrance to the upper parking lot on your right.

From this parking lot you can head west a couple hundred yards on a straight, flat path to the roofed stone gazebo, with wall benches, views, and a picnic bench and barbecue grill nearby. Alternatively, find a signboard with a map of the area at the east end of the parking lot. From here the 0.1-mile, wheelchair-accessible Mission View

Trail (completed in fall 2013) takes you to a couple of new lookout points with informative photo plaques describing Tucson's history. Also from here, various signed trails lead the way to "A" Mountain, to the highest point of Sentinel Peak, and to a city overlook. None of these trails is more than 0.2 mile long, and despite the signs it's easy to become confused by the decades of footprints that have been made by past visitors. Don't worry—you can't get lost.

Nearby Attractions

Downtown Tucson has experienced a renaissance after a streetcar linked the University of Arizona with downtown via Fourth Avenue in 2014. Fourth Avenue prides itself on having numerous local eateries, drinking establishments, and eclectic shops without having one chain outfit. It completely closes to traffic twice a year for spring and winter street fairs (usually March and December), which seem to attract most of Tucson.

Congress Street also boasts fine, offbeat restaurants, as well as music venues and the beautifully refurbished Fox Theatre, which looks the way it did when it opened in 1930. Streets nearby lead to the Tucson Convention Center, the Tucson Museum of Art and other museums, several theaters, and historic districts. The **Tucson Visitor Center** (811 N. Euclid Ave., 800-638-8350, visittucson.org) is a source of local information.

Directions

From central Tucson, drive west on Broadway Boulevard. Where Broadway becomes one-way eastbound, cross downtown on Congress Street, one-way westbound. Continue on Congress under I-10 and, 0.75 mile beyond the freeway, turn left (south) on Cuesta Avenue. Drive 0.6 mile to the lower parking lot, on your right. Here Cuesta becomes Sentinel Peak Road, which goes to the upper parking lot.

If you're approaching downtown along I-10, take Exit 258 (Congress Street); drive west to Cuesta Avenue and continue as described above.

Tucson Mountain Park:
Brown Mountain Loop

SCENERY: ★ ★ ★ ★
TRAIL CONDITION: ★ ★ ★ ★
CHILDREN: ★ ★
DIFFICULTY: ★ ★ ★
SOLITUDE: ★ ★ ★ ★

CHOLLA CACTI AND BROWN MOUNTAIN

GPS TRAILHEAD COORDINATES: N32° 13.778' W111° 08.706'

DISTANCE & CONFIGURATION: 4.5-mile loop

HIKING TIME: 2.75 hours

HIGHLIGHTS: Ridge hike with views of desert and mountains

ELEVATION: 2,700' at trailhead, 3,098' at Brown Mountain

ACCESS: Open daily, sunrise–sunset; no fee

MAPS: National Geographic–Trails Illustrated 237–*Saguaro National Park*, Green Trails Map 2910S–*Saguaro*

FACILITIES: The Brown Mountain Picnic Area has 4 picnic ramadas and grills; no water or restrooms. A small parking area at the trailhead accommodates 6 vehicles; other small pull-outs are spread out over a few hundred yards along the road. The Juan Santa Cruz Picnic Area has about a dozen picnic tables in varying states of repair, some shaded; restrooms and water fountain about 50 yards behind. It has parking for 8 vehicles.

WHEELCHAIR ACCESS: Picnic areas only

COMMENTS: Horses are permitted but rarely seen; no dogs allowed. This is a good hike from fall to spring, but it gets darned hot in the long Sonoran summer. Bring plenty of water—there is none available except at the Juan Santa Cruz Picnic Area.

CONTACTS: Pima County Natural Resources, Parks and Recreation, 520-724-5000, pima.gov/nrpr

Overview

It is satisfying to hike over and around an outlying mountain of the Tucson Mountains. You get to summit a minor peak, enjoy great views, and see plenty of desert plants, with a bonus of spring flowers in March and April. Trail signs are adequate, but occasionally you need to use your route-finding skills.

Route Details

The mountain was named for C. B. Brown, first chairman of the Pima County Parks Commission. The commission was set up to oversee Tucson Mountain Park, which was established in April 1929.

I describe this hike clockwise, starting from the Brown Mountain Picnic Area, beginning with the gentle climb and traverse of Brown Mountain and finishing with a valley walk. You can pick up the trail near the Juan Santa Cruz Picnic Area as well.

The Brown Mountain Picnic Area has four picnic ramadas spread over a few hundred yards; the trailhead is behind the third ramada if you've driven from Tucson. The trail leaves from behind a Tucson Mountain Park map sign, heading approximately west (bearing right, first northwest then soon southwest). After 150 yards you'll cross a small wash (almost always dry), and a few yards later you'll reach an unsigned T-junction with the ribs of a dead saguaro overlooking it. This is the Brown Mountain Trail; turn left (south). After a few hundred yards, you'll see a sign reading Cougar Trail 1.1, where you turn right and begin climbing roughly north. (If you cross the wash again, 20 yards beyond this sign, you've missed the turn.)

The trail climbs and switchbacks past saguaros in all stages of life, ranging from young ones less than a foot high to massive,

Tucson Mountain Park: Brown Mountain Loop

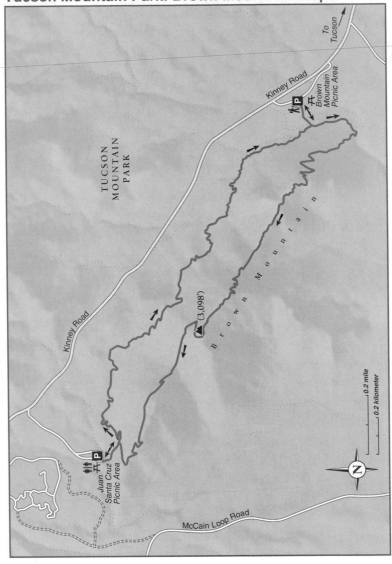

many-armed monarchs. Underfoot, multihued rocks are brownish purple and salmon-colored. When you reach the wide summit ridge, you'll find an open area to the left of the trail where you can pause and take in the view to the southeast.

Old Tucson (see Nearby Attractions) lies to the east-southeast, with Gates Pass Road climbing above it. To the south-southeast is the Gilbert Ray Campground (the only one in Tucson Mountain Park, suitable mainly for RV campers), and gazing beyond it to the horizon you'll see the Santa Ritas and Mount Wrightson.

From here, the summit ridge climbs briefly north and then swings northwest, with super views on either side. Off in the distance to your left, about 40 miles to the southwest, you can see Kitt Peak with its telescopes; south of it is the distinctive triangular shape of Baboquivari Peak, a sacred site on the Tohono O'odham Reservation. On the other side of the ridge are the Tucson Mountains. The highest of several peaks along the ridge is marked as 3,098 feet on most maps, and from here you can see the Arizona-Sonora Desert Museum to the northwest.

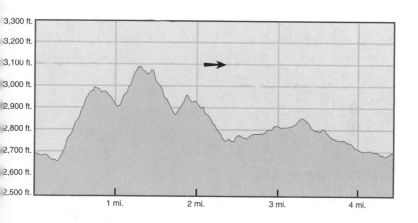

After the highest peak, the trail drops and turns southeast for a short distance before hairpinning back northwest. The trail then climbs around the right (east) side of a final peak, without climbing it, then drops to a sign that appears seemingly in the middle of nowhere, directing you to the Gilbert Ray Campground, back the way you came, and the Juan Santa Cruz Picnic Area, which is your route.

About 200 yards beyond this sign, you reach a T-junction. There is no sign here, but there is a flat rock slab about 2 feet square. Going right (east) continues along the base of the mountain to the Brown Mountain Picnic Area; going left (west) descends about 200 yards to the Juan Santa Cruz Picnic Area, which provides a restroom and a place to eat your snack or packed lunch. You've hiked almost 2.5 miles to this point. Some hikers prefer to retrace their steps from the northwest end of the mountain to enjoy the ridge views again.

Continuing east from the junction with the flat rock slab, follow the valley at the base of Brown Mountain. The trail meanders pleasantly east and then generally southeast, with the mountain looming to the right. Desert flowers abound in spring, and vegetation is fairly thick year-round, so the trail never goes far in a straight line, instead twisting and turning around clumps of cactus or large rocks.

Almost 2 miles from the Juan Santa Cruz Picnic Area, a hard fork left (north) goes over a tiny, broken concrete dam—don't take this trail. Continue southeast, with your eyes open for the dead cactus you saw near the beginning of the hike. It's on the right side of the trail, about 100 yards beyond the fork over the dam. At the cactus, turn left (northeast) and return to the parking area, which is less than 200 yards away but not visible until you are almost back to your car.

Nearby Attractions

The movie studios at **Old Tucson** (201 S. Kinney Road; 520-883-0100, oldtucson.com) have been active for more than 70 years. John Wayne and many other actors shot their way to fame in Westerns made here. Today the studios are still used for filming and are also open as a tourist attraction, with actors performing stunts and mixing with the crowds. Gold-panning, stagecoach rides, Wild West gunfights, and an old-time saloon are among the attractions. Admission: $19.95 for guests age 12 and up, $10.95 for kids ages 4–11, free for kids age 3 and younger (various discounts available); check the website for specific days and hours of operation.

See Hike 31 (next page), Hike 26 (page 182), and Hike 27 (page 189) for other nearby attractions.

Directions

From I-10, take Exit 257 (Speedway Boulevard) and drive west on Speedway 4.8 miles, where Speedway becomes Gates Pass Road. Continue on Gates Pass Road 4.6 miles, crossing Gates Pass (no RVs or trailers allowed). Where Gates Pass Road intersects Kinney Road, turn right on Kinney and drive 0.8 mile to the Brown Mountain Picnic Area, on your left.

If you have an RV or trailer, access Kinney Road from Ajo Way (AZ 86). Ajo Way intersects I-10 at Exit 263 or I-19 at Exit 99; drive west from these exits and turn right from Ajo Way onto Kinney. From here it's about 6 miles to the Brown Mountain Picnic Area.

YOUNG SAGUAROS WITH A VIEW OF GOLDEN GATE MOUNTAIN

Tucson Mountain Park:
Yetman Trail

SCENERY: ★ ★ ★ ★
TRAIL CONDITION: ★ ★ ★
CHILDREN: ★ ★ ★ ★
DIFFICULTY: ★ ★ ★
SOLITUDE: ★ ★ ★ ★

RUINS OF THE BOWEN HOUSE SEEN FROM THE TRAIL

GPS TRAILHEAD COORDINATES: N32° 13.045' W111° 06.176'

DISTANCE & CONFIGURATION: 6-mile point-to-point with car shuttle, 12-mile out-and-back

HIKING TIME: 3 hours one-way

HIGHLIGHTS: Lowland Sonora Desert scenery with appealing cactus-covered mountains; following the steps of a TV personality

ELEVATION: 2,975' at western trailhead, 3,184' at high point, 2,662' at eastern trailhead

ACCESS: Open daily, 7 a.m.–8 p.m.; no fee

MAPS: National Geographic–Trails Illustrated 237–*Saguaro National Park,* Green Trails Map 2910S–*Saguaro*

FACILITIES: None except for parking (about 12–14 cars at west or east end; no RVs or trailers)

WHEELCHAIR ACCESS: None

COMMENTS: This relatively flat desert trail is popular but not crowded with mountain bikers, many of whom know it well and are a good source of information. Horses are permitted but rarely seen. Dogs are prohibited, but that rule is frequently ignored. This is a good hike from fall to spring, but it gets darned hot in the long Sonoran summer. Bring plenty of water—there is none available anywhere.

CONTACTS: Pima County Natural Resources, Parks and Recreation, 520-724-5000, pima.gov/nrpr

Overview

There are no must-see views on this hike, which perhaps is what makes it attractive. The reliable views of thick stands of saguaros, prickly pears, cholla cacti (the "jumping" kind), ocotillos, palo verde and mesquite trees, and spring flowers, with a backdrop of numerous cliffs and crags at the south end of the Tucson Mountains, make this a wild-looking place. It's a hike that somehow grows on you.

Route Details

This route is described from the western Yetman Trailhead, slightly west of Gates Pass, hiking east to the Camino de Oeste Trailhead, which is 300 feet lower. Tucson Mountain Park trail signs tend to face the hiker leaving from the Yetman Trailhead, which makes it easier to navigate from this direction. The signs are not as high-quality as those found in state and federal areas and are subject to vandalism, so carry a map and compass if you don't know the trail well. There are numerous intersections with mapped and unmapped trails.

David Yetman worked to protect the environment as a member of the Pima County Board of Supervisors from 1977 to 1988, and this trail was named in his honor when he retired from politics. Since then he has worked with the Audubon Society and the University of Arizona, has authored numerous books, and has for several years served as the quirky host of the PBS television series *The Desert Speaks* and *In the Americas,* in which he explores the geology, wildlife, and inhabitants of American deserts from Arizona to Argentina.

Grab your water bottles and leave the southeastern corner of the parking lot on a wide, rocky trail that climbs gently southeast

Tucson Mountain Park: Yetman Trail

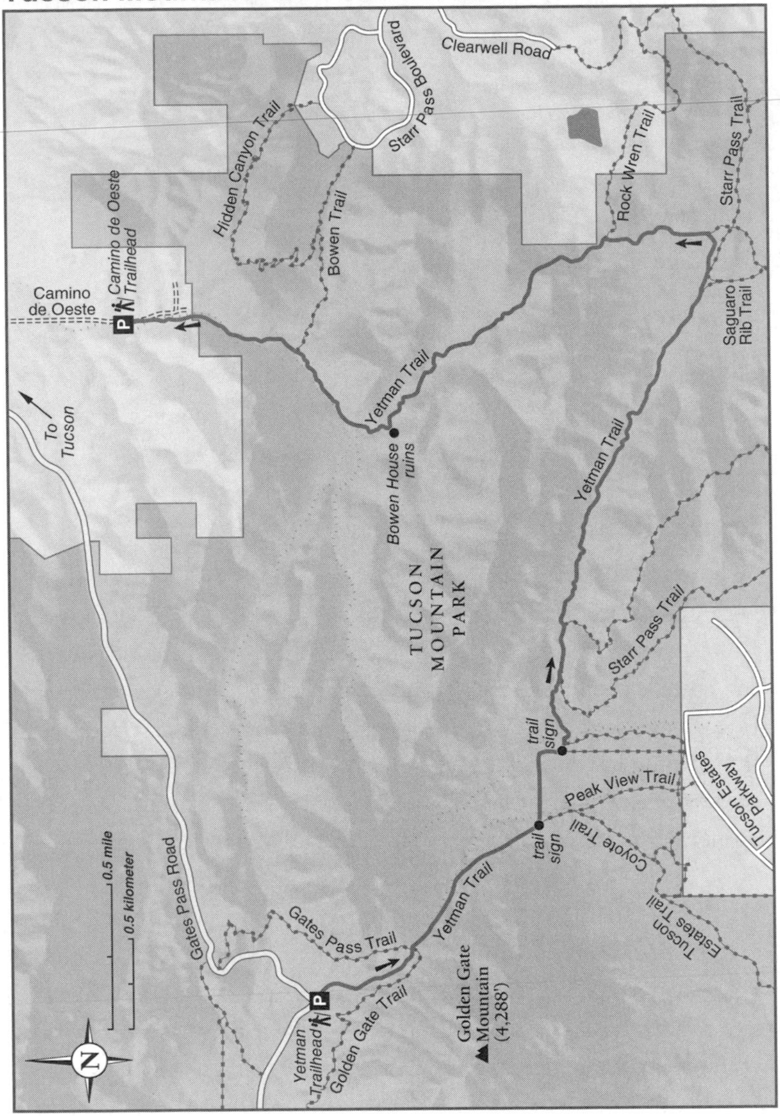

Clearwell Road

Starr Pass Boulevard

Hidden Canyon Trail

Bowen Trail

Rock Wren Trail

Starr Pass Trail

Camino de Oeste

Camino de Oeste Trailhead

P

To Tucson

Yetman Trail

Bowen House ruins

Saguaro Rib Trail

Yetman Trail

TUCSON MOUNTAIN PARK

Starr Pass Trail

trail sign

Peak View Trail

Tucson Estates Parkway

trail sign

Coyote Trail

Gates Pass Road

Gates Pass Trail

Yetman Trail

Golden Gate Trail

Tucson Estates Trail

Yetman Trailhead

P

Golden Gate Trail

Golden Gate Mountain (4,288')

0.5 mile

0.5 kilometer

N

past a couple of trail signs. After 0.45 mile you'll conquer a pass—the high point of the trail, 3,184 feet on my GPS but marked variously on maps. Signs indicate the Golden Gate Trail to the right (returning to Gates Pass Road) and the Gates Pass Trail to the left (not shown on the maps I used).

The Yetman Trail forges on southeast, descending slowly. The peak to your right (west) is Golden Gate Mountain (4,288'), the highest point in the southern half of the Tucson Mountains. Ahead (southeast) in the distance is the Tucson Estates housing development, beyond which the Santa Ritas lie on the horizon.

Thick stands of teddy bear cholla accompany the next section of trail. More than a mile from the trailhead, you'll angle left (east) at a sign for the Yetman Trail (going straight takes you to the Tucson Estates), and almost 1.5 miles from the trailhead another sign indicates that you fork left (east) again on the Yetman Trail. Just beyond here is an unsigned fork; bear left again.

The trail undulates and passes a sharp backward turn to the right, which you ignore; the route continues mainly east and is fairly flat. In this section of typical lowland desert scenery, a rare cristate

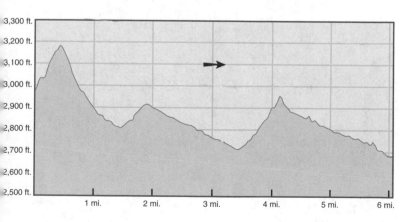

saguaro cactus stands on the left. If you're one of those experienced (lucky?) hikers who can somehow both look around and keep your eyes on the rocky trail, you'll see it.

Almost 2 miles of rolling hiking, parts of it following a sandy wash that's almost always dry, bring you to the signed intersection with the Starr Pass Trail, where you bear left. Some maps indicate the Starr Pass Trail as the short Saguaro Rib Trail, which quickly brings you to the Starr Pass Trail. The trail is flat now and, about 200 yards later, reaches another sign for Starr Pass Trailhead 1.1, quickly followed by a sign for 36th Street Trailhead 0.9. (These trailheads provide access to equestrians.) The Yetman Trail bears left at both of these, heading east-southeast.

Soon the trail swings north and begins to climb gently, with super views of the southern end of the craggy Tucson Mountains to

WEATHERED SIGN AT THE YETMAN TRAILHEAD

the left. About 0.6 mile from the previous signs, you reach a small pass with three trail junctions and a vandalized sign. Look for the thin, poorly marked Yetman Trail to the left (northwest). (Right, southeast, follows the Rock Wren Trail to an equestrian trailhead. Straight on, northeast, is an unmapped trail that goes to a golf course.)

Climbing on the narrow Yetman Trail, you get glimpses of Tucson to the northeast. These views soon disappear as you hike up a quiet valley then drop generally northwest until about a mile from the previous turn, where you'll see a ruined stone house to the left. You can either ignore the building and see it from the trail or hike up and through it and resume the trail a few hundred yards along.

If you hike through the house, the solid stone walls give you the impression that this was a good-size place and would have been a comfortable home at one time. It was built in the 1930s by Sherry Bowen, an editor of the *Arizona Daily Star* who moved with his family to New York City in 1944. The sturdy stone walls endured and are known today as the Bowen House.

Soon after the Bowen House, the trail swings northeast and follows a wide wash. In this area are several small signs that simply say TRAIL. Look for an unmarked trail leaving from the right side of the sandy wash, which follows the right bank on a narrower but firmer footing. After a few hundred yards, this trail crosses the wash to the left bank, and four more crossings follow. Most of the year the wash is sandy and dry, so you could walk along it, but hiking along the banks is easier.

Eventually the trail on the left side of the wash crosses an iron-pole gate indicating that you're leaving Tucson Mountain Park and entering private property. Buildings are visible. The trail soon crosses the wash one more time before arriving at the Camino de Oeste trailhead.

Nearby Attractions

Gates Pass (3,120') was named after Thomas Gates, a Western pioneer whose well-rounded résumé included professional gambler, saloonkeeper, political lobbyist, historian, prison superintendent, and mine owner. His profitable carbonate mine, in the Waterman Mountains about 30 miles west of Tucson, led him to establish a route over a pass through the Tucson Mountains to shorten the journey from his claim to Tucson. The city was unable to come up with the funds to build a road, so in 1883 Gates funded it himself at a cost of $1,000.

The **Gates Pass Overlook** is a popular stop for drivers and hardy cyclists following the historic route. Heading west from Tucson, the overlook is on the right (north) side of the narrow, winding road (no commercial vehicles, trailers, or large RVs) just before the crest of the pass. Here you'll find a sizable parking area (no charge); a restroom; and, at the highest point, a stone gazebo providing superb views into the Avra Valley west of Tucson; all are wheelchair-accessible. Highlights from the overlook include thick stands of saguaros, distant views of Old Tucson and the Arizona-Sonora Desert Museum, and romantic sunset vistas.

See Hike 30 (page 206), Hike 26 (page 182), and Hike 27 (page 189) for other nearby attractions.

Directions

From I-10, take Exit 257 (Speedway Boulevard). Drive west 4.8 miles to where Speedway becomes Gates Pass Road at Camino de Oeste. If you're doing a car shuttle, turn left (south) on Camino de Oeste and drive 0.7 mile to the Camino de Oeste Trailhead, where you will leave a car. *Note:* The last 0.2 mile is unpaved and has one-way sections, so use caution.

Back where Speedway becomes Gates Pass Road, continue west on Gates Pass. Drive over the pass (the overlook is about 2.5 miles beyond Camino de Oeste), and then carefully descend to the first parking lot on your left (south) for the Yetman Trailhead, 3 miles along Gates Pass Road.

32

Wild Burro Loop

SCENERY: ★ ★ ★ ★ ★
TRAIL CONDITION: ★ ★ ★ ★
CHILDREN: ★ ★ ★
DIFFICULTY: ★ ★ ★
SOLITUDE: ★ ★ ★

PURPLE ARROWS SHOW THE WAY THROUGH DENSE DESERT VEGETATION.

GPS TRAILHEAD COORDINATES: N32° 28.529' W111° 05.455'

DISTANCE & CONFIGURATION: 8.5-mile balloon loop

HIKING TIME: 4 hours

HIGHLIGHTS: Dense desert flora, spring flowers, views of several mountain ranges

ELEVATION: 2,804' at trailhead, 4,092' at high point

ACCESS: Dawn–dusk; no fee

MAPS: Free *Tortolita Mountain Trail Guide* at trailhead; download at maranaaz.gov/trails.

FACILITIES: Large parking area with restrooms, water, and shaded picnic bench

WHEELCHAIR ACCESS: None on trail

COMMENTS: Horses, mountain bikes, and leashed dogs permitted. The first 0.5 mile is easy enough for toddlers and can be crowded; continue for a harder climb and fewer people.

CONTACTS: Marana Parks and Recreation, 520-382-1950, maranaaz.gov/recreation

Wild Burro Loop

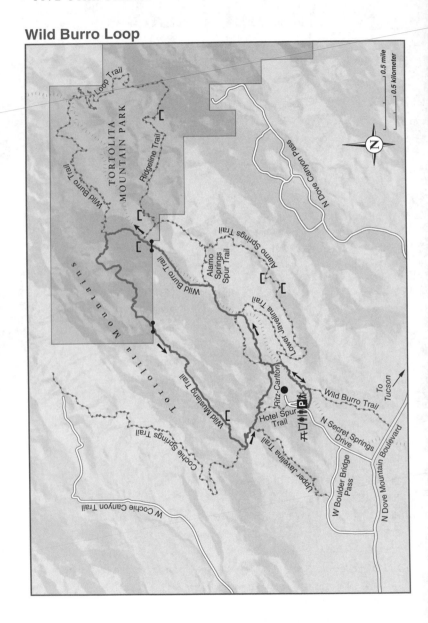

Overview

The lovely Tortolita Mountains are an almost-forgotten fifth mountain range northwest of Tucson with rugged canyons and peaks reaching 4,696 feet elevation. In 2004 the town of Marana (which adjoins Tucson to the northwest) began constructing a trail network centered on Wild Burro Canyon, and in 2009 home sales began in the upscale Dove Mountain residential community, which surrounds the Ritz-Carlton resort and spa. New road construction and a spacious trailhead area built in 2012 have now opened the Tortolitas to easy exploration on well-maintained trails that penetrate some of the densest cactus and desert tree forests in the region.

Route Details

The Wild Burro Trailhead is the major access point to a 30-mile network of a dozen trails, which can be combined into numerous loops or out-and-back hikes. Each trail is color-coded on the trailhead map and well-signed with appropriately colored arrows, so it is straightforward to make up your own loop. A nice feature of this

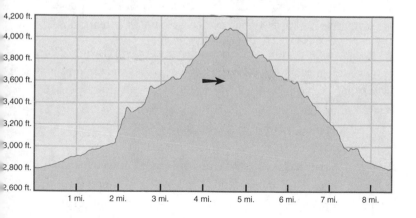

THE SETTING SUN LIGHTS UP A RIDGE OVERLOOKING THE WILD MUSTANG TRAIL.

well-designed network is that the trail signs are reflective—a boon if you get caught taking longer than you expected and are finishing up your hike in the dark. (Yup. It happened to me here as I spent too long admiring a sunset. Remember to always pack a headlamp!)

All loops begin with the Wild Burro Trail, and I describe a loop via the Wild Mustang and Upper Javelina Trails. Immediately after leaving the trailhead, you'll cross the sandy (and almost always dry) Wild Burro Wash and within 0.1 mile reach a T-junction for the Wild Burro Trail where you turn left (northeast). The almost flat trail recrosses the wash a couple of times while meandering through thick vegetation. The extensive Ritz-Carlton resort is visible to your left. Some hikers just walk up the sandy wash until, after 0.5 mile, you reach a notice board, a trail register, and a sign indicating Alamo Springs Trail heading right; this is a popular alternate loop that returns to the Wild Burro Trail farther up the canyon.

After signing in at the register, head left (north) to continue on the Wild Burro Trail, which climbs gently while passing signs for the Upper and Lower Javelina Trails in quick succession. You'll follow the purple arrows for the Wild Burro Trail, which rises almost imperceptibly through lush desert vegetation until reaching the signed Alamo Springs Spur Trail, 1.8 mile from the trailhead. Turn left (north) and start climbing a rocky trail past the ruins of a small stone ranch house (I wonder who built it); continue climbing another 0.9 mile to the signed end of the Alamo Springs Trail. Views down into the Wild Burro Canyon are excellent on this section.

About 100 yards beyond the Alamo Springs Trail, a sign indicates LUNCH OVERLOOK, and a very short side trail leads left to a bench where you can rest, enjoy the view, and eat lunch while reading a plaque explaining the area. Just beyond the lunch area, the Wild Burro Trail goes through a fence and wire gate with a PLEASE CLOSE THE GATE sign. Beyond the fence, you are in Tortolita Mountain Park, and the route continues through a shallow, wide mountain basin with a great display of spring flowers in a good year.

The Wild Burro Trail reaches the signed end of the Wild Mustang Trail 2.3 miles from the trailhead. If you wish, you can continue on the Wild Burro Trail 2.4 miles to a cattle water tank and the remains of a windmill, which attest to the fact that this was a former ranch. Sharp-eyed hikers may also spot petroglyphs etched into rocks more than 1,000 years ago by the first inhabitants of the area.

To follow the loop described here, turn left (west) onto the less-frequented and rougher Wild Mustang Trail, marked with orange arrows. This trail is not recommended for horses, is a tough ride for mountain bikers, and gives hikers the chance for greater solitude. Wild mustangs? I've read that there is a herd of about a dozen wild horses in the Tortolitas—maybe you'll be lucky enough to spot some. Bobcats, javelinas, and deer have also been reported, but the reality is that you'll probably see plentiful bird and reptile life but rarely catch sight of a mammal. The plants and views of several mountain ranges will keep your camera busy.

Soon after you enter the Wild Mustang Trail, you'll go through another wire PLEASE CLOSE ME gate and continue rising and falling partially along a ridge for almost 3 miles until you reach another rest bench on the left. Informative signs here help you identify the surrounding mountains and downtown Tucson in the distance. You reach the signed beginning of the Cochie Springs Trail 3.5 miles along the Wild Mustang Trail and, 0.4 miles beyond, arrive at a T-junction for the Upper Javelina Trail, which is signed with red arrows. Turn left (east) and descend over the rockiest and hardest part of the loop. Views of the Ritz-Carlton resort dominate to the right and below. Fortunately the brown buildings blend into the landscape. A 0.9-mile descent will bring you back to the Wild Burro Trail, which you can follow back to the trailhead or, to shave a few yards off your return, just follow the wash and look for the trailhead sign to the parking area.

Nearby Attractions

The trailhead parking area is part of **The Ritz-Carlton Dove Mountain** (520-572-3000, ritzcarlton.com/en/hotels/arizona/dove-mountain), one of Arizona's premier luxury resorts, with over 250 balconied rooms, a 27-hole Jack Nicklaus golf course, and a state-of-the-art spa. Rates are upwards of $200 a night during the summer and closer to $500 during choice winter dates.

Directions

From downtown Tucson take I-10 north to Exit 244 (West Twin Peaks Road). Turn right, drive 3.9 miles to Tangerine Road, and keep straight onto Dove Mountain Boulevard. Follow Dove Mountain 4.6 miles to Secret Springs Drive. Turn right and go through the Ritz-Carlton resort guardhouse (tell them you are going to the hiking trailhead); continue 0.8 mile to the parking area.

STATELY SAGUAROS ACCOMPANY YOU ALONG THE WILD BURRO TRAIL.

Madera Canyon Area

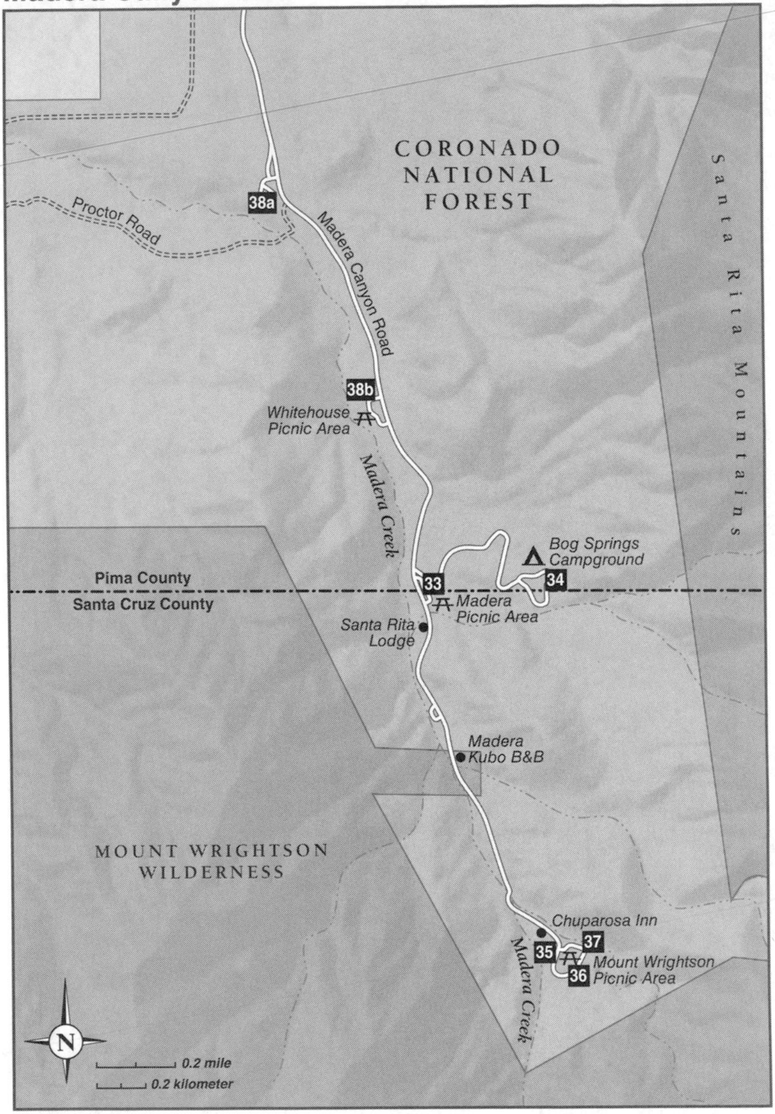

CORONADO
NATIONAL
FOREST

Santa Rita Mountains

Proctor Road

Madera Canyon Road

38a

38b

Whitehouse
Picnic Area

Madera Creek

Bog Springs
Campground

33

34

Pima County

Santa Cruz County

Madera
Picnic Area

Santa Rita
Lodge

Madera
Kubo B&B

MOUNT WRIGHTSON
WILDERNESS

Chuparosa Inn

37

35

Mount Wrightson
Picnic Area

36

Madera Creek

N

0.2 mile

0.2 kilometer

Madera Canyon Area

THE ROUGH ROAD NEAR THE BEGINNING OF THE BOG SPRINGS–KENT SPRING
LOOP, WITH MOUNT WRIGHTSON IN THE BACKGROUND

227

Bog Springs—
Kent Spring Loop

SCENERY: ★★★★
TRAIL CONDITION: ★★★
CHILDREN: ★★★
DIFFICULTY: ★★★
SOLITUDE: ★★★★

TINY WATERFALLS TEASE THE HIKER ON KENT SPRING TRAIL.

GPS TRAILHEAD COORDINATES: N31° 43.606' W110° 52.810'

DISTANCE & CONFIGURATION: 5.8-mile balloon loop

HIKING TIME: 3.75 hours

HIGHLIGHTS: Mountain and valley views, thick forest, 3 springs

ELEVATION: 4,840' at trailhead, 6,660' at Kent Spring

ACCESS: Open daily, 6 a.m.–10 p.m. Coronado Recreation Fee: $5/$10/$20 for day/week/year for up to 4 occupants of 1 car, available at picnic areas and at Santa Rita Lodge (see page 258); all National Park Service annual passes accepted

MAPS: Green Trails Maps 2962S–*Santa Rita Mountains;* free trail map from Friends of Madera Canyon available at trailheads and at the website below

FACILITIES: Restrooms, picnic tables, and water at trailhead

WHEELCHAIR ACCESS: Restrooms and picnic tables at trailhead

COMMENTS: Leashed dogs and hikers only. There are 3 possible trailheads. I describe the route from Madera Picnic Area, with brief mentions of the trailheads at Bog Springs Campground and the Nature Trail and Amphitheater Parking Area.

CONTACTS: Friends of Madera Canyon, friendsofmaderacanyon.org; Coronado National Forest, Nogales Ranger District, 520-281-2296, fs.usda.gov/coronado

Overview

This loop takes you far from the desert and into thick and beautiful forests of sycamores, oaks, and pines. The Santa Rita Mountains are riddled with springs and streams that provide year-round moisture and support healthy woodlands. You pass three springs on this trail, at least two of which should have water year-round, but carry drinking water as the spring water is not clean. The streams are somewhat more intermittent, but they're gorgeous when they flow after snowmelt and after monsoon rains.

Route Details

The trailhead, with a map board, is on the east side of the Madera Picnic Area. Climb a narrow, rocky trail through mixed oak–juniper forest with agaves and yuccas scattered about. After 100 yards, join a wider trail and bear right (southeast); after another 100 yards, the trail keeps heading east.

About 0.3 mile from the trailhead, the trail reaches a very rough, rocky, narrow unused road. If you take the road left (north),

Bog Springs–Kent Spring Loop

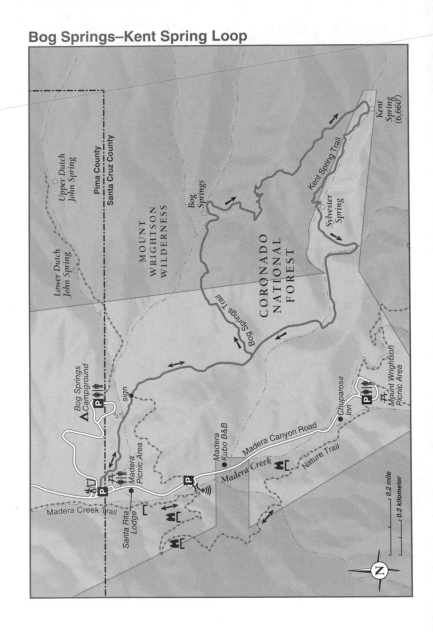

you'll drop down into the dry draw and hike up to Bog Springs Campground, 0.1 mile away. If you're camping, there is a signed trailhead with a map board for Bog Springs Trail at the campground, and you could begin from there.

If you wish to avoid the campground, keep heading east on the rough road. About 0.1 mile farther, you'll come to a metal sign on your left indicating that Bog Springs and Kent Spring are ahead. The narrow, unsigned trail to the right (south) goes 0.6 mile to the Nature Trail and Amphitheater Parking Area on Madera Canyon Road, the third trailhead for this hike.

Beyond the metal sign, the going is much less complicated now that hikers from all three trailheads are on the same rocky road, which was originally built to reach Kent Spring but hasn't seen a vehicle for years. The woodlands on either side of the road are thin, and deer roam the area—I saw a pair. Soon Mount Wrightson looms on the horizon to the southeast, and at some points it's dead ahead on the road.

About 0.5 mile beyond the last sign, you reach a signed fork where you can go either way on the ensuing 4-mile loop. Left goes to Bog Springs first; right, to Kent Spring first. I prefer the clockwise

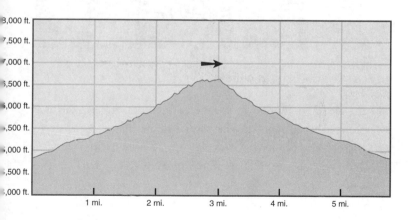

SYLVESTER SPRING IS CACHED IN RECTANGULAR CONCRETE BASINS ALONG THE BOG SPRINGS–KENT SPRING LOOP.

loop: the section between Bog Springs and Kent Spring has the narrowest, steepest trail, and I like to climb it rather than descend it.

The left trail is a narrow one, and after a few hundred yards of climbing, views open to the left to the town of Green Valley to the northwest, 2,700 feet below and 12 miles away. Green areas around the town are pecan orchards, and the metallic-blue lake behind it is part of a mining operation. If conditions are clear, you might see Kitt and Baboquivari Peaks on the distant horizon.

The trail enters thicker forest and, 0.8 mile from the beginning of the loop, a sign indicates Bog Springs to the left on a 0.1-mile dead-end trail that drops into and crosses a minor ravine before arriving at the spring. The spring water is cached in a small, rectangular concrete basin surrounded by a lovely glade of pines and whitish Arizona sycamores, inviting further exploration. The water in the basin is greenish from fallen leaves and would require a good filter or several minutes of boiling to make it potable—typical for the springs in these mountains. If you explore farther back, you'll find more water caches, which is why "Bog Springs" is plural. Once you're done, head back to the main trail.

Continue climbing briefly through tall, shady trees before emerging on a steep and exposed section, switchbacking up. You lose the shade but gain wonderful views of Mounts Wrightson and Hopkins. If you have a good eye (or binoculars), you can pick out Bog Springs Campground below. Eventually, the switchbacks end and the trail contours around to the south and then southeast, entering shade trees again. Kent Spring, reached 1.2 miles after Bog Springs, has a round concrete basin of dirty water. Just before it, a seasonal trickle is cleaner.

Our trail now turns hard right; drops west-northwest into a fern-filled little valley; and within a few yards becomes a steep, rough, and rather slippery shale-surfaced road—watch your step. The seasonal stream may accompany you to your right if it was flowing just before Kent Spring. After a few hundred yards, the trail crosses the streambed and becomes less steep. Trees bend over and provide a lovely shaded bower through which to continue your descent.

Soon you reach the third spring on the trail, Sylvester Spring, cached in two rectangular basins. The trail recrosses the streambed and climbs briefly before dropping to another stream, this one flowing from left to right across your route. An unsigned trail climbs to your left if you want to explore the source of this stream. The Kent Spring Trail continues down, following the left bank of the stream through a gorgeous riparian area. At times, the stream disappears underground and pops up again a minute later.

About 0.1 mile before the Kent Spring Trail rejoins the Bog Springs Trail, a dirt road to your left (west) goes to the Kent Spring Center, a 110-year-old house that's occasionally used for nature projects. Continue straight, but don't forget to look over your shoulder for views of Mount Wrightson lit by the afternoon sun. When you reach the sign for the Bog Springs Trail, continue north-northwest and then west 0.9 mile, retracing your steps to the Madera Picnic Area.

Nearby Attractions

Bog Springs Campground (520-281-2296, fs.usda.gov/coronado) has 13 first-come, first-served sites, each featuring a picnic table and a fire ring with a barbecue grill. Drinking water and vault toilets are available; RV hookups aren't. Maximum vehicle length is 22 feet. Fees are $10 per night (the Forest Service is proposing to double them). During weekends, especially in spring, summer, and fall, the campground can be full by lunchtime. On a recent camping trip here, I saw deer and wild turkeys near my tent, in addition to the ever-present jays, woodpeckers, and squirrels. (There was also one small RV that insisted on running its loud generator at night until I had a quiet word with the owner.) Bearproof boxes are provided for your food; black bears may amble through every year or so.

Directions

From Tucson, follow the directions to the Visitor Information Station and Proctor Parking Area, as detailed in Hike 38 (page 259). Continue south on Madera Canyon Road 1.1 miles to the Madera Picnic Area and trailhead. The road to Bog Springs Campground is on the left, just before the picnic area, and it's 0.5 mile to the campground. Signage is excellent.

34

Dutch John Spring Trail

SCENERY: ★ ★ ★ ★
TRAIL CONDITION: ★ ★ ★
CHILDREN: ★ ★ ★
DIFFICULTY: ★ ★ ★
SOLITUDE: ★ ★ ★ ★

HIKING PAST THREE ARIZONA SYCAMORES ON THE DUTCH JOHN SPRING TRAIL

GPS TRAILHEAD COORDINATES: N31° 43.602' W110° 52.489'

DISTANCE & CONFIGURATION: 2.6-mile out-and-back

HIKING TIME: 2 hours

HIGHLIGHTS: Lovely woodlands, relative solitude on the upper trail

ELEVATION: 5,060' at trailhead, 6,000' at upper spring

ACCESS: Open daily, 24/7. Coronado Recreation Fee: $5/$10/$20 for day/week/year for up to 4 occupants of 1 car, available at picnic areas and at Santa Rita Lodge (see page 258); all National Park Service annual passes accepted

MAPS: Green Trails Maps 2962S–*Santa Rita Mountains;* free trail map from Friends of Madera Canyon available at trailheads and at the website below

FACILITIES: Restrooms and water at the trailhead

WHEELCHAIR ACCESS: Restrooms at trailhead

Dutch John Spring Trail

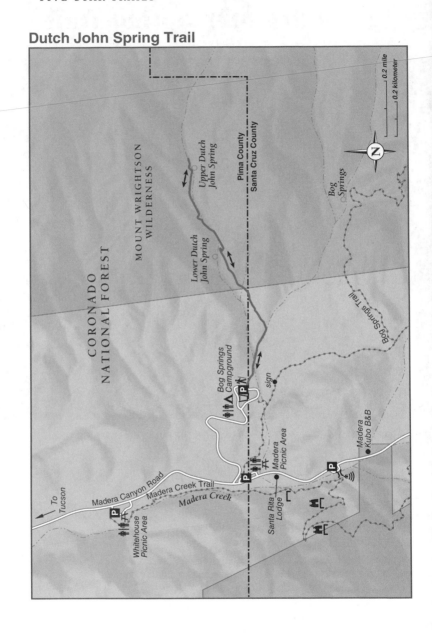

COMMENTS: Leashed dogs and hikers only. To make this hike almost a mile longer, begin from the Madera Picnic Area and follow the first two paragraphs of Route Details in the previous hike.

CONTACTS: Friends of Madera Canyon, friendsofmaderacanyon.org; Coronado National Forest, Nogales Ranger District, 520-281-2296, fs.usda.gov/coronado

Overview

This lovely woodland trail is just far enough away from Tucson that it gets few hikers. Most stop at the lower spring, and those continuing to the upper spring will either get lost or find solitude. (Audrey and I managed to do both!)

Route Details

The trailhead, which has an informative map board, is on the east side of Bog Springs Campground, behind the one restroom in this delightful little campground. If you aren't camping here, four parking spaces by the trailhead are designated for hikers only. If you're hiking in from the Madera Canyon Picnic Area, when you get to the campground, follow the road around to your right a couple hundred yards to the restroom and trailhead.

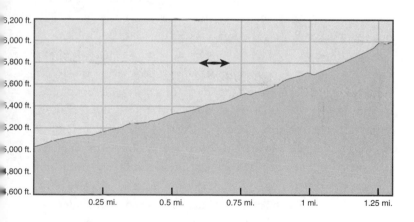

From the trailhead, you go east up a rocky trail between two campsites. After less than 0.1 mile you encounter a gate, which will let you through but keep horses out. Soon after, you'll cross a small ravine that looks like it should have water in it but rarely does. The trail, now pleasantly earthen instead of rocky, climbs gently through mixed woodland, soon reaching a four-strand wire fence on the right that marks one of the few areas of private land left in the canyon.

The plant life consists mainly of different kinds of oak trees, with agaves, yuccas, and the occasional lost-looking prickly pear cactus scattered through the woodland. Many of the oak species don't have the familiar deciduous, lobed leaves. Southern Arizona's plant life is enhanced by species that are mainly found in Mexico, such as Emory oaks, whose elongated, evergreen leaves can be smooth or toothed. These are shed but quickly replaced, and there are usually leaves on the ground year-round, not just in the fall. In several places along the trail, the oaks form a lovely bower overhead.

About 0.3 mile beyond the gate, the trail crosses the usually dry creekbed again and continues generally east or northeast. A quarter-mile farther brings you to a signed fork to the left indicating Dutch John Spring, just a few yards below you. A bathtub-size metal trough here may be dry for much of the year. A half-dozen pale-barked Arizona sycamores surround the area, making for a very pretty glade.

Once you've finished exploring this area, which I call Lower Dutch John Spring, you can continue climbing on a narrow trail to the east-northeast, following the right side of the small ravine. Soon you'll cross to the left side under three Arizona sycamores and come to a 12-foot-square dirt platform shored up by a few rocks—I don't know what this is. About 0.3 mile from Lower Dutch John Spring, look for an unsigned fork that goes steeply right. (If you miss the turnoff and continue straight, staying on the left side of the creekbed, you'll be on a trail that swings north and peters out after a few hundred yards.)

The steep fork to the right soon becomes a gentle climb up the left side of another drainage. After a few hundred yards this becomes greener, and you may glimpse pools of water to your right, steeply but not far below. A mossy, glistening cliff on the far side appears to be the spring. If you cross the drainage to the right and start climbing a steep rock face, you've gone about 100 yards beyond the upper spring. There are no signs here.

So who was Dutch John? A locally respected historian, writer, and hiker spins a story about a murderous German gunslinger named John who worked in the Santa Rita Mountains in the 1920s, and whom locals thought might be Dutch. Perhaps they mistook his Deutsch for Dutch. (Truth be told, I found no history behind the name of this spring, so you're welcome to make up your own.)

Nearby Attractions

See the previous hike and Hike 37 (page 252) for details about camping or staying in Madera Canyon.

Directions

From Tucson, follow the directions to the Visitor Information Station and Proctor Parking Area, as detailed in Hike 38 (page 259). Continue south on Madera Canyon Road 1.1 miles to a turnoff to the left for Bog Springs Campground, and drive 0.6 mile to the campground.

35

Nature Trail and Madera Creek Trail

Nature Trail:
SCENERY: ★ ★ ★ ★ ★
TRAIL CONDITION: ★ ★ ★ ★ ★
CHILDREN: ★ ★ ★
DIFFICULTY: ★ ★ ★
SOLITUDE: ★ ★ ★ ★ ★

Madera Creek Trail:
SCENERY: ★ ★ ★ ★
TRAIL CONDITION: ★ ★ ★ ★ ★
CHILDREN: ★ ★ ★ ★ ★
DIFFICULTY: ★ ★ ★
SOLITUDE: ★ ★ ★

ARIZONA SYCAMORES AND HORSETAILS GROW ALONG MADERA CREEK.

GPS TRAILHEAD COORDINATES: N31° 42.792' W110° 52.498'

DISTANCE & CONFIGURATION: 2.8-mile point-to-point with car shuttle, 5.6-mile out-and-back

HIKING TIME: 1.5 hours one-way

HIGHLIGHTS: Superb views of the mountain crest leading to Mount Wrightson; woodlands; riparian walk; bird-watching

ELEVATION: 5,420' at trailhead, 4,650' at trail's end

ACCESS: Open daily, 6 a.m.–10 p.m. Coronado Recreation Fee: $5/$10/$20 for day/week/year for up to 4 occupants of 1 car, available at picnic areas and at Santa Rita Lodge (see page 258); all National Park Service annual passes accepted

MAPS: Green Trails Maps 2962S–*Santa Rita Mountains;* free trail map from Friends of Madera Canyon available at trailheads and at the website below

FACILITIES: Restrooms, picnic tables, and water at trailhead

WHEELCHAIR ACCESS: Restrooms and picnic tables at trailhead

COMMENTS: Leashed dogs and hikers only. The steeper Nature Trail joins the easier Madera Creek Trail.

CONTACTS: Friends of Madera Canyon, friendsofmaderacanyon.org; Coronado National Forest, Nogales Ranger District, 520-281-2296, fs.usda.gov/coronado

Overview

The upper section of the Nature Trail seems almost forgotten by hikers who are heading for the adjoining trailheads leading to the summit of Mount Wrightson, and there are relatively few people to be seen. Along the high trail, wooden benches are strategically placed for a relaxing rest and some of Madera Canyon's best views of Mount Wrightson. After undulating high above the valley, the route plunges down to Madera Creek, where a very popular trail parallels both the creek and the road but is just far enough away from the latter for birdsong to be heard.

Route Details

Begin from the west side of the extensive Mount Wrightson Picnic Area, at the southern terminus of the Madera Canyon Road. The trailhead is in the first parking lot on the right as you enter the picnic and parking area; you'll find a map board at the beginning of the trail. (Several trails depart from this parking area, so make sure you're on the right one.)

Nature Trail and Madera Creek Trail

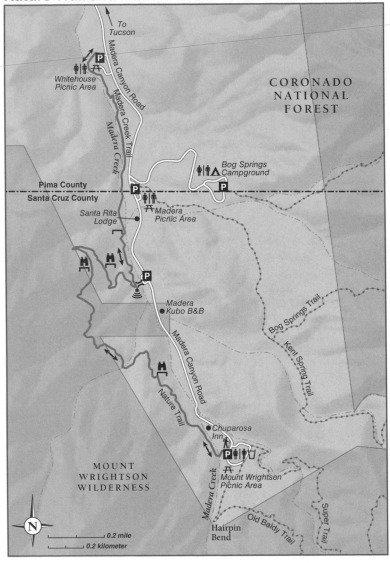

From the trailhead, turn left (south), walk about 10 yards to cross a usually dry streambed, and then switchback to the north, with the streambed below to your right. After 100 yards, climb to your left away from the stream on a broken concrete trail. Soon you'll see the Chuparosa Inn across the stream to your right as you climb a little higher.

The trail quickly flattens and contours northwest, with Madera Creek dropping away below you. Although it seems fairly flat, the route actually undulates as it makes its way through mixed oak–juniper woodlands, with impressive yucca plants embellishing the trailside.

After about 0.6 mile, past the first of several wooden benches, the Madera Creek valley opens below. Occasional plaques identify trees growing alongside the trail. I like to stop at the second bench, a little over a mile from the trailhead, where there's a particularly impressive view of the Santa Ritas and a nearby plaque neatly shows the peaks and landmarks stretching from McCleary Peak to Mount Wrightson. The greener area surrounding Dutch John Spring is easy to make out and, with binoculars, Audrey and I were able to pick out our little blue-and-silver tent nestled in Bog Springs Campground. Fun stuff!

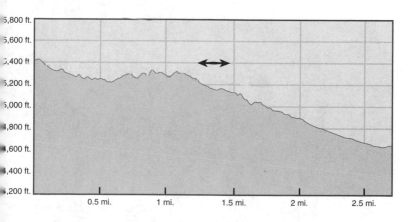

Shortly beyond the second bench, the trail hairpins and begins zigzagging down the hills toward the creek, with continuing great views. You pass a third bench. More signs interpret the geology and natural history of the canyon. Eventually, 1.8 miles from the trailhead, the route flattens and passes a small outdoor amphitheater used for ranger-led presentations and talks. Just before the amphitheater, to the right, a footbridge crosses Madera Creek and leads to the Nature Trail and Amphitheater Parking Area on Madera Canyon Road.

At this point, the Nature Trail becomes the Madera Creek Trail. With Santa Rita Lodge a short walk from the parking area, this segment of the trail is especially busy with walkers and bird-watchers. Water flows in this part of Madera Creek for much of the year, and frequent benches along the trail allow you to rest and enjoy the riparian scenery or listen to the sounds of birds and water. If you wish, you could return to the trailhead the way you came for a 3.6-mile out-and-back hike.

Continuing north from the amphitheater, the Madera Creek Trail starts by following the left bank and descending almost

WILD TURKEYS ARE COMMONLY HEARD AND SEEN IN MADERA CANYON.

imperceptibly. Almost 0.5 mile from the amphitheater, the trail crosses the stream and passes through the west section of the Madera Picnic Area. (The east section, across the road, is the trailhead for the Bog Springs–Kent Spring Loop, page 228.) After the picnic area, the trail passes through a very green, moist section with many horse-tail plants. You cross the creek a couple of times via wooden bridges before arriving at the Whitehouse Picnic Area, 0.6 mile beyond the Madera Picnic Area, where one of the Wheelchair-Accessible Loops in Hike 38 begins (see page 259).

If you left a second vehicle here, you're finished; if not, return the way you came. Walking back along the road to the Mount Wright-son Picnic Area is a shorter return trip, but I don't recommend it because there's no sidewalk and the road is narrow.

Nearby Attractions

See Hikes 33 and 37 (pages 228 and 252, respectively) for details about camping or staying in Madera Canyon.

Directions

From Tucson, follow the directions to the Whitehouse Picnic Area, as detailed in Hike 38 (page 259)—leave a car here if you're doing a one-way hike. To reach the Mount Wrightson Picnic Area and trailhead, continue south on Madera Canyon Road 1.6 miles. Observe speed limits and drive carefully on this narrow road, which has one-lane bridges and pedestrian traffic.

36

Old Baldy Trail to Mount Wrightson

SCENERY: ★ ★ ★ ★ ★

TRAIL CONDITION: ★ ★ ★ ★ ★

CHILDREN: ★ ★

DIFFICULTY: ★ ★ ★ ★ ½

SOLITUDE: ★ ★ ★

THE BOY SCOUT MEMORIAL AT JOSEPHINE SADDLE

GPS TRAILHEAD COORDINATES: N31° 42.757' W110° 52.423'

DISTANCE & CONFIGURATION: 10.8-mile out-and-back

HIKING TIME: 7 hours

HIGHLIGHTS: Summiting the highest peak in the Tucson area; beautiful forest and increasingly spectacular views

ELEVATION: 5,450' at trailhead, 9,453' at summit

ACCESS: Open 6 a.m.–10 p.m. Coronado Recreation Fee: $5/$10/$20 for day/week/year for up to 4 occupants of 1 car, available at picnic areas and at Santa Rita Lodge (see page 258); all National Park Service annual passes accepted

MAPS: Green Trails Maps 2962S–*Santa Rita Mountains*; free trail map from Friends of Madera Canyon available at trailheads and at the website below

FACILITIES: Restrooms, picnic tables, and water at trailhead

WHEELCHAIR ACCESS: Restrooms and picnic tables at trailhead

COMMENTS: Leashed dogs and hikers only. U.S. Forest Service signs, available maps, and other sources agree on a 10.8-mile out-and-back distance; my GPS tracked it at less than 10 miles.

CONTACTS: Friends of Madera Canyon, friendsofmaderacanyon.org; Coronado National Forest, Nogales Ranger District, 520-281-2396, fs.usda.gov/coronado

Overview

This is the oldest, shortest, and steepest route to ascend the 4,000 feet from the trailhead to the summit. Hikers can experience pleasing pine-forest smells, scenery, and shade while taking a break from the heat. The trail is popular and occasionally becomes overrun with large hiking groups. With the exception of a few short rocky sections near the summit, the trail is well maintained and makes the ascent surprisingly manageable, although the steep descent may take a toll on older knees. On a clear day, views stretch from northern Mexico to north of Tucson.

Route Details

Begin from the southeast end of the extensive Mount Wrightson Picnic Area, at the southern terminus of Madera Canyon Road. You'll find an Old Baldy Trail map board at the beginning of the trail. (Several trails depart from this picnic and parking area, so make sure you're on the right one.)

The first 0.25 mile follows a rough road (no vehicles) as it climbs southwest through thick forest to an intersection marked by two welded metal signs and a bench. One sign points the way southwest to Agua Caliente Saddle with the less-than-encouraging words VERY STEEP TRAIL. Although this isn't our route, it is noteworthy that the first section of this trail, before it gets very steep, is popular with birders looking for the elegant trogon, a parrotlike bird from Central America. The trogon's northernmost limit is a few canyons in southeastern Arizona and southwestern New Mexico, with Madera Canyon

Old Baldy Trail to Mount Wrightson

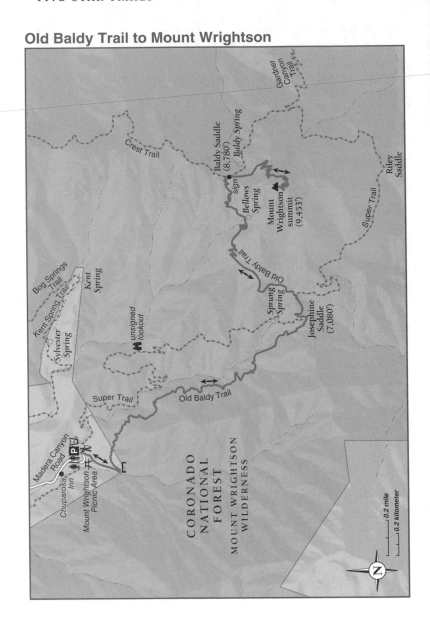

being a hot spot; this trail section is among the best places to see it. The birds nest here from April to August and head as far south as Costa Rica in the fall and winter. The male's striking red, white, and green plumage is unmistakable, and it is only one of many species that make a bird-watching expedition to the canyon a memorable event.

Another sign at this intersection points out the Old Baldy Trail, which makes a hairpin bend left and climbs steadily but gently, swinging around from northeast to southeast and following the right (west) side of the Madera Creek valley. Once, when Audrey and I hiked up this trail, we saw a black bear browsing in that valley, about 100 feet below. We quietly kept climbing and it ignored us, but we finished that day with a great story to tell.

There are no especially difficult or remarkable stretches on the 2.5-mile climb from the trailhead to Josephine Saddle, at 7,080 feet. The lower parts traverse mixed deciduous oak forests with the occasional conifer, but when you reach Josephine Saddle evergreens begin to dominate. The trail, climbing steadily with occasional flattish sections, is mainly comfortably earthen with a few roots and

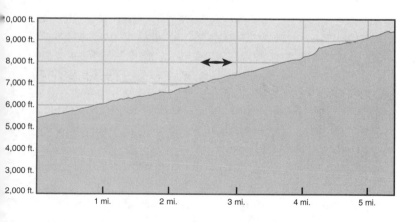

rocks. You'll glimpse Mount Wrightson to the southeast and east, but mostly you'll enjoy forest hiking.

At Josephine Saddle stands a rustic cross, a memorial to three teenage boys—members of Boy Scout Troop 249, who were caught by an unseasonably early winter storm on November 15, 1958, and died of hypothermia. Passing hikers and Scouts leave tributes, and the memorial looks slightly different from month to month.

Six trails meet at Josephine Saddle, and there are several signs to sort them out. Old Baldy Trail and the Super Trail (see next hike) follow the same route for a short section heading left (northeast) on the trail signed for Mount Wrightson. About 40 yards beyond the Boy Scout cross, the trail forks and you go left to climb a couple of switchbacks. There are good views of the observatories on Mount Hopkins just south of west, and the distinctively triangular peak of Pete Mountain to the northwest. About 0.2 mile above Josephine Saddle, the Super Trail goes off to the right and Old Baldy Trail goes more or less straight east and then swings north. It's 4.2 miles to Mount Wrightson via the Super Trail or 2.7 miles via Old Baldy.

As the trail climbs, views open to the northwest of the town of Green Valley, with a metallic-blue lake—the result of a mining operation—behind it. Soon after, the trail becomes rockier, the gradient increases, and you begin switchbacking through thinning trees, some of which show evidence of past forest fires. Just over a mile beyond the intersection with the Super Trail, the trail flattens and you'll pass Bellows Spring to your right, at 8,170 feet elevation. A small, verdant cliff above the trail shines with water seeps, which are collected in a little stone-and-concrete basin right by the trail. This water should be filtered or boiled before drinking.

After Bellows Spring, the trail continues switchbacking through a mixture of pine trees and bare, colorful rock cliffs, some of which are rusty with iron ore. Another 0.7 mile of climbing takes you to the 8,780-foot Baldy Saddle, where expansive views open of distant mountain ranges to the east and Gardner Canyon below. Back to the west-southwest, you're now looking down on observatory-topped

Mount Hopkins; to the south, the bald cliffs of Mount Wrightson appear an impossibly steep 0.9 mile away. You can see how the mountain got its original name of Old Baldy.

About 100 yards south of Baldy Saddle, a metal sign points to Gardner Canyon down to the left (southeast)—this is the descent via the Super Trail. The Super and Old Baldy Trails now follow the same route to the summit, climbing gently south and contouring around the northeast side of the mountain through pine forest. The final push to the top begins suddenly, with a long series of rocky switchbacks that end equally suddenly at the summit.

There used to be a fire lookout perched on top, but only foundations remain, accompanied by a couple of waterproof ammo boxes that hold trail registers. An informative plaque tells the history of the lookout. The views can be awesome on a clear day. Unfortunately, there are more and more hazy days when the horizon is totally obscured by smog or smoke—hopefully you'll be here on a pristine day with jaw-dropping vistas.

Nearby Attractions

See the next hike and Hike 33 (page 228) for details about camping or staying in Madera Canyon.

Directions

From Tucson, follow the directions to the Visitor Information Station and Proctor Parking Area, as detailed in Hike 38 (page 259). Continue south on Madera Canyon Road 2.3 miles to the Mount Wrightson Picnic Area and trailhead. Observe speed limits and drive carefully on this narrow road, which has one-lane bridges and pedestrian traffic.

37 Super Trail to Mount Wrightson

SCENERY: ★ ★ ★ ★ ★
TRAIL CONDITION: ★ ★ ★ ★ ★
CHILDREN: ★ ★
DIFFICULTY: ★ ★ ★ ★ ½
SOLITUDE: ★ ★ ★ ★

MOUNT WRIGHTSON IN THE AFTERNOON SUN

GPS TRAILHEAD COORDINATES: N31° 42.811' W110° 52.392'

DISTANCE & CONFIGURATION: 16.2-mile out-and-back

HIKING TIME: 10.5 hours

HIGHLIGHTS: Beautiful forests; great views of the high crest leading north of Mount Wrightson; summiting the highest peak in the Tucson area

ELEVATION: 5,425' at trailhead, 9,453' at summit

ACCESS: Open daily, 6 a.m.–10 p.m. Coronado Recreation Fee: $5/$10/$20 for day/week/year for up to 4 occupants of 1 car, available at picnic areas and at Santa Rita Lodge (see Nearby Attractions); all National Park Service annual passes accepted

MAPS: Green Trails Maps 2962S–*Santa Rita Mountains;* free trail map from Friends of Madera Canyon available at trailheads and at the website below

FACILITIES: Restrooms, picnic tables, and water at trailhead

WHEELCHAIR ACCESS: Restrooms and picnic tables at trailhead

COMMENTS: Leashed dogs and hikers only. U.S. Forest Service signs, available maps, and other sources agree on a 16.2-mile out-and-back distance; my GPS tracked it at 15.4 miles. There is a section where scratchy graythorn bushes encroach on the trail, so you might want to wear long pants.

CONTACTS: Friends of Madera Canyon, friendsofmaderacanyon.org; Coronado National Forest, Nogales Ranger District, 520-281-2296, fs.usda.gov/coronado

Overview

This is a newer, longer, and more gradual route to ascend the 4,000 feet from the trailhead to Mount Wrightson's summit. But what it gains in being less steep is lost in distance—it's not an easier trail. The lower sections have some attractive riparian areas, and pine forests provide shaded hiking up to Josephine Saddle, where the Super Trail coincides briefly with the Old Baldy Trail. Then the Super Trail almost circumnavigates the mountain as far as Baldy Saddle, where it again overlaps with the Old Baldy Trail for the last 0.9 mile to the summit, including the steepest section of this route.

Using the intersection with Old Baldy at Josephine Saddle, hikers can create a number of loops or a figure-eight, so that several ascents can be made without repeating exactly the same path.

Route Details

Begin from the northeast end of the extensive Mount Wrightson Picnic Area, at the southern terminus of the Madera Canyon Road. When you enter the picnic and parking area, drive almost all the way around it to a restroom at the northeast corner. The trail begins behind this restroom; you'll find a Super Trail map board at the trailhead. (Several trails depart from this parking area, so make sure you're on the right one.)

Head east from the parking lot and soon follow the right bank of Madera Creek about 0.3 mile. Here the trail crosses the creek at a

Super Trail to Mount Wrightson

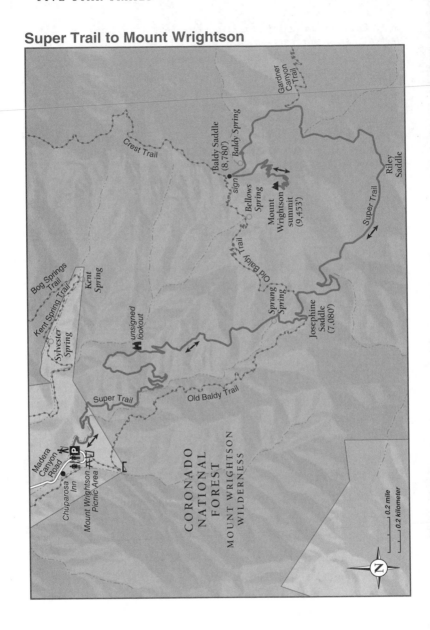

Gardner Canyon Trail

Crest Trail

Baldy Saddle (8,780')

sign

Baldy Spring

Bellows Spring

Mount Wrightson summit (9,453')

Riley Saddle

Super Trail

Bog Springs Trail

Kent Spring Trail

Kent Spring

unsigned lookout

Old Baldy Trail

Sprung Spring

Josephine Saddle (7,080')

Sylvester Spring

Super Trail

Old Baldy Trail

Madera Canyon Road

Chuparosa Inn

Mount Wrightson Picnic Area

CORONADO NATIONAL FOREST
MOUNT WRIGHTSON WILDERNESS

0.2 mile
0.2 kilometer

N

point marked by three majestic Arizona sycamores, then continues up the other side, heading west briefly. (There probably won't be any water in the creek from late spring until the monsoon season.) The trail switchbacks up the far side of the creek in long, gentle ascents, which change direction to all points of the compass. Deciduous forest begins to give way to coniferous as you climb, and you get frequent glimpses of Mount Wrightson to the southeast and Mount Hopkins to the southwest.

About 2 miles from the trailhead, you'll have climbed about 1,000 feet. Views open to the left of the trail and between the trees of the main crest of the Santa Ritas, including the three highest peaks in these mountains. Mount Wrightson is the farthest southeast. Mount Ian (simply marked as 9,146 on most maps) is to the east, and to the northeast an unnamed peak (marked 8,853) is the third highest. Somebody needs to come up with a fitting name for this significant summit! If you're trying to get the best views between the trees, keep your eyes open for a flat, unsigned lookout on the left side of the trail.

The next landmark, about 1.5 miles farther, is the delightfully named Sprung Spring, which fills a round metal basin on the right

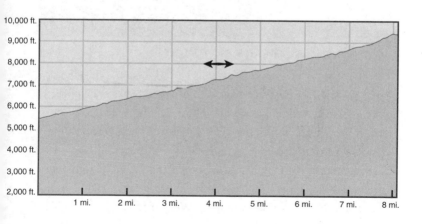

MOUNT WRIGHTSON AS SEEN FROM BALDY SADDLE

side of the trail. The water looks clear but should always be purified. You're now just 0.25 mile from Josephine Saddle, which is 3.7 miles from the trailhead. The Super Trail enters the saddle opposite the Boy Scout memorial cross (see page 250) and turns left, following the same route as the Old Baldy Trail for 0.2 mile. A metal sign clearly marks where the Super Trail turns off Old Baldy to the right (south). From this fork, it's 4.2 miles to Mount Wrightson via the Super Trail or 2.7 miles via Old Baldy.

The next section swings around the southwestern side of Mount Wrightson, climbing occasional switchbacks and yielding excellent views of Mount Hopkins to the west. You'll encounter a few brief loose sections as the trail crosses small, rocky landslides, but none are a problem. About 1.4 miles of hiking from the previous trail fork will bring you to the 8,000-foot contour and Riley Saddle, on the south side of the mountain. A signed but poorly maintained trail from here goes south toward Josephine Peak, which has tree trunks scattered on it like matchsticks. No one seems to know who Josephine was, but she has the fifth-highest peak in the Santa Ritas, a saddle, and a canyon named after her.

The Super Trail continues swinging around the south and southeast sides of Mount Wrightson. The next section is notable for the thick, scratchy graythorn bushes encroaching on the trail—you might want to wear long pants. As you climb around to the east side, you'll see increasingly burned-out areas, remnants of the Florida Fire of 2005. The signed junction with the Gardner Trail is 1.1 miles beyond Riley Saddle. By this point you're surrounded by a surreal landscape of burned, dead trees.

From this junction it's a 0.8-mile climb to Baldy Saddle. Much of this section has fallen trees across it, so your ascent is slowed as you make your way around or over the obstacles. About 0.15 mile before the saddle, you'll pass Baldy Spring, which used to be a reliable source of water; since the fire, however, the bathtub-size green metal basin used for catchment is often dry.

The Super Trail terminates at Baldy Saddle. The familiar metal sign indicates that Mount Wrightson is 0.9 mile to your left, and you follow the same route as Old Baldy Trail to the summit. To reach the heart of Baldy Saddle, turn right and walk 100 yards.

The mountain used to be called Old Baldy because of its rocky, treeless summit but is now named after William Wrightson, a mining surveyor who was killed by Apaches in 1865. Nearby Mount Hopkins is named after Gilbert Hopkins, a mining engineer who was killed in the same attack.

A remarkable natural feature of the summit is ladybugs. Most of the year you won't see any, but in early summer (around June) these familiar red insects with the black spots swarm the summit by the thousands to breed. Don't worry—they don't bite!

Nearby Attractions

While it's possible to climb Mount Wrightson with a dawn departure from Tucson, some hikers prefer to spend the night nearer the mountain. You can camp (see Hike 33, page 228) or stay in one of three rustic lodges in Madera Canyon. These offer standard rooms with kitchenettes, and guests bring their own food (there are no restaurants). None of them are luxurious, but they do offer a pleasant getaway from the desert. The nearest stores and restaurants are in Green Valley, 15 miles away. During the spring and early-summer birding seasons, reservations are advised.

The largest and best-known lodge is **Santa Rita Lodge** (520-625-8746, santaritalodge.com), with about 15 rooms and cabins, mostly in the $115–$225 range (varies by season). A small store sells souvenirs, maps, books, drinks, and snacks, and a bird-watching station is open to the public. The tiny **Madera Kubo B&B** (520-625-2908, maderakubo.com) has four Hobbit-size cabins (two with spiral stairways) and a souvenir shop; rates are $125 for one night or $110 for multiple nights and include a self-serve Continental breakfast. The **Chuparosa Inn** (520-393-7370, chuparosainn.com) has four nice rooms in the $200–$275 range, requires a two-night minimum stay, and serves a Continental breakfast.

Directions

From Tucson, follow the directions to the Visitor Information Station and Proctor Parking Area, as detailed in the next hike. Continue south on Madera Canyon Road 2.3 miles to the Mount Wrightson Picnic Area and trailhead. Observe speed limits and drive carefully on this narrow road, which has one-lane bridges and pedestrian traffic. Drive all the way around the large parking area to the trailhead.

38 Madera Canyon:
Wheelchair-Accessible Loops

SCENERY: ★ ★ ★

TRAIL CONDITION: ★ ★ ★ ★ ★

CHILDREN: ★ ★ ★ ★

DIFFICULTY: ★

SOLITUDE: ★ ★ ★

OCOTILLOS AND ELEPHANT HEAD SEEN FROM PROCTOR LOOP TRAIL

GPS TRAILHEAD COORDINATES: Proctor: N31° 44.467' W110° 53.215';
Whitehouse: N31° 44.026' W110° 52.950'

DISTANCE & CONFIGURATION: 0.8-mile loop from Proctor Parking Area Trailhead;
0.5-mile loop from Whitehouse Picnic Area Trailhead; 1.5-mile figure-eight

HIKING TIME: As long as you want

HIGHLIGHTS: Wheelchair access; nice mix of mountain views, high desert woodlands, and
historical markers

ELEVATION: 4,450' at Proctor Parking Area, 4,650' at Whitehouse Picnic Area; no
significant rise

ACCESS: Open daily, 6 a.m.–10 p.m. Coronado Recreation Fee: $5/$10/$20 for day/
week/year for up to 4 occupants of 1 car, available at picnic areas and at Santa Rita Lodge
(see page 258); all National Park Service annual passes accepted

Madera Canyon: Wheelchair-Accessible Loops

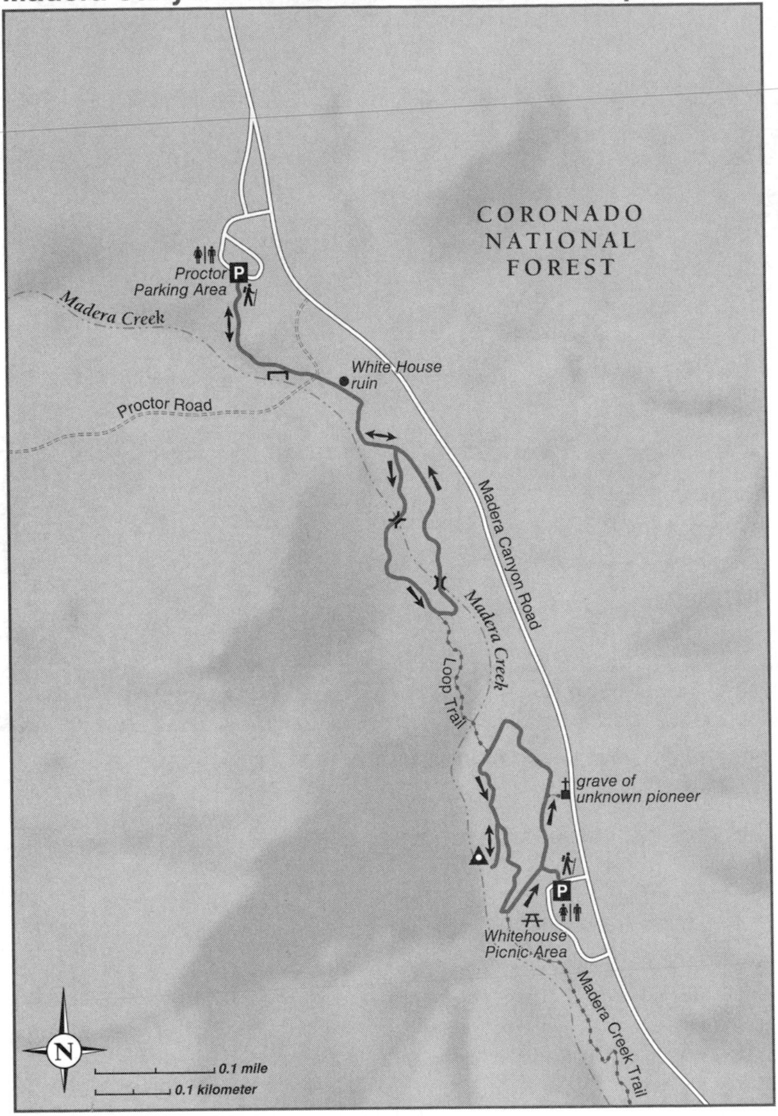

CORONADO
NATIONAL
FOREST

Proctor
Parking Area

Madera Creek

Proctor Road

White House
ruin

Madera Canyon Road

Madera Creek

Loop Trail

grave of
unknown pioneer

Whitehouse
Picnic Area

Madera Creek Trail

N

0.1 mile
0.1 kilometer

MAPS: Green Trails Maps 2962S–*Santa Rita Mountains;* free trail map from Friends of Madera Canyon available at trailheads and at the website below

FACILITIES: Restrooms, water, and shaded picnic tables at both trailheads

WHEELCHAIR ACCESS: Restrooms, picnic tables, and on both loop trails but not the short connector trail

COMMENTS: Leashed dogs and hikers only. The 2 paved loops are at least 42" wide.

CONTACTS: Friends of Madera Canyon, friendsofmaderacanyon.org; Coronado National Forest, Nogales Ranger District, 520-281-2296, fs.usda.gov/coronado

Overview

These two loops are lovely. Folks in wheelchairs will get a real out-doors experience with fine mountain views, bird-filled woodlands, and historical sites. The trails are also recommended for slower hikers who use a cane or don't want to climb. Bird-watchers and visitors with limited time enjoy the easy hike and the informative signs. The Proctor Trailhead has an informative shaded ramada detailing the history and natural history of Madera Canyon, along with a visitor center that's open most weekends.

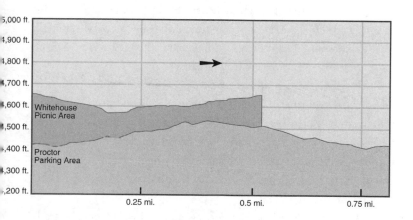

Route Details

Proctor Loop

From the Proctor Parking Area, the paved trail goes south. After 100 yards, a plaque on the right identifies the mountains to the west, visible on a clear day. A hundred yards farther, on the left, a narrow footpath leads to the whimsically decorated grave of Benita Morales and her infant son (see below). A hundred yards farther, a 20-yard-long side trail takes you to a huge Arizona sycamore that shades a bench. This is one of many benches found along the trail.

Back on the main trail, you'll cross the unpaved Proctor Road (a brief inconvenience to wheelchair users) and soon reach a signed left turn to the White House ruin, easily reached on a very short paved trail. A century ago, these adobe walls were whitewashed, and the house was a major landmark—indeed, the original name of the canyon was White House Canyon. According to the book *A History of Madera Canyon,* published by the Friends of Madera Canyon, the house was built around 1880 and had several owners and inhabitants. The last full-time inhabitants were Alcaro Morales, who moved here in 1911 with his bride, Benita. He helped his wife give birth to four children, but sadly, she and their fifth child died in childbirth in 1921. The family continued to live here, supporting themselves by selling vegetables, cheese, pine nuts, and mescal, until shortly before Alcaro's death in 1942. Today, only part of one wall remains.

Just beyond the White House trail, the Bat House exhibit is on your left. Four bat houses have been placed on tall poles, and a well-illustrated plaque explains that 17 of the 45 bat species found in the United States and Canada have been recorded in Madera Canyon. The best time to see bats is at sunset, when they become active, especially in the spring and summer. Please don't disturb the bats, and stay on the trail.

A few yards past the bat houses and 0.24 mile from the trailhead, the trail forks into a 0.35-mile loop that you can take either way. Going right, you'll quickly come to a wooden bridge crossing

Madera Creek, which will be dry in late spring and summer. About halfway around the paved loop, you'll reach the signed intersection with the unpaved Loop Trail. This 0.2-mile-long trail links with the Whitehouse Loop, and hikers can use it to make a figure-eight excursion. Wheelchair users will continue around the paved loop, crossing another wooden bridge over Madera Creek and returning to the Proctor Parking Area.

Whitehouse Loop

It's a 0.7-mile drive from the Proctor Parking Area to the Whitehouse Picnic Area, where the second paved, wheelchair-accessible loop begins. Heading right from the trailhead, you'll pass a short, paved side trail to the grave of an unknown pioneer; a short way farther are three bat houses with an informative plaque. The trail is surrounded by the pine–oak woodlands typical of this elevation.

Roughly halfway around the paved loop, the signed, unpaved Loop Trail takes hikers 0.2 mile to the Proctor Loop for a figure-eight. Wheelchair users continue around the paved loop to a fork that gives access to a Madera Creek overlook, to the right via a short paved trail. The main loop trail passes a few remnants of a Depression-era Civilian Conservation Corps camp, where hundreds of young men were housed and employed by the national forest. The end of the loop coincides with the last few yards of the Madera Creek Trail.

Nearby Attractions

See the previous hike and Hike 33 (page 228) for information about camping and lodging in Madera Canyon.

Directions

From Tucson, take I-19 S. This short freeway begins in south Tucson at I-10 and continues to the US–Mexico border at Nogales, with distances marked in kilometers. From the I-10 exit, it's 38 kilometers (about 24 miles) along I-19 to Exit 63 (Continental Road). Take Continental

Road east 1.2 miles to White House Canyon Road. Turn right and drive 7.2 miles to Madera Canyon Road, where you turn right again and drive 3.5 miles to the Visitor Information Station (open most weekends, 10 a.m.–2 p.m.) and the adjoining Proctor Parking Area.

The Proctor Parking Area is the trailhead of the first wheelchair-accessible loop. To get to the second loop, turn right out of the Proctor Parking Area and drive 0.7 mile south to the Whitehouse Picnic Area.

THE SHADED LOWER PROCTOR LOOP TRAIL

Appendix A:
Outdoors Shops

Perhaps because the weather here is so ideal and folks don't need down jackets, four-season tents, and snowshoes, Tucson has surprisingly few outdoors stores that sell high-quality hiking equipment. Here are some that do.

MILLER'S SURPLUS   millerssurplus.com
Old-fashioned army surplus—you never know what they might have!

406 N. Sixth Ave.
Tucson, AZ 85705
520-622-4777

REI   rei.com
160 W. Wetmore Road
Tucson, AZ 85705
520-887-1938

SUMMIT HUT   summithut.com
In business since 1969, this is Tucson's oldest—and only—independent outdoors retailer, and warmly recommended.

5251 E. Speedway Blvd.	7745 N. Oracle Road
Tucson, AZ 85712	Tucson, AZ 85704
520-325-1554	520-888-1000

WESTERN NATIONAL PARKS ASSOCIATION (WNPA)   wnpa.org
The hiking gear is limited, but the WNPA sells Tucson's widest selection of books and gifts for the outdoors enthusiast.

12880 N. Vistoso Village Drive
Tucson, AZ 85755
520-622-9999

Appendix B: Map Sources

U.S. Geological Survey (USGS) topo maps are accurate but often lack trails. I like Green Trails maps—three cover the Santa Catalina Mountains, Santa Rita Mountains, and Saguaro area—and National Geographic's Saguaro National Park maps, which are based on USGS topographical information and show hiking trails as well. The U.S. Forest Service map of Pusch Ridge is also useful.

The stores in Appendix A and the visitor centers listed for hikes in Saguaro National Park, Sabino Canyon, and Catalina State Park sell all of the above; you can also buy them at the sources below.

GREEN TRAILS MAPS   greentrailsmaps.com

NATIONAL GEOGRAPHIC MAPS   nationalgeographic.com/maps

U.S. GEOLOGICAL SURVEY   nationalmap.gov, usgs.gov

Appendix C:
Hiking Clubs

Local hiking groups meet online as well as on the trail.

SIERRA CLUB–GRAND CANYON CHAPTER, RINCON GROUP
arizona.sierraclub.org/rincon
738 N. Fifth Ave., Ste. 214
Tucson, AZ 85705
520-620-6401

SOUTHERN ARIZONA HIKING CLUB
sahcinfo.org
P.O. Box 32257
Tucson, AZ 85751
520-330-4647

THE TUCSON HIKING MEETUP GROUP
meetup.com/tucsonhiking

TWISTED PINE TREES NEAR THE SUMMIT OF MOUNT WRIGHTSON (HIKE 36, PAGE 246, AND HIKE 37, PAGE 252)

Index

DEAR CUSTOMERS AND FRIENDS,

SUPPORTING YOUR INTEREST IN OUTDOOR ADVENTURE, travel, and an active lifestyle is central to our operations, from the authors we choose to the locations we detail to the way we design our books. Menasha Ridge Press was incorporated in 1982 by a group of veteran outdoorsmen and professional outfitters. For many years now, we've specialized in creating books that benefit the outdoors enthusiast.

Almost immediately, Menasha Ridge Press earned a reputation for revolutionizing outdoors- and travel-guidebook publishing. For such activities as canoeing, kayaking, hiking, backpacking, and mountain biking, we established new standards of quality that transformed the whole genre, resulting in outdoor-recreation guides of great sophistication and solid content. Menasha Ridge Press continues to be outdoor publishing's greatest innovator.

The folks at Menasha Ridge Press are as at home on a whitewater river or mountain trail as they are editing a manuscript. The books we build for you are the best they can be, because we're responding to your needs. Plus, we use and depend on them ourselves.

We look forward to seeing you on the river or the trail. If you'd like to contact us directly, visit us at menasharidge.com. We thank you for your interest in our books and the natural world around us all.

SAFE TRAVELS,

Bob Sehlinger

BOB SEHLINGER
PUBLISHER

American Hiking Society

PROTECT THE PLACES YOU LOVE TO HIKE.

Become a member today and
take $5 off using the code **Hike5**.

AmericanHiking.org/join

American Hiking Society is the only
national nonprofit organization dedicated
to empowering all to enjoy, share, and
preserve the hiking experience.

About the Author

Photographed by Todd Jones

ROB RACHOWIECKI was raised in London and climbed his first mountain by accident while on a school biology field course in Scotland. After a day of dissecting newts, he walked to the top of a windswept hill behind the outdoor studies center, looked around at miles of wilderness, and had an "I'm the king of the world!" revelation.

Rob crossed the pond in 1974, planning on traveling around the world, but he ended up living and traveling throughout the Americas, from Alaska to Argentina. He has authored hiking and climbing guides to Central America and the Central Andes, as well as travel guides to Peru, Ecuador, Costa Rica, and the American Southwest for publishers ranging from Lonely Planet to National Geographic. He has been an active member of the Society of American Travel Writers since 1997.

From 1983 to 2008, Rob worked as an adventure-travel guide, leading treks in the Andes and adventures on the Amazon. Since 1990 he has lived in Tucson, where he earned a master's degree at the University of Arizona and where he enjoys the area's varied ethnic restaurants, theaters, and outdoor music festivals. He is often found hiking the many desert, canyon, and mountain trails surrounding Tucson, following the seasonal changes and usually doing a spot of bird-watching, as Brits are wont to do.

After earning a respiratory therapy degree in 2006, Rob worked three days a week in local rural community hospitals until he retired in 2016. Now he travels the world, often accompanied by his partner, Audrey. His wanderlust has led to a four-month backpacking trip to Southeast Asia, visits to the lesser-known countries of Europe, and several adventures in various African countries. To avoid baggage fees, he wears hiking boots on international flights.